ALSO BY JULIE SUMMERS

Henry Moore and the Sea

The Caros: A Creative Partnership

Fearless on Everest: The Quest for Sandy Irvine

The Colonel of Tamarkan: Philip Toosey and the Bridge on the River Kwai

Remembered: A History of the Commonwealth War Graves Commission

Stranger in the House: Women's Stories of Men Returning from the Second World War

Remembering Fromelles

British and Commonwealth War Cemeteries

When the Children Came Home: Stories of Wartime Evacuees

Rowing in Britain

JAMBUSTERS

The Story of the Women's Institute in the Second World War

JULIE SUMMERS

SIMON & SCHUSTER

London · New York · Sydney · Toronto · New Delhi

A CBS COMPANY

First published in Great Britain by Simon & Schuster UK Ltd, 2013
A CBS COMPANY

1 3 5 7 9 10 8 6 4 2

Simon & Schuster UK Ltd
1st Floor
222 Gray's Inn Road
London WC1X 8HB

www.simonandschuster.co.uk

Simon & Schuster Australia, Sydney
Simon & Schuster India, New Delhi

A CIP catalogue record for this book is available from the British Library.

ISBN: 978-0-85720-046-4
EBOOK ISBN: 978-0-85720-047-1

Typeset by M Rules
Printed and bound by CPI Group (UK) Ltd, Croydon, CR0 4YY

In affectionate memory of Ga
and to all the unnamed WI members
who made the countryside tick
during six long years of war

CONTENTS

FOREWORD

In June 1939 the Women's Institute held its annual general meeting in London. The weather was glorious. Many of the delegates who came to London from all over the country had never been to the capital before. Cicely McCall, who was responsible for the WI's national education programme, observed the scene with fascination. She met one excited seventeen-year-old from Cumberland who had slept with her train ticket under her pillow for a month before the meeting, so thrilled was she to have been asked to represent her institute. Dressed in their best suits and dresses, wearing hats, gloves and sensible shoes, more than 8,000 women, many fanning themselves in the heat, crowded into the magnificent Empress Hall in Earls Court. The seating was arranged in alphabetical order by county beginning with Berkshire, Buckinghamshire, Cambridgeshire, Cheshire and so on. Stewards dressed in cream overalls with broad green and red ribbons over one shoulder showed people to their seats. There was a buzz of conversation and an air of eager anticipation.

The national committee members walked up onto the stage. Everybody stood up. Miss Nancy Tennant from Headington raised her right hand to conduct. The organist played the opening bars of 'Jerusalem' and 8,000 women lifted the roof with the well-known anthem. The great theatre reverberated to Parry's beautiful tune and the voices rose and rose. As the music faded, the delegates took their seats.

Lady Denman, dressed formally and wearing a green hat, stood up and welcomed her delegates. She then asked Miss Hadow to greet their honoured guests from the Associated Countrywomen of the World, who had gathered in London for a mass rally. Twenty-three countries were each represented in the Empress Hall by a woman delegate, many in national dress. Miss Hadow stood up. Tall, thin, every bit the vision of a blue-stocking academic, she addressed the meeting: 'Lady Denman and Fellow Countrywomen, we are met here today in our great parliament to welcome our sisters from other lands. In the first place, we are country women; we live on the land and serve the land. And in the last resort, it is not by armed force, or even by industrial prosperity, but it is by the land itself that men live.'

There was loud applause and appreciative murmuring from the delegates. She went on:

> In the second place, we are women, we belong to the constructive sex, whose whole instinct is to reserve and to foster life, to build homes in every land. In the hands of women, of wives and mothers, and I will even dare to say of sisters, daughters and spinster aunts, the health and happiness of mankind very largely is laid. Those two things, the unity of the land, the unity of our common womanhood, speak a universal language. It is in that tongue that in the name of 328,000 English and Welsh women I do indeed say to our guests from other countries – You are Welcome!

The applause swelled. As she sat down the foreign delegates stepped up onto the stage one by one. Some neither spoke nor understood English but all of them understood the applause and the smiles that greeted each fresh announcement. America, Sweden, India . . . One by one by they came forward, made their bow, and sometimes said a few words. Latvia, Norway . . . Germany. Miss McCall was in the hall and watched as the German delegate walked onto the stage.

> She was a tall woman. Her shoulders were flung back, her face set as she stepped on to the platform. There was a second's tense silence, as though suddenly eight thousand pairs of lungs had contracted, and their hearts too. Then came deafening applause. It rang round the hall tumultuously. It fell, then grew again increasing in volume as though each perspiring delegate on that very hot June morning could not enough say: 'Welcome! We are all country women here today. We are non-party, non-sectarian. We wish for peace, goodwill and cooperation among nations. You have had the courage to come here in spite of rumours of wars. We bid you welcome!'

Countess Margarete Keyserlingk was overwhelmed. The look of strain on her face disappeared and pleasure and amazement replaced it. She spoke in German: 'It is with great pleasure and thanks to you all and to my delegation that I am able to be here today to bring you greetings from my country, in the hope that this meeting will lead us all to a greater understanding of one another.' As she stepped off the platform she hesitated and almost stumbled. We shall never know what message she took back to Germany because within three months Poland had been invaded and Britain had declared war on her country.

*

When I set out to write a history of the Women's Institute in wartime I had in mind an historical overview with anecdotes from village institutes about jam-making, vegetable-growing, salvage-collecting, knitting and other activities we associate with the Second World War. As I have gone along I have realised that this is not what lies at the heart of this book. There are many top-down biographies of the Women's Institute but what I was interested in was the bottom-up story, the ordinary country-women who were at the heart of the village institutes. What has grown out of my research is a picture of the remarkable role played by ordinary women in rural Britain during the war. Unpaid, unsung, to a large extent uncomplaining, these women quietly and often with humour, made the countryside tick. The role of the WI was crucial in two ways: on the one hand, the government relied on its links with the National Federation of Women's Institutes to make direct requests of countrywomen to look after evacuees, collect everything from National Savings to bones for the munitions industry and to care for the nation's larder; on the other hand, the WI at institute level offered women a safety valve. At their monthly meetings, after they had completed their business and agreed on the many requests for their help towards the war effort, they could let their hair down. And they did. Singing, dancing, sketches and readings, beetle drives, musical bumps, and 'identify the ankle' competitions all helped to lighten the mood and send them on their way to take up the tasks set for them.

This book is a tribute to these women. Some were grand county ladies, others were farm labourers' wives and daughters. The majority were somewhere in between. In the institute there was no differentiation between their backgrounds. Though it would be foolish to suggest that all social boundaries were broken, they were, however, porous. The story of how they all buckled to and helped out is of more interest to me than who was the president or secretary on any given committee. The WI bound them together. Sybil Norcott, a WI member for nearly seventy years, summed it up: 'The WI is in my heart. It is in all our hearts. It is a way of life.'

I have been fortunate enough to interview a number of women who joined the WI during the war, albeit as very young members, or whose mothers, aunts or other family members were involved. Their personal perspectives give the historical material its colour and they are the only ladies in the book who are referred to by their Christian names. Peggy Sumner joined her WI before the war and is still a member. Her county, Cheshire, honoured its nonagenarian members in 2011 with a service in Chester Cathedral. Sybil Norcott, also a Cheshire member, was a child during the war but her mother belonged to her local institute and Sybil used to go to meetings as her mother was afraid to walk through the woods to the hall on her own.

Ann Tetlow and Dorcas Ward have known each other since they were a few months old. Dorcas's mother and grandmother were founder members of Bradfield WI in Berkshire. Her mother was secretary throughout the war and her minute books are amongst the most colourful and descriptive I have read. Ann's mother was also a very active member of the institute and used to allow Ann and her brother to attend the social half-hour of their afternoon meetings.

Caroline Dickinson's mother, Ruth Toosey, was my great aunt. She was on the committee of her WI in Barrow for several years during the war and she also held an ambulance licence with the Women's Voluntary Service, as well as being responsible for the girls of the Women's Land Army in her village. Dr Gwen Bark was a doctor who ran baby clinics in Tarporley, while bringing up her own young family and being an active member of her WI. She was outspoken on matters to do with child health, milk and the Beveridge Report but was also keen to encourage young mothers to find something of interest beyond the home in order to keep them mentally alert.

And Edith Jones, the wife of a farmer from Smethcote in Shropshire, whose great niece, Chris Downes, has given me access to Edith's wartime diaries. These offer a view of the war as well as the activities of her village and her farm-life during those years. In 1938 she wrote on the first page of her diary: 'It is interesting to keep a diary. To look back on past events. Things often work out for our good. Ups and downs have been worthwhile. With God's help let us make this year worthwhile for each other in our family life.' The great beauty of her diaries is that they were written without a view to being seen by anyone else and are at once personal but objective. She recorded everyday life: 'The weather is spring like, so I prune "my" apple trees. 6 of them. I like being out on these bright days but feel stiff after being on the steps and reaching! We move the pullets from the cabin to the big house. They look healthy and red. Geoff and Jim are ferreting.' But she also noted events out of the ordinary: 'Jack saw the "Northern Lights" last night. He said there was a very red sky like a fire, but it had faded when I looked out. He was pleased when I heard on the wireless that it had been seen all over England and that he too had seen it.' Edith was secretary of her WI from the day it was set up in 1931 and in addition to her monthly and annual minutes, she wrote an article about life in rural Britain in the early twentieth century that helps to cast a contemporary light on the benefit the WI brought to rural communities such as hers. I will introduce each of these women at an appropriate point in the narrative and some, notably Edith, will appear in more than one chapter.

All the other stories come from minute books, contemporary

records held by the National Federation in its archives at the Women's Library in London, letters, diaries and anecdotes that have been passed on to me. The women in these stories are referred to, as they would have been during the war, by their title and surnames. Traditionally the married women would have used their husband's Christian names to identify them if more than one member of the family belonged to an institute. So Mrs Peter Walker was the sister-in-law of Mrs Trevor Walker and the mother of Edith Walker, addressed of course as 'Miss Walker'.

One other woman will feature: Clara Milburn of Balsall Common WI near Coventry. Her diaries were published in 1979, an edited version of the fifteen exercise books she had filled with daily observations about life during the war. Peter Donnelly, who edited the diaries, described how they began: 'In the early uncertain days of 1940 Clara Milburn took time off from her loved (and sometimes loathed) garden and sat at her desk to begin a task she'd thought of starting for some time now. Opening a cheap soft-backed exercise book, she wrote "Burleigh in Wartime" on the first thin blue line, underscored it, and set to work on a project without any foreseeable end.' Mrs Milburn wrote mostly of things that concerned her and other women: first and foremost the fate of her son, Alan, who was a prisoner-of-war in Germany, but also of her dismay at the ever-increasing price of what little was available in the shops, the terrible plight of the people of Coventry during the bombings there, and of her clothes, her garden and her institute.

The Women's Institute covered England and Wales. Scotland had its own organisation called the Scottish Rural Women's Institute, which was independent of the WI and although it functioned on broadly the same lines as its English and Welsh equivalent, it does not come under the umbrella organisation and therefore will not feature in this book. Not every village in

England and Wales had a WI during the war years. In fact only one in three had an institute but often they would cover more than one village, such as Edith Jones's Smethcote Institute, near Shrewsbury, that also catered for Picklescote, Woolstaston, Leebotwood and Lower Wood. WIs were encouraged to involve those without institutes in communal activities such as fruit-canning and bottling or running market stalls so that the spread of its organisational reach was larger than that of any other organisation in the countryside. Its membership was ten times that of the Women's Voluntary Service at the beginning of the war and twenty times the size of the Townswomen's Guild. The WVS expanded to half the size of the WI during the war but with a proportionally smaller number of members in the country villages than in the towns. Many WI members belonged to other voluntary organisations, some sat on rural district or parish councils, others ran Guides or Brownies while others still were school governors or members of charity committees local to their areas. Some women worked full time, others were housewives or farmers' wives whose domestic life was their work. The spread was enormous and the energy equalled it.

The Second World War was the backdrop to the lives of Britons for six years. For children who were five or six at the outbreak it shaped their childhoods; for young women it coloured their adolescence and the formative years of their adulthood; for middle-aged and older women it came as an all too grim reminder of the Great War that had ended just a generation earlier and cost the country nearly a million lives. As Peggy Sumner reminded me, the women who were members of her WI were the wives, sisters, fiancées and young widows from that war.

At the outbreak of the Second World War the population of the countryside almost doubled. Key workers, evacuated families, unaccompanied schoolchildren and military camps resulted in unprecedented pressure on rural life. Food, housing, transport, schools, local services were all affected. As the country adapted to wartime conditions it was women who were at the forefront of helping with the adjustments needed. This was an era when wives were chattels and women made up a quarter of the workforce. Their lives in the countryside were not easy. When the war began over two thirds of rural housing had no access to electricity and main drains, a large number had only one tap or a pump in the kitchen to supply water. Some women even had to get their household water from a village well and privies were the norm. Washing was done in a copper, usually on Mondays, fires had to be laid daily in cold weather and some women still cooked on an open fire rather than a range or stove. Contraception was twenty years in the future and pain-relief for childbirth was unavailable except in hospitals. And yet this was the post-First World War generation of women who generally had less help in their homes than their grandmothers had.

The title for this book, *Jambusters*, was the inspired suggestion of my brother, Tim. He deserves credit for a very clever pun, though I suspect he did not know at the time he suggested it just how apposite it would be. During the war the WIs bust logjams, circumvented bureaucracy and improvised in many different ways. They wrote a major report on evacuation, were involved in advising eleven ministries, including the Treasury, and as a result influenced government thinking about children's health and education, housing and post-war reconstruction. They ran canteens for troops, baked pies for farm workers, and collected hundreds of tons of rosehips and herbs for the pharmaceutical industry. By their joint effort, members contributed millions of knitted garments to keep troops and refugees in Europe warm. They made 12,000,000 lb. (5,445,000 kilograms) of jam and preserves, helped to set up over 1,000 pig clubs and made more than 2,000 fur-lined garments for Russia. And in amongst all this major activity they sang, put on plays and organised parties to entertain their villages and keep their spirits up. The Second World War was the WI's finest hour.

In her speech to the annual general meeting of the Women's Institute held in the Albert Hall in 1943, Queen Elizabeth thanked the women for their enormous contribution to the war effort. As joint president of Sandringham WI with her mother-in-law, Queen Mary, where her daughter, Princess Elizabeth, became a member in 1943, and as a regular visitor to other institutes, she had first-hand experience of the WI's work. She said:

> When we have won through to peace, a great page in the history of Britain's war effort should be devoted to the countrywomen in this dear land of ours, who, left to carry on in the villages, tackled their job quietly and with wonderful efficiency: and institutes up and down the country have given a grand demonstration of how women can work together cheerfully and lovingly for the good of all. I am so glad to have this opportunity of paying my tribute to the NFWI and to all my fellow-members.

It will take a whole book, not just one page as suggested by Queen Elizabeth, to pay tribute to and celebrate their extraordinary achievements on the Home Front during six long years of war.

Jambusters opens with a brief history of the WI and introduces a small number of the key players who ran the organisation at national level. Then we follow the course of the war, seen through the eyes of women who have all been involved in or associated with the WI in one way or another at institute level. We will look at some of the large variety of activities women undertook at the behest of the government and its national body, such as jam-making, food production and knitting. The book ends with a brief summary of the post-war lives of those women whose personal stories have featured.

All the stories in this book have been checked as far as possible for accuracy, and if there are any errors in the narrative, I take responsibility for them. No names have been changed but a small number of stories have been told anonymously so as not to cause offence to relatives who might still be alive. To every woman who has helped to bring this book to life I offer my warmest thanks.

The village of Milton in Cambridgeshire had a wartime motto which I think sums up the contribution made by the WI: 'Say little, serve all, pass on. This is the true greatness – to serve unnoticed and work unseen.' Women did not trumpet their achievements and many of them were unquantifiable anyway since the aim was to keep going, and make life a little easier for others.

Julie Summers
Oxford

I

LET THE SUNSHINE STREAM IN

> A friend said, 'Come along with me.' I said, 'No, I'm not.' But she kept bothering me and my husband said, 'For goodness sake go with her and stop her worrying.' So I went with her and that was the best day's work I ever did.
>
> *A WI member, 1919*

Not every woman in the countryside joined her WI, but for those who did it probably presented the only opportunity for them to socialise outside the home and to learn about life beyond their immediate environs. Edith Jones was one such woman. She described her village in the early part of the twentieth century:

> Life in the truly rural areas could be rather humdrum before the motor transport came into its own. Some of us lived 10–12 miles from the market town and 3–5 miles from the nearest railway station depending on where our houses were situated. We were in a scattered area, mostly farmers and connected with farm work and the women had a full time job in the home for there was no electricity nor piped water or any other

> modern convenience and everything was 'made at home'. We seemed to have little time or cause to visit our next village unless it was for a fresh sitting of eggs in the spring or a jar or two of honey in the autumn ready for winter colds. The menfolk generally managed the cattle auctions, touching each other for a lift in the farmers' gigs but if the farmer's wife went too they knew they'd have to be sober to touch a ride back.

Edith married John Cecil (Jack) Jones on 10 July 1914, less than a month before the outbreak of the First World War. They moved to Red House Farm in Smethcote as tenant farmers, with milking-cows, sheep and poultry on some sixty acres. It was not a large farm, even in those days, and they had little money. They milked morning and evening with the help of Jack Middleton, who lived in nearby Picklescote. Jack was an ex-soldier of the Great War. He never married but lived with his elderly mother and earned his living by catching rabbits and working for Mr Jones, earning five shillings for eight hours' work, Edith noted. The cows came into the milking shippon opposite the house to be milked but that building had no water so the cows had to be driven down to the pond at the end of the farmyard to drink after milking. In addition to the cattle and sheep there were Edith's chickens, of which she was extremely fond. She sold eggs at the farm gate as well as taking them into Shrewsbury market on Saturdays. When there were tasks on the farm, such as caring for sick animals, Edith invariably helped out. She wrote about drenching and hand-feeding a calf that was poorly. For three days she looked after it but, she wrote, 'at a quarter to one on Saturday morning the calf died. The men buried it. It had tried hard to rally.' Although she was clearly touched by the calf's death Edith was unsentimental about animals. Farming was a way of life and there would always be deaths as well as births in the countryside.

Jack Jones was a quiet man committed to his farm and the community. A rural district councillor who also served as a churchwarden, he was a regular pall-bearer at funerals. He went to market weekly to buy or sell stock and he enjoyed the quiet life of the country with its seasonal rhythms. His wife was different. Edith was extraordinarily industrious and gifted at turning her hand to mending and making almost anything. She was also an avid reader, and despite her busy life as a farmer's wife would try to set aside an amount of time each afternoon to reading or studying. She loved the wireless and used to note programmes that she had listened to in her diaries. In March 1938 she wrote: 'Sowed antirrhinums and sweet peas in boxes. Listened to the Parliamentary discussion on the unrest in Central Europe.' Six months later Chamberlain returned from Munich: 'The European Peace Pact was signed! May it be a lasting pact and for our good. War has threatened and been hanging over us and the relief when peace was declared was immense.' That year, on Armistice Day, she remained hopeful: 'Nice morning. I gather and clear up wood under yew trees. Chop some then Len comes and finishes them. There is now a good supply in the shed and it looks tidy. We keep the two minutes silence and feel thankful for peace in the country.'

Her great-niece, Chris Downes, remembered how Edith always wanted to know more about the world she lived in.

> She had a passionate belief in the value of education and she read widely on any number of topics. I remember when she was in hospital in her eighties having had a hip replacement. We visited her and she was astonished that other women in her ward were just sitting in their beds. 'You wouldn't believe it, Christine, they just sit there and do nothing. They're not even interested in reading or playing Scrabble.' As a young woman

> she had studied butter-making at Radbrook College in Shrewsbury. She was very skilled and achieved top marks for her butter-making.

The Joneses were childless but in 1926 they were asked to look after Edith's nephew, Leonard Manley. The Manley family had moved from Shropshire to Staffordshire, to a farm near the river. Leonard suffered from rheumatic fever and his parents were told that if he remained in the house by the river he would die. Leonard believed he was going to spend the summer with Aunt Edith and Uncle Jack at Smethcote but in fact he stayed with them for the rest of his childhood and became for them the son they never had. He remained close to his parents and siblings and there were regular family visits but his home was Red House Farm. When he was old enough he went to Rodbaston Agricultural College in Staffordshire and did a one-year course just before the outbreak of the war. The relationship between Leonard and his aunt was close, so that when Chris was born she called Edith 'Gran Jones'. 'I told my friends at school that I had three grandmothers, my mother's mother, my father's mother and Edith. The teachers said that was not possible but it was true. I regarded all three women as my grandmothers and I saw a great deal of Gran Jones. She and Jack retired down the road to Church Stretton in 1947 when Leonard married my mother, Gwladys Hughes.'

In the late 1920s a local bus service started, described by Edith as 'a red letter day indeed'. This meant that women could take the bus to Shrewsbury market on Saturdays to sell produce and do their own shopping:

> Some had baskets of eggs, butter, cheese and chickens, also rabbits and flowers for the market. On the bus they could meet

> with their neighbours and get to know the women from the other places of call, for [the driver] had a circular round to pay his way and fill the bus. At times overfill it! It was an entertainment just to sit and listen to the conversations, exchanging recipes and how they managed their homes. An eye-opener indeed at times. Something to keep our minds amused for several days. Then there was the next time to prepare for and look forward to.

Not long after the local bus service had brought women a degree of freedom a new rector, Mr Tuke, arrived in Smethcote. He was different from the previous incumbent and people were delighted that he and his wife seemed to take a genuine interest in the life of the parish. 'When visiting the people they heard about the 'local bus' on all sides and how much difference it had made in our lives. The rector's wife thought it would be a good idea to form a branch of the Women's Institute movement and was warmly supported by most of the women though some still shied at any new ideas.' Edith was an enthusiast for the new institute. She relished any opportunity to improve her knowledge of the world beyond Smethcote and at the first meeting she was elected to the committee and given the role of secretary. Mrs Tuke, who had been the first president, died at the end of 1931, which was a great sadness but the institute kept going. In May 1934 Edith wrote in her diary: 'Have heard that Rev Tuke and Miss Hollier are engaged (shock).' Miss Hollier, treasurer under the first Mrs Tuke, married the rector later that year. The shock wore off and she soon became accepted as part of the community. In time she was elected president of Smethcote WI and continued to have an interest in the institute until her death at the age of a hundred in 2001.

Smethcote Women's Institute had fifty members from the

surrounding villages of Picklescote, Woolstaston, Leebotwood and Lower Wood. There were farmers' wives, local women who had lived in the villages for years and Mrs Tuke, new to the parish. At the first meeting they had a demonstration on how to make slippers from old felt hats. The meetings were to be held on the second Wednesday of each month at Smethcote, Woolstaston and Leebotwood alternately. As the Joneses had no car, Edith had to walk or later cycle to all the meetings. Chris remembered that she walked long distances, thinking nothing of covering the two and a half miles to Leebotwood for a meeting in the winter. The first annual report of Smethcote WI recognised this as an issue, noting that 'the average attendance is 34. The district being very scattered, many members have a long distance to come.' This theme runs through all the annual reports, especially during the war when members had to resort to walking or cycling as petrol rationing limited car use for those who had them. The early reports are full of colour and optimism for the future and there is a real sense of the energy that the WI released in these women. For many it was the first time they had had an opportunity to be creative, to try singing in a choir or to hear lectures on diverse topics from home dyeing and boot repairing to a visit to the Stork margarine works, which seems to have been of particular interest to the members in 1934.

Edith remembered the early days when not everyone thought the WI was a good thing:

> The men were not used to the women having a 'cause of their own' and were rather up in arms about it. The bus service had spoilt them, now the WI. What would be the next move? What indeed. Well, we started the WI meetings combining three villages in rotation to make it fair for all and soon became popular

and we'd arranged to have afternoon meetings to be home again for the family meal and to attend to the fowls and dairy work.

Our local bus driver was willing to support us and took us to the group and other area meetings. That was something else we had to get used to: 'competing with the outside world' as it seemed to us. Standing up in public and giving our views when asked and in the competitions we well held our own for the women had been brought up to home-made crafts and some were really skilled at it and only now could it be brought to light. The men folk were sheepishly proud of their women when they returned home with prizes and gradually could admit the WI was a good idea. Well it grew and thrived until 1938. The war seemed imminent and much thought was given to what might be necessary. We had first-aid classes and came home proudly with our signed certificates. We had talks and demonstrations to be of help in time of need, and of course the war happened and many of our men folk joined the forces and often the women had to take their place on the farms as well as do their housework.

Alongside her WI minutes and annual reports for Smethcote WI Edith kept annual diaries. She wrote just a few sentences a day in the little books, which had seven days and an eighth section for memoranda per double-page spread. In January 1938, for example, she wrote: 'I have had 6 letters for my Birthday. I appreciated the remembrance. Although I am getting older I do not feel it much because (I suppose) I keep so fit and well, for which I am always thankful. Good health helps one to enjoy and keep an interest in life. Such a blessing.' The books were bound in soft leather and several of her wartime diaries were 'The Electricity Supply Diary and Handbook', which is ironic considering Red House Farm, where she lived, did not have electricity until long after the war. The diaries provide a glorious insight into the life of a middle-aged countrywoman, emphasising the repetitive nature of her highly structured week but also offering glimpses into her personal life, such as buying blouses in Shrewsbury after she had had a good sale at the market, as well as juxtapositions of war news and home life such as 'one day [WI] school for chutney and jam making. I go with Mrs Muckleston, held at Church Stretton. City of Rome taken by our troops.'

Over the eight years leading up to the war, Smethcote WI members concentrated their efforts on learning dress-making skills, baking cakes and learning about child welfare. Edith took part in the competitions and frequently won with her Victoria sponges. Len told Chris years later that he loved it when Edith entered the WI cookery competitions because she always practised beforehand so that he and his uncle were then treated to excellent cakes. In 1938 she won second prize for her fancy dress costume 'Departed Spirit' and at the annual meeting that year she noted: 'Prizes for competitions for the year were awarded to Mrs Langley 1st with 20 marks, I was 2nd 17 marks and M Langley and G Gretton tied for 3rd with 9 marks each. My prize being a coloured tablecloth.' In addition to the competitions the committee organised outings and sent delegates to county meetings, often with the assistance of the bus driver, who would obligingly take a group of women to Shrewsbury or further afield to attend group meetings.

In 1937 they sent three members to London to see the Coronation decorations. The following year it was Edith's turn to go to London for the WI's annual general meeting. It was her second visit. This time she travelled with several other women from Shropshire and they stayed at a hotel in the West End. Her diary entry for that day recorded: 'Arrive at 2:15 after leaving luggage at Cora hotel. Three of us go over the Tower, St Pauls, (All Hallows modern church). Meet others at the Strand Corner

House for tea (Lyons) then to Coliseum for show, which we all enjoyed. Then walked down Regent St to see shops lit up and call at milk bar then turn in at 12:30! Wet afternoon. Very wet at Smethcote.' The following day she attended the meeting. 'Meeting in Albert Hall is crowded. Lasts all day . . . Some were interesting, others dry,' she noted about the speakers, adding that she hoped to write an interesting report about the meeting for her institute. Len met her off the 10.15 p.m. train with the pony and trap and brought her back to the farm. 'So pleased to see him', she wrote. The following day she was tired. Her entry was brief: 'Fine generally, wet later. Do not have a busy day.'

Just over a year later the war broke out. Edith's annual report from 1939 had a quite different flavour: 'From the beginning of the year until September the Institute seemed to be making steady progress but the outbreak of war and the extra work thrown on members by evacuees in the district has made it difficult to adhere to our programme.' In her private diary, on 2 September 1939 she wrote: 'Yeomanry called up for National Service. Len goes off this morning. We feel sad at this vital passing and shall pray for his safe return.'

The war changed the lives of those women. Numbers dwindled at the institute as people found they had too many other responsibilities but Edith was pleased to see that by 1940 new people had moved into the villages from the cities and were delighted to be invited to WI meetings. This gave the institute a new impetus and energy because, as she wrote, these women brought new ideas and introduced fresh blood. She believed that the WI had helped her and others 'to appreciate people to whom otherwise we wouldn't have given two thoughts'. When the war came and people had to work together, Smethcote, like other villages, had a ready-made organisation that could be called upon to coordinate whatever response was required.

What was unique about the WI was its extraordinary reach. From early on it existed at three levels: national, county and village. The London-based National Federation of Women's Institutes had serious lobbying powers and a reputation as a powerful force that was well organised, passionate and clear in its aims. It had already brought about changes in a whole variety of matters from district nurses to railway lavatories, from venereal disease (it submitted a report on this to the Department of Health in 1922) to water pollution on Britain's beaches. On the other hand the WI had the largest grass-roots membership of any women's organisation in the country and was bigger, in its total number, than all but the largest of the men's Trades Unions. In 1939 there were 5,546 Women's Institutes in England alone, totalling 328,000 members. The middle level, equally active and useful, comprised the Voluntary County Organisers who looked after groups of WIs within their county and were often women who held posts in local government offices or had the ear of council officials. At the outbreak of war the fifty-eight county committees were used by the National Executive to reach the individual institutes with astonishing rapidity. One way and another, the WI reached almost every corner of the countryside.

The WI was, and remains today, independent. It runs its own affairs, finances itself and educates its members at its own college. But it is also well connected: government representatives sit on WI committees and WI representatives sit on government committees. That has been the case since the earliest days and at almost no time in its history was that more relevant than during the Second World War.

The Women's Institutes set out to cross class barriers as well as those of religion and party. At the outset there was some resistance from the lady of the manor, or, more often, the lord of the manor, but these hurdles were overcome surprisingly quickly and stories abounded of goodwill between women who would not otherwise have spoken to each other, much less joined forces to help one another. One early member wrote:

> The institute has brought together in our very rural village women of all classes in true friendships, women who have lived in the same village for many years as total strangers to each other, not perhaps from any unkind or class feeling but from sheer want of opportunity for meeting and making friends. Women who have never ventured out to church or chapel or village entertainment . . . now come eagerly to our meetings, forget their shyness in opening up their minds to new ideas and welcome opportunities for developing their hidden talents.

The WI is democratic. Members vote for their committees in a secret ballot, which has had the result that no single person or faction has been able to manipulate the WI to a minority purpose. It is not a secret society or religious organisation. Church, chapel, atheist or agnostic, anyone can join the WI and be sure her beliefs will not be attacked. Every difference is respected. It is not political, nor it is affiliated to any party. This has been one of its greatest assets. Since party politics play no part in the WI this means the institute can comment without prejudice on government legislation. The WI is the village voice and encourages its members to speak out on decisions that affect their lives. The only qualification for setting up a women's institute is that a village has to have a population of less than 4,000.

The first Women's Institute in Britain was formed in the Welsh village of Llanfairpwllgwyngyllgogerychwyrndrobwllllantysiliogogogoch, on the Isle of Anglesey, on Wednesday 16 June 1915, the day that Lloyd George took the oath as Minister of Munitions. Although seen by many as a quintessentially British phenomenon, the WI was started in Canada nearly twenty years before Mrs Stapleton-Cotton became president of the first WI in England and Wales.

So what had inspired Canadian countrywomen to come together and form women-only institutes and what were they for? The answer was education. 'Not education for education's sake' . . . though 'very beautiful in theory', asserted Mrs Adelaide Hoodless, the founder of the WI movement in Canada, 'but when we come down to facts, I venture to say that 90 per cent of those who attend our schools seek education for its practical benefits.'

Mrs Hoodless had married John Hoodless of a prosperous business family in Hamilton, Ontario, in 1881. She bore four children, two boys and two girls. In 1889 their youngest son died at the age of fourteen months, due to an intestinal infection as a result of drinking contaminated milk. Infant and child mortality was prevalent, with up to 20 per cent of babies and infants dying before they reached their fifth birthday, the majority as a result of bacterial infection. Mrs Hoodless appears to have blamed herself for her baby's death and for the rest of her life she devoted herself tirelessly to promoting ideas about domestic hygiene. She believed that while girls should be educated at school in academic subjects, they also needed to learn the practical skills they would require to run a home and a family when they grew up and married. This, after all, was the future for the overwhelming majority of women of that era.

Domestic science was a new concept to the audiences at Adelaide Hoodless's lectures given as part of her promotion of the importance of home economics. She defined it as 'the application of scientific principles to the management of the home. It teaches the value of pure air, proper food, systematic management, economy, care of children, domestic and civil sanitation and the prevention of disease.' She urged her listeners to consider the importance of respecting domestic occupations and giving value to the education of the woman as a homemaker, concluding: 'The management of the home has more to do with the moulding of character than any other influence, owing to the large place it fills in the life of the individual during the most plastic stage of development. We are therefore justified in an effort to secure a place for home economics or domestic science in the education institutions of this country.' Most importantly, she believed in 'elevating women's work to the level of a profession and putting it on a par with a man's work'.[1]

Her appeal did not fall on deaf ears. At that time in North America women's issues were beginning to come to the fore. The International Council of Women had been formed in 1888 in the United States, advocating women's human rights and working across national boundaries. At their first conference in Washington DC in March and April of that year there were eighty speakers and forty-nine delegates, representing women's organisations from nine countries. Britain was represented by Lady Aberdeen, wife of the Governor General of Canada, who became the council's president in 1893. At the conference of the Canadian National Council of Women in the same year, Mrs Hoodless succeeded in persuading them to back her campaign to introduce domestic science into the school curriculum.

Her conviction that things would only change if women could bring basic scientific knowledge into their homes convinced her to tackle the issue at the grass roots as well as at the national level. 'Is it of greater importance that a farmer should know more about the scientific care of his sheep and cattle, than a farmer's wife should know how to care for her family, or that his barns should have every labour saving contrivance, while she toils and drudges on the same old treadmill instituted by her grandmother, perhaps even carrying water from a spring, a quarter of a mile from the house, which I know has been done?'[2] The emphasis on raising the status of women's work to that of men was a key part of her message.

A speech she gave at a conference of the Farmers' Institute at the Ontario Agricultural College in Guelph was heard by Mr Erland Lee, secretary of the Farmers' Institute of Wentworth County. He immediately invited her to speak at their next Ladies night at his institute in Stoney Creek. Some thirty-five farmers' wives were present at the talk. They received enthusiastically her suggestion that as the men had a Farmers' Institute so the women should consider having one of their own. The farmers' wives were so keen that they invited her to return the following week, on 19 February 1897. That night the idea of a women's institute was born and a week later what became known as the 'Stoney Creek Women's Institute' was called into being and its first meeting was held. Its motto, chosen five years later, became 'For Home and Country'.

Mrs Hoodless continued to lecture on girls' education while the movement of women's institutes grew and flourished throughout Canada. She herself was credited with founding the movement but it was the women who set up the individual institutes who were its champions. They set to work with Mrs Hoodless's words ringing in their ears: 'What must be done is to develop to the fullest extent the two great social forces, education and organisation, so as to secure for each individual the highest degree of advancement.'[3]

Women alone were not responsible for the success of the Women's Institute movement in Canada any more than they would be in England and Wales two decades later. The movement needed the approval of the male-dominated establishment and it had Mr Erland Lee and members of the Farmers' Institute and the Canadian Ministry of Agriculture firmly behind it. Both bodies could see the value of motivating and empowering rural women in their plan to improve life in rural villages. They threw their support behind institute initiatives, both at a local and national level, so that by the early years of the twentieth century, just a decade or so after the first meeting at Stoney Creek, there was a pool of speakers, a list of topics for discussion and training colleges for teachers as well as short courses for institute members on cookery, home nursing, food values and sewing. One report concluded with satisfaction: 'We have learned so much now that if we have typhoid fever or scarlet fever, we do not say "This is the Lord's will", but examine drains, sinks, cellars, walls and backyards where we know there may be conditions favourable to the development of these germs. We have learned that the best way to get rid of them is to let the sunshine stream in.'[4]

More than anything else the Women's Institutes, of which there were 3,000 in Canada by their twenty-first year, gave women who had lived isolated lives the opportunity to meet together regularly, providing a network of friendship as well as expertise and education, which few had ever experienced in their lives. It was enormously empowering.

Why did it take until 1915 for this movement to catch on in Britain? After all, Norway had independently formed the House Mothers Association in 1898, which spread throughout Scandinavia and had a membership, within two decades, of 70,000. Belgium formed Cercles des Fermières (Circles of Farmers' Wives) in 1906 and the United Irishwomen were formed in Ireland in 1910. To some extent it was the conservative nature of the British that meant that change came only very slowly. Life in the countryside was shaped by tradition and an unwillingness to exchange the familiar, however imperfect, with the new and unknown. A typical village at the beginning of the twentieth century would have a manor house, inhabited by the squire and his family, who might be resident full time or who might only come down for the hunting. Then there would be the farmers, some owning their own farms, others as tenant farmers but many of very long standing. These families, headed by the men, might have been working the land for many decades, if not centuries. Resistance to change, and in particular to book learning, was strong amongst this group. They had learned from their forebears and from experience. There were no short cuts to be had when it came to farming and managing the land. The main body of the village would comprise farm labourers and their families, who again might have been living in the village and serving the big house for generations. Some villages had a doctor and he, as a man of learning with knowledge of science, was viewed with awe and suspicion in equal measure. The vicar or priest was accorded equal respect. A few villages could boast an artist or two but they were generally on the periphery of village life and not part of the hierarchy.

Rural Britain in the early twentieth century was in decline. In the last thirty years of the nineteenth century in excess of 2 million acres of arable land had been allowed to go out of production. An exodus to the cities in search of an easier way of life had left agriculture a bereft and flagging industry. Many farmers had gone bankrupt and unemployment among agricultural labourers was high. This in turn brought great hardship to their wives, children and other family dependents. Many rural communities were under-populated and impoverished, not just financially but also educationally. Most of the poorest children did not have the opportunity to attend school as they were needed for labour. Often the only education available was at Sunday school. A vicar in Kent described how the children of the poorer part of his parish were taught to read and 'to be instructed in the plain duties of the Christian religion, with a particular view to their good and industrious behaviour in their future character as labourers and servants'.[5] Village life was also riven by class and an attitude amongst the gentry that it was not necessarily wise to educate the servant class in the same way that it would not be sensible to teach a cow her value or a horse its power. Abhorrent as it now seems, this attitude prevailed. Yet there were some people who were determined to make a difference to rural communities in spite of the opposition they met.

The government was sufficiently concerned by the situation in the countryside that it set up the Board of Agriculture in 1889 which brought together all government responsibilities for agricultural matters under one department.

Twelve years later, in 1901, the Agricultural Organisation Society (AOS) was formed. It grew from a voluntary body into an organisation to help to stem the decline in agriculture. The AOS had the specific brief to encourage the formation of local societies of farmers, smallholders and growers who could work cooperatively. Initially the cooperatives concentrated on the supply of fertilisers, mixed feed and seeds; the development of trading came later. The forming of these groups created a structure which had political representation at a high level. England, Wales and Scotland each had branches with chairmen and committees. Its secretary was a man of great determination and vision, who would play a role in the setting up of the Women's Institute. His name was John Nugent Harris, but on the eve of the First World War he was still dealing with the resuscitation of a depressed agro-economy.

As early as 1904 Edwin Pratt, author of *The Organisation of Agriculture in England and other Lands*, proposed that women's institutes might be a good way to educate British countrywomen. The suggestion received little acknowledgement and no interest. Eight years later, Robert Greig, who had worked as a staff inspector at the Board of Education, pushed rather harder. He had been tasked to carry out an investigation into agricultural instruction in other countries and was impressed by the WIs he saw on his visits to Poland, Belgium and across the Atlantic in Canada. Most importantly he saw the value not only of the educational talks geared towards child-rearing and homemaking, piggery and poultry, gardening and dairy work but also the purely entertaining topics, including music and literature. He wrote a pamphlet which explained the great work being done in other countries by Women's Institutes, concluding that: 'perhaps the most profitable outlet for the expenditure of energy and public money in the improvement of agriculture will be found in widening the mental horizon of the farmer's wife and especially the wife of the labourer, smallholder, and working farmer . . .'[6] He stressed the fact that women in the countries he had visited had risen to the challenge of setting up institutes and had been aided by their governments through generous grants. He urged 'energy, enthusiasm and bold optimism' from women who should be encouraged to follow the lead of those in other countries.

There was still no reaction from anyone in rural Britain. As Mr Robertson Scott concluded in his history of the WI, written in 1925: 'Unfortunately Mr Greig did not go a-gospelling with his pamphlet. Nothing was done to forward this plea for Women's Institutes, the case for which has seldom been more effectively made.'[7] The WI movement needed an advocate to sow the seed and fertile soil in which to flourish. Two things coincided to bring this about: the champion was Mrs Margaret Rose 'Madge' Watt; and the fertile environment was the First World War.

Mrs Watt was Canadian born although her parents were both of Scottish descent. She was highly educated, having obtained a first class honours degree in modern languages at the University of Toronto in 1889 and gone on to do postgraduate work in history and pedagogics. She worked as a journalist in New York and wrote literary criticism for American and Canadian newspapers. In 1893 she married Alfred Tennyson Watt, who was the medical officer of health for British Columbia. In 1909 Mrs Watt became a founder member of the Metchosin Women's Institute on Vancouver Island and was soon involved in developing the movement in British Columbia. In 1913 her husband died and she decided to move to England in order to educate her two sons.

From the moment she arrived in Britain she began promoting the idea of women's organisations. She spoke at public meetings and private gatherings but there was little interest. Some listeners felt she was out of tune with English village life and the comparison with Canada, with its more progressive views, jarred. Her breakthrough came when she wrote a pamphlet explaining how Women's Institutes could function as a valuable part of the war effort by encouraging countrywomen to take responsibility for increasing and safeguarding the supply of food. Mr Nugent Harris, then general secretary of the Agricultural Organisation Society, met her at a conference in London in February 1915. She introduced herself and said she wanted to talk about Women's Institutes. He had never heard of such a concept but he was impressed by her and invited her to talk to him at his office.

Mr Nugent Harris had been looking for a way to involve women in the cooperative agricultural societies and indeed he even succeeded in persuading some groups to allow women to attend the meetings. However, it was not a successful experiment as the women never spoke at the meetings, although afterwards they would talk to him and criticise or comment on this or that decision. When he asked them why they would not speak up they replied: 'We dare not because our husbands and sons would make fun of us.'[8] He was frustrated by the reaction but refused to give up: 'I would not rest until I could establish some movement that would give the women-folk a chance to express themselves free from the fear of being ridiculed by the men. By the merest chance, I met Mrs Watt. I felt I had come in touch with the very movement I wanted.'[9] With permission from the AOS he appointed Mrs Watt to start Women's Institutes in July 1915.

Mrs Watt found people in the country villages in England and Wales a great deal more conservative than the pioneer communities of Canada where the first institutes had taken off so successfully eighteen years earlier. Life in Canada was harder but it was also socially more equal. 'Rural Britain was a very narrow society, hidebound and with groups who were suspicious of each other,'[10] wrote WI archivist Anne Stamper. Allegiances ran along predetermined lines. If parents were conservative then children joined the Conservative Association. If they were liberal they joined the Liberal Association and 'the Other Party if their parents were Otherwise'. The same applied to church or chapel as well as where people shopped. In short, there were sections of society who had no idea how the people who worked for them lived, or vice versa.

The impact of the First World War on rural Britain was enormous. Hundreds of thousands of young farmers, farmhands and village boys signed up in a patriotic haze. The workforce was badly depleted and as the greedy war machine consumed ever more men, the situation for working farmers became increasingly difficult. Women were called on both privately and by the government to help to provide food for the nation. The Women's Land Army was brought into being in 1915 to fill the gaps left by farmworkers who had been called up. According to official records there were some 250,000 women working as farm labourers by the end of 1917, though just 20,000 of them, less than 10 per cent, were members of the Land Army. This pointed to the huge pool of potential labour in the countryside. In the face of the mounting casualties on the Western Front, and the call of the Army and Navy for more men, party politics and class distinctions seemed much less important than they had before the war. People were forced into cooperation and sacrifice for the common good. Robertson Scott wrote: 'Men saw new merits in other men, women discerned new merits in other women, and men and women beheld new merits in each other. Women, whose enfranchisement had justly come, but before the nation was wholly in favour of it, had their great chance of showing their quality and proving their right.'[11]

Mrs Watt was invited by Mr Nugent Harris to speak at a conference at the University of Bangor and it was here that her message made an impression and started the WI ball rolling. Two of those present were Sir Harry Reichel, Principal of University College at Bangor, and Colonel the Hon. Stapleton Cotton, Chairman of the North Wales branch of the Agricultural Organisation Society. The colonel and his wife invited Mrs Watt to come and speak at a village meeting in their village, Llanfairpwll, the following day.

Thus, Britain's first Women's Institute was formed with Mrs Stapleton Cotton as the president. This small institute was to meet monthly on Tuesdays at two o'clock in the afternoon in a room kindly lent by Mrs W.E. Jones 'until such time as the Women's Institute has its own building'. The colonel admitted later to Mrs Watt that he had not shared his wife's belief that a women's institute would work. He wrote to her six months later that he had been 'one of the many who had doubted the capacity of women to conduct even their ordinary business with success but I have learned more about women than I have learned in forty years . . . I see and believe that women can and will bring all classes, all denominations, all interest, all schools of the best thought together in that common brotherhood of love . . . which every man and every woman longs for in his or her innermost heart.'

There were two factors that ensured the survival of the Llanfairpwll institute. The first was the support of Sir Harry Reichel and his willingness to supply speakers on rural matters, as Erland Lee had done in Canada twenty years earlier. The second was the approval of the Marquis and Marchioness of Anglesey, who provided the patronage that would ensure enduring success. Lady Anglesey became their patron, setting a model that was copied in villages throughout the country.

As Anne Stamper wrote in her book *Rooms Off the Corridor*: 'in the early days if the "big house" did not support the formation of a WI (and often the lady of the manor became the president) then the WI was either not formed or did not flourish.' Rural Britain was perhaps not quite as ready for equality as Mrs Watt might have hoped but the fact that a farm labourer's wife and the lady of the manor could sit in the same meeting and discuss sewerage or child welfare, join in a song or a beetle drive or listen to a lecture on the latest agricultural ideas was something radical and new. Not every woman was confident enough to speak up at meetings but simply being there and being part of a new community movement, of having a monthly event to look forward to and on which to reflect, gave a large number of women something precious to hold on to.

Three more institutes were set up in North Wales before Mrs Watt moved back into England: Cefn, Trefnant and Criccieth. Which was the first WI to be formed in England is disputed. Singleton in Sussex and Wallisdown in Dorset both claimed the honour and when Mr Robertson Scott wrote his *Story of the Women's Institute Movement* in 1925 he gave the palm to Wallisdown. He summarised the success of the WI: 'The Institute movement is wide enough to include women who fought passionately for the suffrage, women who loyally accepted votes when women's suffrage became the law of the land, and women who are still opposed to the participation of women in politics.' Mr Nugent Harris agreed, writing: 'The suffragists made the pot boil, the Institute movement showed how some things could be got out of the pot.'[12]

Mrs Watt was very anxious that the institutes were set up on the same lines as they had been in Canada, adopting the rules and principles. These defined clearly the non-sectarian, non-political character of the Women's Institutes, which was such an important aspect of their character, most especially in the early days. News spread quickly and soon institutes were springing up all over the country. By the end of 1915 there were twelve institutes in England and Wales. This grew to 37 in 1916 and 187 in 1917. At the end of the First World War there were 773 institutes and over the next three years that figure went up by nearly 600 a year. In Scotland things moved a little more slowly and the first institute was formed at Longniddry in East Lothian 1917. They called themselves the Scottish Women's Rural Institutes and were run under the auspices of the Board of Agriculture for Scotland until they became independent in the late 1920s.

While no democratic organisation would ever wish to be defined by the personality of its chairman there is no doubt that Lady Denman had a very great impact on the way the WI developed. She chaired what became the National Federation of Women's Institutes from 1917 until 1946, seeing it through two world wars, the great depression and many teething problems. She was also the honorary director of the Women's Land Army from 1939 to 1945 and chairman of the Family Planning Association, which was something she was passionate about. As an able sportswoman she was president of the Ladies

Golf Union from 1932–38, vice president of the Royal College of Nursing from 1933 until her death in 1954 and chairman of the Cowdray Club, for the nation's nurses and professional women, from 1937 until 1953. She was described as 'attractive, very intelligent, [she] had a fine stride in walking, was good at sport and expert in tree felling, a capable business woman, a good housekeeper, shy, devoid of sentimentality, and full of sympathy for those in trouble. She believed in success and demanded a high standard of work in everything and never spared herself.'[13]

Born the Hon. Gertrude Mary 'Trudie' Pearson on 7 November 1884, she was the second child and only daughter of the Liberal MP and later first Viscount Cowdray, Weetman Dickinson Pearson. Her mother, Annie Cass, was a charitable worker and political hostess. Educated at a day school in London and then at a finishing school in Dresden, Trudie Pearson supplemented her education by reading books on economics and philosophy in her father's library. Her parents were often abroad on business so that she grew up as a wholly independently minded but somewhat shy young woman, a trait which she later overcame by hard work and enthusiasm. She was brought up to believe that being born to great wealth and privilege came with a duty to give something back by service to the community and she did not avoid what she considered to be a lifelong obligation.

In November 1903, at the age of nineteen, she married Thomas Denman, ten years her senior. He was the third Baron Denman, an army officer and a Liberal peer. Her mother was happy with the marriage but it would appear that her daughter was less so and it was no secret that the couple lived separate lives, though remained on friendly terms, within a few short years of their wedding. They had two children. Thomas was born in 1905 and Judith in 1907. In 1908 Lady Denman served on the Executive Committee of the Women's Liberal Federation. With a membership of 100,000 and the main business being women's suffrage, the lessons she learned during her two years on the committee gave her a valuable introduction to large organisations as well as an interest in women's issues. Three years later Lord Denman was appointed Governor General of Australia and she accompanied him to Canberra as First Lady. They spent three years in Australia but the climate did not suit her husband, whose health was frail, and they returned to Britain in June 1914, just before the outbreak of the First World War.

In the early years of the war she was a moving spirit and chair of the Smokes for Wounded Soldiers and Sailors Society but it was her interest in smallholdings that introduced her to the newly formed subcommittee of the Women's Institutes, still under the aegis of the Agricultural Organisation Society, that was to change her life. Already convinced that making use of waste scraps was a responsible and sensible way to save on food imports, she began a scheme to start backyard hen-keeping. She and a friend, Nellie Grant, took an office in Pimlico and commissioned another friend to make designs for a model hen house which could be set up in small gardens, on allotments and in backyards. She started her own poultry farm at Balcombe in Sussex, the house and estate that had been given to her by her father in 1905, and made plans for a cooperative poultry colony of smallholders at Balcombe.

During the First World War she had been appointed to the Board of Agriculture as assistant director of the women's branch of food production. The board had responsibility for the early Women's Institutes and Lady Denman's job was to bolster those as well as look after the Women's Land Army. She believed that women were at least as capable as men at running their own affairs as well as producing food for the nation. She came to the attention of the subcommittee of the Women's Institutes in 1916. Her name was put forward to be approached if Lady Salisbury, the first choice of leader, were to refuse. In the event Lady Salisbury did turn down the offer and Lady Denman accepted. 'By this chance and as second choice the Institute movement had acquired the Chairman whose ability and personality were to colour, enliven, and hall-mark the growing organisation,'[14] wrote Inez Jenkins in her history of the Women's Institute in 1953.

The experience of living in Australia, where she had seen for herself the great difficulties endured by countrywomen, most especially in the suffering caused by too-frequent childbirth, combined with her practical approach to problems and her contacts and experience gathered partly from her standing in society but also in her work for the Women's Federation, made her well qualified for the task of running the WI. She knew that they would need someone who had a good understanding of rural issues, as well as an entrée into the older, established families. A note in the WI files read: 'I can see that if rightly worked, we are going to get the pick of the county ladies in support of our movement. You know that I am naturally democratic, but so much depends on getting that ear of the ladies in the counties . . .'[15] She knew that these contacts would be key to the success or failure of the WI and she was determined that there would be success. She had strong feelings about the difference between life in London and in the country. On one occasion she invited a candidate to come down to Balcombe for an interview. 'How shall I recognise you at the station?' she asked the woman. 'I shall be wearing pink' came back the reply. Lady Denman was perturbed by this and felt certain that the woman would be completely out of place. When the train arrived the candidate disembarked and was greeted warmly by Lady Denman who shook her hand and said: 'What very smart pink tweed.'

Tall, slim but not beautiful, Lady Denman cut an impressive figure. She looked like a leader and was sometimes feared. Her friends explained that her shyness often led to the impression that she was standoffish yet she was always keen for people to challenge her views. One county voluntary organiser met Lady Denman at a meeting in London. She was nervous and told her that she would be no use on the committee as she was so uneducated. Lady Denman retorted that 'education doesn't mean a thing. It is experience that counts. We go down the village streets and see all the nice doorways but we don't know what goes on behind them. This is what you can tell us.'

Robertson Scott summed up her leadership qualities: 'Lady Denman had the invaluable faculty of devotion, and, what is much needed along with devotion, humour and a sense of perspective . . . She had the faculty of order, the knack of detaching herself, and she was fair. She had the leader's ability to hit hard or tap gently until the nail was driven home.'[16]

Lady Denman was admired for her firm belief in democracy as well as her mastery of the rules and public procedure. She never went onto the platform at an annual general meeting without her copy of the *Chairman's Handbook* and she once told a conference that 'It is better for a meeting to make the wrong decision it wishes to make than the right decision which its chairman wishes to make.' She was also admired by those who knew her well for her loyalty to her friends and colleagues, her unfailing sense of justice and 'her gaiety and odd unexpected twists of humour that enlivened the proceedings of every meeting at which she presided'.[17]

She was equally impressive when it came to putting her point of view over to the government. She told the delegates at the 1938 AGM about her experience when the WI launched a campaign for free milk for children:

> I do know that very many WIs did write to their MPs, for I was one of your representatives who met the Nutrition Group of Members of Parliament in the House of Commons. On that occasion more members came than we expected. One MP suggested that he would have been saved a lot of work if he had received one letter from the Country Federation rather than fifty from individual WIs. I suggested in reply that it was always possible for one letter to be overlooked, whereas fifty were bound to receive attention. Judging by the way this remark was greeted by a chorus of 'Hear Hear' and laughter, most of the Members of Parliament entirely agreed that there is strength in a united attack.[18]

Another MP commented that she was worth ten men on a committee.

If Lady Denman brought administrative experience and expertise to the Women's Institute movement, the woman elected to be vice-chairman in early 1918 brought academic excellence, outstanding communication skills and a kind personality. When Miss Hadow's name was put forward Lady Denman said: 'If she will accept, I will scrub her office floor for her!' They were different in almost every way but they complemented each other well and they had a very warm relationship. Inez Jenkins, who was on the National Executive in the 1920s, wrote: 'One can't say too much or expatiate too long on the extraordinary fortune which put the movement in their hands. The very contrast in manner and style and dress, as one observes them side by side on the platform at the Annual Meeting, illustrates the widely divergent gifts and qualities they bring to the movement, and the importance of both.'[19]

Grace Hadow was an Oxford-educated college tutor, social worker and tireless campaigner for adult education, particularly for women. Like Lady Denman, she had a great flair for organisation. Born in 1875, a decade before Lady Denman, she was the youngest child and fourth daughter of a vicar from South Cerney, near Cirencester. She loved the countryside and understood and appreciated rural life. She knew how hard it could be for many of her father's parishioners but she also understood that their lives could be improved through education. This knowledge, combined with her intelligence and curiosity, made her a valuable member of the WI executive and a good second in command to Lady Denman. She was educated in Stroud and Truro but spent a year in Trier in Germany, studying music and languages, before going up to Oxford in 1900 to read English at Somerville College. She overcame an early shyness by 'simply pouring herself into college life and developed skills and interests which remained throughout her life, including her quick wit and charm as a speaker'.[20] After gaining first-class honours she took up a teaching post in Pennsylvania, returning to Oxford in 1906 when she was appointed tutor of English at Lady Margaret Hall. It was during this time at the university that she edited with her brother, Sir William Henry Hadow, *The Oxford Treasury of English Literature* and *Chaucer and His Times*. Amongst her other writings was a translation of Berthold Litzmann's biography of Clara Schumann, again in collaboration with her brother.

This academic work did not take her away from her interest in social problems. All her life she had a very strong sense of public duty. During the First World War, while carrying on with her writing and caring for her widowed mother, she worked with Belgian refugees in Oxford. In 1917 she heard Mrs Watt lecture on Canadian institutes and immediately formed an institute in Cirencester. She actively engaged her local county council, urging them to put on lectures, and proposed setting up several more local institutes in her area. After the death of her mother later that year she resigned her lectureship at Lady Margaret Hall and went to run the department of extramural welfare for the Ministry of Munitions, where her job was to organise women's work in the factories, crèches, housing and lodgings. Miss Hadow was described by an admirer as having not only intelligence and friendliness but fibre. He wrote: 'I have heard that all her aeroplaning has been done in the open air alongside the pilot. It is told of Miss Hadow that when her services were later on accepted at the Ministry of Munitions, her chief said to somebody, "Well, she won't cry!"'[21] She was also an intrepid mountaineer, becoming one of the first British women to climb to the summits of the Matterhorn, the Finsteraarhorn and the Fletschhorn, the latter by an unclimbed route. During the descent she developed pulmonary oedema and nearly died. By this time she was already in her late forties.

After the war she took up a post as secretary at Barnet House in Oxford, which at that time was developing as a centre for social and economic studies and social-work training. She liked the emphasis on self-government and social service and was able to pioneer the development of rural adult education, 'fostering village industries, libraries, lectures, and classes on social and economic questions, music and drama'. So successful was this scheme that it became a prototype for rural communities on a national scale. She explained that it was not her aim to 'take folk dancing and travelling cinemas to villages' but 'to get people to formulate their own demands and tackle problems' and 'to take their own place in local government or voluntary organisations, and future development can be left in their hands'.[22] She believed that the keystone of the WI arch was a combination of personal self-expression and social service. She played a leading part in negotiating with government departments but also helped and encouraged a broader outlook amongst the WI in the villages. She said: 'Members must learn to realize their responsibility toward the community in which they live and, from an interest in their own village and their own county, come to see the connection between their affairs and those of the nation at large.'[23]

With these qualifications and interests, in combination with her outstanding abilities as a speaker – she was remembered after her death as one of the best women speakers in Britain – she was an ideal vice-chairman to Lady Denman. 'Miss Hadow brought the great social force of education to the Women's Institutes to complement Lady Denman's great social force of organisation.'[24] At an annual meeting in the 1920s Miss Hadow had to take the place of Lady Denman, who was unable to attend. Mrs Inez Jenkins, then the general secretary, had lost her voice. Miss Hadow had a sudden attack of nerves before the meeting and turned to Mrs Jenkins on the stage and said 'If you see me getting into a muddle over procedure, you will shout, won't you?', Mrs Jenkins grabbed a pencil and wrote on a piece of paper: 'I can't, I've lost my voice.' She remembered how Miss Hadow was about to get to her feet when she saw what Miss Jenkins had written, and took the pencil out of her hand and added two words 'please hiss'.[25]

Miss Nancy Tennant, who succeeded Miss Hadow as vice-chairman in 1940, summed up the early pioneers of the National Executive:

> Lady Denman had clear judgement and great precision . . . she was immensely respected. She was looked up to enormously and was very valuable . . . Miss Hadow was an academic. She looked like a bean pole, very tall and angular with pince-nez,

> but attractive and funny, and gay and sweet. Lady Denman and Mrs Watt worked in totally different ways, but they were both absolutely necessary, and I think that Miss Hadow was a sort of king pin in between, because she was more approachable than Lady Denman, by a long chalk, but had all the precision of an academic.[26]

As the WI continued to expand so decisions had to be taken about the nature of the way it should be governed and also how to manage the ever-growing number of individual institutes. Lady Denman favoured self-governance and eventual financial independence, which was achieved within a decade.

The middle tier of the WI was born in 1918 with the introduction of the Voluntary County Organisers. Mrs Watt was in charge of the first training school, held at Burgess Hill in Sussex, where twenty-three students spent three weeks. She explained that as well as choosing the ladies for their suitability to carry out this work she also felt 'that the new organisers would require not only training and information but being put absolutely on the right lines. I felt they must learn from others as well as from me, that they must have practical demonstrations as well as lectures, that there must be ample time for discussions and questions and help, and that all of this should be given in an atmosphere impregnated with institute work and ideals.'

This set the trend for the Voluntary County Organisers (VCOs), who, Anne Stamper maintained, 'have done more to sustain and mould the WI than anybody or anything else'.[27] Mrs Watt emphasised the role of the WI, which was to stimulate interest in the agricultural industry and develop cooperative enterprises; to encourage home and local industry; to study home economics and to provide a centre for educational and social intercourse and for all local activities.

But the overriding message to the students was to promote the technical knowledge of agriculture and to give the housewife the information and confidence to work in partnership with her husband. 'The farmer will say that the science of farming is not a woman's job, but it is exactly what she ought to know about. So we want the farmer's wife to attend the Women's Institute; we want her to get into the habit of seeing books and papers on the science of farming, and to link up her own home interests with her husband's business interests.'[28]

This was ambitious and exciting. It was potentially liberating and certainly different from anything most of the countrywomen who came to those first institutes had ever experienced. One member from a village WI told one of Mrs Watt's students: 'I am only a girl in service, but I cannot tell you what help Wivelsfield WI is to me. I learn so much there, and when I am married and have a house of my own I can put it all into practice.'[29]

Mrs Watt returned to Canada in 1919, well pleased with her work in England and Wales. Before she left she had the satisfaction of starting a WI at Sandringham of which Queen Mary became president. In a report on the institutes and their achievements she wrote: 'A great movement has been set going. The results are out of all proportion to the energy expended. I feel quite uplifted. Rural womanhood, touched by the magic wand of opportunity, has blossomed as we knew it would. It has all been womanly, kindly and homely.'[30] There is no doubt that her energy and zeal helped to form the firm roots of the Women's Institutes and set them on the course that they were to follow. On Mrs Watt's departure Mrs Nugent Harris took over the running of the VCO schools and by the end of 1919 VCOs had become a permanent feature, with 89 operating in 26 counties with responsibilities for 1,405 institutes.

Over the next twenty years the WI grew in stature and confidence. It learned how best to lobby ministers and furthered its aim to educate the membership and set up guilds to teach and confer qualifications. Above all, the WI learned how to make democracy work. Lady Denman spoke on the twentieth anniversary of her appointment as chairman of the NFWI in 1937: 'To my mind the greatest of all achievements of the Institutes is that we really have learnt to govern ourselves. We do not believe in dictators; we believe that each member should be responsible for her institute and should have a share in the work.'

By 1939 the Women's Institute was as well organised and prepared as it could be to take on anything that was asked of it. And they knew that they would be asked in the event of a war.

2

THE GATHERING STORM

> How can we who must carry on in our own villages best serve our country.
>
> *Lady Denman*
> *October 1939*

Peggy Sumner joined Dunham Massey Women's Institute in 1938 with her older sister, Marjorie, and her mother. The family came from Hale and Peggy was the family's driver. Her car was one of perhaps six used to get to the meetings in those pre-war days. Dunham Massey had been founded in 1919 by the Countess of Stamford, who called a meeting of the members of the War Working Party which, according to Marjorie Sumner's brief history of the institute, 'had been disbanded the previous autumn leaving a heartfelt gap in village life'. The countess was elected the first president and Dunham Massey became the first institute to be formed in Cheshire. The WI undertook all the regular lectures, activities and business but they were also involved in the local library scheme. 'Books were presented by members and Miss C. Perkins was the first Librarian. After a time it had to be closed – some of the books being thought unsuitable for young girls. Most undesirable.' After censorship it continued but following several complaints, the librarian was given permission to burn any she herself thought unsuitable. In 1936 all books were sent to the hospital.

By the time Peggy joined the WI, Mrs Hardy, who presided over the institute for twenty-six years, was president and the membership had to be capped at 120, which was a comparatively large institute with a varied social strata. Dunham Massey did not have its own hall so they used to meet in the school room, which is now the village hall, converted in the 1960s. The school had been erected in 1759 'for the benefit of the township of Dunham Massey according to the will of Thomas Walton Gent' and the handsome red-brick building still has the fine black and red details over the tall windows. 'We paid our entrance fee of 2d to the treasurer, Mrs Hughes, which was for a piece of cake and a cup of tea. Biscuits were not acceptable in those days. In fact even during the war we tried very hard to keep making home-made cakes for our meetings.'

The room was always laid out in the same way: low school chairs were set in a C shape around the president's table. They were fortunate to have indoor loos at the school; many other institutes had to use outside privies, but they were the children's toilets so were very small, which was not easy for everyone. Mrs Hardy sat at the front of the hall with her secretary and treasurer. Peggy recalled her first impressions:

> Everyone was wearing heavy coats, hats, gloves, good solid thick stockings and well-soled shoes or boots. The predominant colour was black or navy blue and these were top coats that had been bought to last a lifetime. People were still in

mourning from the Great War which had ended twenty years earlier and some of the coats dated from that era. The room itself was always cold. You had to push the emergency bar on the inside of the school room door to get into our room, which brought with it an icy blast of cold air in the winter. There were heating pipes around the room but they could not compete with the draughts, so we all kept our coats, gloves and hats on throughout the meetings.

Mrs Hardy ran a tight ship. Members greeted their neighbour on arrival but there was no talking during the meeting except when someone raised a point or had a question, put through the chair, of course. 'The only time we talked was when the tea came round and the cakes were handed out. If you were at the end of the row you had to hope that a nice-looking cake you had spotted would not have been taken by the time it got to you.' Meantime, Mrs Hardy kept strictly to the timetable, and Mrs Hutchinson, who was on the tea committee and known to everyone as Mrs Hutch, used to hurry everyone to drink up quickly so that they could get on with the washing up. 'We weren't chatty, really, even during the social half-hour which was programmed by the committee. There were readings, plays and sometimes singing. The only chatting we did was during the brief tea-break. I didn't find it intimidating. I just accepted it like you did when you went to church.' And as with church, there was an unspoken hierarchy and plenty of hats.

A year after Peggy had joined the WI, on 3 September 1939, Britain declared war on Germany, who two days earlier had invaded Poland. With this began the most widespread and destructive war in history. By the end some 50 million people, military and civilians, had lost their lives and some of the worst atrocities ever recorded had been perpetrated. When Peggy heard the declaration of war announced by Neville Chamberlain on the wireless she was not surprised. 'We had all been expecting it,' she said.

So had Mrs Miles and her fellow institute members in Shere near Guildford. In August 1939 Constance Miles, the daughter of Sir William Robertson Nicoll, founder of the *British Weekly*, decided to write a journal for her son as a record of her wartime experiences. She was married to Major Elyston Miles, who had retired, and they lived in a large house in Surrey. Mrs Miles was fifty-seven at this point and wrote that she felt 'rather at a loss and useless in this one' having worked through the First World War. The journal takes the form of a diary with long excerpts copied out from newspapers and books that she was reading, providing a rich backdrop to the war and great detail for her son. Unlike the diaries of Edith Jones, these journals were written with a view to being read by others, and in 1947 she lodged a set at the Imperial War Museum in the hope that they might be of interest in the future.

Her early entries give a sense of the panic felt by people at the outbreak of war. Her fear was one expressed by many: 'doubtless the refugees and the air raids will be the worst home feature of this next war' she wrote on 24 August 1939. She spent a week busily packing up clothes, precious china and other treasures into boxes and storing them. She worried about who would come to the house, and fretted over how much should be packed away. And in all this activity and concern there was the constant theme of the horrible news coming from Poland.

On the evening on 3 September she wrote: 'The Prime Minister, in the most delightfully English voice, told us just after 11 that we were at war. It seems incredible! As I write, the sad day has gone by. The evening sun is glowing on the garden and Edie's border shows her African and French marigolds still beautifully fresh and golden. The King spoke on the radio. Curiously slow and sad and with much lack of vitality. Better far that the Queen had spoken.'

As the country was numbed by the fear of aerial bombardment and possible gas attacks on civilians, so the WI was briefly paralysed as it tried to decide what its role should be. Throughout the 1920s and 30s it had been actively promoting the League of Nations. An NFWI representative was appointed to the women's committee of the union and within a few short years some 600 institutes, over 10 per cent of the total number, had become 'study associates' of the League of Nations. In 1929 the annual meeting had passed a resolution that the movement consider how best to further the cause of world peace and in 1934 they passed the following resolution:

> We desire to affirm our faith in the League of Nations Union and to urge His Majesty's Government to do their utmost to secure a real measure of world disarmament; and further, we authorise co-operation where advisory between the NFWI and other organisations with a view to every possible effort being made to attain this end. Further, we recommend that all Women's Institutes should endeavour during the next year to introduce into their programme something that would interest their members in the activities and outlook of other nations.[1]

Their pacifist stand would cause the National Federation a great deal of worry in the early weeks of the war. How should the WI respond?

Miss Hadow, with her usual clear thinking, wrote in the WI's monthly magazine, *Home & Country*:

> It is for every individual to decide for herself how best she can serve her country in peace or war, but the fact that Institutes were called into existence in 1915 because such an organization was needed and that it was a government department which fostered their growth at such a time, should make all of us consider whether possibly this work in our own villages and our own county, work for which we have been specially trained may not be that for which we are best fitted and in which we can be of most use . . . Here is a great organization ready to be used, but it will cease to be an organization if all its most efficient members are drained away . . . No one would wish to restrain people from volunteering for National Service, but National Service may lie in simple things, and to help to keep up morale and to prevent life in an emergency from becoming wholly disorganized is in itself work of no mean value.[2]

She was concerned about membership numbers declining and indeed she was right to do so. Membership fell by nearly 40,000 between 1939 and 1943 at the height of mobilisation. In the early months of the war younger women left the WI to sign up for the forces or were drafted into war work. Others felt that they had an obligation to take on a more active role and joined the Women's Voluntary Service and this clashed with the WI's principles. But there were a number, such as Ruth Toosey of Barrow near Chester, who felt that in a time of war there was no need for such sensitivities and continued to be members of their local WI as well as the WVS.

The October edition of *Home & Country* was almost entirely devoted to the outbreak of hostilities. The editor, Miss Margaret Jackson, asked for forbearance as the issue was late and cut down in size owing to 'difficulties', a word which became the byword for the war in many institute minute books. 'We had hoped, every one of us, that war would be averted. But it is with us, and we must each do what we can to maintain that spirit of sanity, friendliness, and corporate activity which has been the distinguishing mark of Women's Institutes since their foundation, now twenty-two years ago, in an earlier time of stress and common danger.'

Members of the WI in Mobberley, Cheshire, were as anxious as anyone else. Gertrude Wright, in her short history of the institute, *The First Thirty Years*, wrote: 'I remember well the Committee Meeting in September [1939] – the sense of fear, the fear of the unknown future – but it was decided that if possible the monthly meetings be held as usual and that the officers carry out the work if it was impossible to hold a Committee Meeting.' By the end of October they could record with satisfaction that they had helped evacuee mothers and children, issuing an open invitation to the women to join their meetings; they had sent a large parcel of clothing to the City League of Help and knitted 144 garments for the forces. They had also decided to reform their choir and to keep up 'the same loyal spirit as thousands of other Institute members in all parts of the British Empire'. The following year their hall was requisitioned by the government so they had to hold their meetings in a large upstairs room at the Bull's Head.

After the initial days of fear and anxiety, evacuation, relocation, mobilisation and confusion, Britain settled down to wait and see what would happen. While the government had been advised and indeed believed that Hitler's Luftwaffe would drop an enormous tonnage of bombs on cities and other targets within hours of the declaration of war, quite the opposite happened. There followed almost nine months of what became known as the Phoney War. The first deployment of troops to the continent was completed by mid-October, at which point the British Expeditionary Force comprised 158,000 men. Six months later it had doubled in size to 316,000. The biggest worry for the first batch of men was not fighting Germans but fighting the cold and boredom. The winter of 1939/40 was the coldest in forty-five years. Ruth Toosey's brother-in-law, Major Philip Toosey, had been sent to Lille with his medium artillery regiment. He wrote later: 'The winter was bitterly cold. The men lived in barns and I kept them busy by digging pits for the guns and building command posts on what was an extension of the Maginot Line. It was a pretty painful experience; before this we had always had permanent cook houses at camp and I well remember the many cooking problems and getting used to the atmosphere of living in the field.' That Christmas his men received parcels sent not only from families but also from the Red Cross. These contained comforts such as gloves, socks, woollen helmets and scarves, which were very welcome. The WI had been busy knitting.

Mass Observation, that brilliant window on everyday life, presented the most valuable of vignettes in its myriad reports, diaries, questionnaires and observations during the early years of the war. Set up in 1937 by three young men, anthropologist Tom Harrisson, poet and journalist Charles Madge, and film-maker Humphrey Jennings, its aim was to document and record everyday life in Britain through the eyes of ordinary people. They recruited some 500 people, who were untrained, to keep diaries and volunteers to work on questionnaires. The initial impetus was to record the public's reaction to the abdication of Edward VIII but in August 1939 they asked the public to send them a day-to-day account of their lives in the form of a diary. They had in place observers who would continue to record their lives during this turbulent time. The value of these observations for historians is inestimable but even at the time Mass Observation's research through questionnaires influenced government thinking. Famously, it was publicly critical of the Ministry of Information's posters, including 'Keep Calm and Carry On', forcing a change of attitude and the production of more appropriate posters.

Muriel Green, who wrote a diary for Mass Observation from August 1939, was the daughter of a garage and village shop owner in Norfolk. By Christmas she had become resigned to living in wartime, though nothing much had happened. Then on 27 December she and her sister heard an aeroplane overhead: 'we both said at once, "I'm sure that's a Nasty." But we both stood and watched, making no attempt to take any precautions. About 5 mins later we heard more aeroplanes and Jenny rushed out and said she saw 3 Spitfires chasing over after the 1st plane.' Muriel was eating her lunch, the dog was barking and jumping around and Mrs Green said she was going to go outside and see what was going on: 'She said we might as well be killed while we were as excited as anytime.'

Other women were less excited by the prospect of war. Mrs Street from Gravesend in Kent wrote: 'I hate the blackout. It makes me feel uneasy. Everything is so dark and I can't do anything for fretting for what might happen in the night.' Stella Schofield, a full-time member of Mass Observation's staff in 1939, wrote a report in January 1940 based on interviews she had carried out with women's organisations in late 1939, in particular looking at the effect of the war on their membership. Her conclusions point to a two-fold reaction: the first that the impact of this war as against the last war was that women were affected from the outset. Women were fatalistic about the inevitability of war, even though by and large they opposed it.

> Inside their organisations women are more consciously critical, more questioningly aware of the war processes. They find themselves once more precipitated into world war by a man-monopolised society. It would be idle to speculate whether or not the present situation could have been avoided had women held executive government positions – there are, of course, women who believe this – but it is very much to the point to realise that, however unorganised the mass of women may be today, they were far less organised in the last war.[3]

The second observation she made was that women accepted there would be change and that they would have to deal with it. Men had gone or were liable to go away to fight or defend; children had been evacuated or had arrived as evacuees; life had been disrupted from the day war was declared by blackout and air-raid warnings. Meeting huts and buildings had been taken over and the rhythm of life thoroughly interrupted and disrupted for almost every woman.

While some women were understandably afraid, others, like Mrs Hurdle in Betchworth in Surrey, took action. She and her husband ran the busy village post office, which had the mail-sorting office and the telephone exchange within the building as well as the general stores. Mrs Hurdle was a loyal committee member of Betchworth WI and when she heard a rumour that the hall where they held their monthly meetings might be requisitioned she became very concerned about the survival of the WI's lovely china, which was kept in a corner cupboard in the main hall. Mrs Hurdle's daughter, Jean Bristow, told the story:

> It was very pretty blue and white china that had been donated by a member. My mother was a very positive character and,

> no doubt after consulting Madam President, came rapidly to the conclusion that, whatever was about to happen in regard to the hall, the china must be rescued promptly and put into much safer keeping for the duration. You will have guessed that Mother was not in the mood to be argued with. Darkness had already fallen and the china had to be rescued with all haste. There was no petrol and in the dark impossible to harness Peter the pony to the trap. The matter was urgent. Time was of the essence. My determined mother hit upon the idea of persuading Father to get between the shafts of the trap (I'll bet he did as he was told!) and set out.

Other members and friends had been urged to come along to help and when Mr Hurdle struggled to negotiate a steep, sharp bend called Parr's Corner there were plenty of hands to help push the trap uphill towards the hall. They reached it safely, though with a great deal of huffing and puffing. The precious china was duly packed up and loaded for the return trip. This was altogether a more tricky journey as the trap was heavier and the road ran downhill so the main danger was of the cart racing out of control round the bend at Parr's Corner. However, the bend was successfully negotiated and the china was saved. In the event the hall was not taken over but Jean Bristow found out sixty years later that the china had survived the war and been returned to the corner cupboard in the hall afterwards and was still in use.

Meanwhile, back in London, the National Executive Committee was struggling with what the WI could and could not do in wartime. Not only had the WI taken a strong anti-war stand but enshrined in the constitution was the principle of non-sectarianism; it was out of respect for the beliefs of pacifist Quaker members that the executive decided to impose restrictions upon the participation of WIs in war work. In practice it meant that the WI could not support or fund any activity that might be construed as assisting the war effort. At the same time it was obvious that women would want to be involved in helping their country and Lady Denman suggested that there were other, practical ways in which they could help. 'WIs can give and are giving the most valuable help with regard to plans for the reception of city children in the villages. It is also obvious that if the great disaster of war should overtake us, the authorities will look to the WIs to give their help in increasing food production and in looking after members of the WLA in addition to caring for evacuated town dwellers.'

Lady Denman knew that the war represented one of the biggest challenges to the Women's Institutes to date. They had to find a role and yet be in a position to continue with their determined crusade to improve rural life, as they had been doing for the last two decades. She sent a message to all institutes in October 1939, urging women to do their bit but not to let go of the spirit at the heart of the institutes:

> Germany is said to count on breaking our nerve. Every person who spreads an atmosphere of cheerfulness and quiet resolution at this time is helping to win the war. We are proud of the cause for which Britain is fighting, and those of us who are not called upon to endure the hardship of actual fighting, will be glad to feel that we have comforts to go without, difficulties to contend with in daily life, and that by meeting such troubles cheerfully and helping our neighbours to do so, we are taking our small share in winning the victory which we believe will come, but which will come only if the whole nation is ready to make willing sacrifice.[4]

Most institutes agreed that keeping going was important and they went to great efforts to hold their meetings, often in temporary accommodation and on new days and at new times, all of which had to be discussed and agreed not only between the membership but also the village police, ARPs and anyone else who had a call on communal premises. As this was being organised in the countryside, Lady Denman was in touch with the government. She had received a letter from the War Office, written to all voluntary bodies on 1 September 1939, explaining that, in the event of war, a Ministry of Information would be set up with the remit to distribute information, instructions, appeals and advice.

Lady Denman replied on 5 September 1939:

> The Women's Institutes of England and Wales will I know be glad to cooperate with the Ministry of Information. There are WIs in 5600 villages, a network which covers the greater part of the rural areas and through them in their journal *Home & Country* the Ministry could disseminate information throughout the country areas . . . I am sure you will agree that using a Society with this large number of branches it is important to make arrangements to ensure that the greatest possible use is made of the organisation.[5]

The person tasked with the responsibility of communicating government messages within the WI was the general secretary, Miss Farrer. The fourth general secretary to take up this paid post, the chief executive of the NFWI, she was the longest-serving (1929–59). She succeeded Inez Jenkins, who moved to help Lady Denman to run the Women's Land Army. The Hon. Miss Farrer, later Dame Frances, was born in 1895, the daughter of a senior civil servant, the second Lord Farrer. She was educated at St Andrew's School, Scotland and at Newnham College, Cambridge, where she graduated in 1917 with a degree in economics. During the last two years of the Great War she worked for the Forestry Commission and was introduced to the women's movements. In the 1920s she travelled to India and returned via Baghdad, after which she renewed her ties with her WI and joined several other committees including the Colonial Social Welfare Committee, the National Savings Committee, the Women's Group on Public Welfare and the Women's Committee of the Economic Information Unit.

Miss Farrer brought to her role of general secretary a rigour and efficiency that earned her the respect of her colleagues and civil servants alike. She had a brisk style and a great sense of humour. She made a point of speaking to ministers on the telephone before breakfast. That way, she explained, she could be sure to reach them and get their attention. Getting government ministers' attention was something that the WI excelled at and Miss Farrer was exceptionally good. Making use of her excellent family connections, she was able to help the National Executive as it became increasingly active in lobbying successive governments. She was an early founder member of her local WI in Abinger, near Dorking, set up in 1920. She was also a major shareholder in the Leigh Hill Musical Competition, becoming the first chairman and president. Through her energies other local gentry became shareholders and Dorking Halls was built as a venue to hold the music festival. The buildings were opened in 1931 and Ralph Vaughan Williams was able to realise his dream of being able to stage Bach's *St Matthew Passion*. Dorking Halls was commandeered by the Meat Marketing Board and the Army in 1939. (Sadly they were in such poor condition after the war that they could not be restored to their former glory.) In August 1939 Miss Farrer had a great deal on her mind, apart from Dorking Halls, as she cut short her summer holiday to return to the office and deal with the outbreak of war. On 25 August she wrote to Lady Denman:

> I came back on Thursday a little earlier than I had planned in case there were any emergency things to do. We have only a skeleton holiday staff here but luckily I found no urgent letters awaiting me. I have offered help to the LCC and the WVS but at present they can manage with their own staff. I could get no reply from the WLA so conclude there is no urgent work to be done there.
>
> I have had a most splendid holiday and feel lucky to have almost finished it before the crisis. Our 'Dug Out' and ARP preparations are all made and everyone here seems quite calm. I expect you are busy preparing for an inundation of children.[6]

As there were no emergency calls on the WI that week, Miss Farrer drew up a letter to send to county chairmen which they then circulated in turn to their institute presidents. It was an efficient way of getting information shared at village level. She wrote:

> It seems clear that the NFWI will be of increasing service to the nation as war goes on. For a time, during the first period of dislocation, it may be necessary to drop a meeting. Everyone will be busy making major adjustments, dealing with evacuees, and settling down to conditions. Very soon, however, in addition to ordinary activities there will be a whole field of new work to cover, and the sooner this is planned the better.

The letter went on to suggest that great efforts should be made to maintain WI meetings in the villages and 'to welcome thereat the evacuated mothers'. She urged members to take the women and children into their bosom. 'The social needs of mothers, teachers and children will make calls on the resourcefulness and ingenuity of every member. It is also hoped that members of the Land Army working in the neighbourhood will be given a warm welcome.'

The WI archives have an almost complete set of the letters sent out by the county chairwomen or county secretaries to the presidents as a result of Miss Farrer's communication. These reflect the differing issues that were raised in each county as a result of the outbreak of war. Cumberland, for example, was much more concerned with food production than Berkshire, which was inundated with evacuees. Northumberland had many mining villages in the south of its enormous county and they knew they would be targeted in aerial attacks, which they later were. Their focus was to concentrate on assisting their local hospitals.

Mrs Skimming, chairman of Buckinghamshire Federation, was heartened by the news that the government had written to the National Federation asking institutes to maintain as active a programme as possible saying: 'We attach great importance to the normal continuation of all types of classes and lectures, however small the group. This recognition by the government of the important work done by even the smallest institutes should be a great incentive and encouragement to us to carry on with renewed vigour.'

The letter she wrote to her presidents listed advice on any number of subjects, from salvage for hospitals to knitting patterns, recipes, speakers, blood transfusion services, books and library facilities, music, gardening, harvesting, keeping livestock and what to do with children with verminous heads. She was able to report that Beaconsfield, Bledlow Ridge, Chalfont St

Peter, The Lee and Taplow had started working parties for the Red Cross while other institutes, such as Haddenham and Iver, had offered a variety of entertainments and diversions for evacuee mothers with young children and unaccompanied schoolchildren. West Wycombe had opened its church hall on Sundays so that parents visiting from London could see their children there rather than in the child's billet, so as not to cause difficulties between parents and hosts. Stokenchurch WI was farsighted in giving some of the evacuee boys spades and forks and was delighted to report that they 'are busy cultivating a piece of spare ground with terrific keenness'.

County newsletters and *Home & Country* were bursting with advice for increasing cultivation in the garden. Cumberland's agricultural committee offered advice about planting spring cabbages '<u>now</u> in case there is a shortage' while members were urged to listen in to the radio programme on 'Vegetable Crops in War-Time'. While most institutes were advised by their county secretaries to dig up every available piece of land, one or two advised against complete destruction of their flower beds. 'Now that the country is at war it is up to all WI members to do their utmost to produce from their gardens and allotments as much of the perishable foodstuffs as possible. Do not, however, in the first rush of energy, tear up every flower border and destroy plants. Many beds, such as narrow front gardens, are not suitable for vegetables, and we shall always need flowers to bring relief from the nervous strain and stress of war-time life,'[7] wrote one chairman.

A number of institutes were thrown into bewilderment in the first few weeks of the war. The outbreak of hostilities coincided with their planning meetings for the winter and spring programmes but with halls commandeered, travel facilities reduced and many members taken up with other duties there was a sense of despondency about how realistic it was to keep going, despite national and county encouragement. Some wondered whether or not they should shut down for the duration of the war and a few even went as far as informing headquarters than they planned to do just that. The confusion soon passed and, as the editor of *Home & Country* wrote proudly in her November editorial: 'The whole spirit of the Institute movement, which was born in times of difficulty, is opposed to despondency.' She encouraged members to continue to practise handicrafts, attend meetings and not lose sight of the public questions they had been so forcefully campaigning about in the 1930s:

> . . . because we are at war, our housing, our water supply, our refuse disposal, our rural education, have not suddenly become perfect. Their flaws, indeed, are increasingly apparent owing to the sudden arrival in the country districts of thousands of extra people. Above all, we need more than ever to try to understand the close dependence of the nations of the world one on another; we must not neglect our study of international affairs.[8]

At institute level the first concern was how and where to hold monthly meetings. In Oxfordshire, East and West Hendred's minute books recorded a typical experience. On 19 September 1939 they met at 3 p.m. at the Parish Room to discuss the future plans of the WI. 'It was decided to suspend all meetings at present as the women of the village were taking up other social work, and some had the care of evacuated children.' At that meeting the president's resignation was tendered and accepted with regret. Two months later they decided to resume and the monthly meeting was held, unusually for wartime, at 6.15 p.m. in the Parish Room. There was no mention of the war but they dealt with the voting in of 1940's committee and the lecture programme.

In January they were still meeting at 6.15 p.m. but it was causing problems for Miss Hope, their cookery demonstrator, as she could not get to the village owing to the blackout, lack of trains and buses and it was too far for her to cycle. Various members offered to have her to stay overnight and in February she 'gave a demonstration of how to cook with economy during these hard times'.[9] It was not until November 1940 that East and West Hendred decided to cave in and hold their monthly meetings in the afternoons rather than the evenings and the reason appeared to be so that they could invite evacuees. This however resulted in a drop in numbers as many members were unable to attend in the afternoons and there was, as they noted ruefully at the end of that year, a drop in membership overall. Juggling with the many demands placed on them both within the WI and outside was evidently difficult. One way to make life easier for themselves was to rely less on outside speakers and more on home-grown talent. Institutes were advised to see what their own membership could supply in terms of lectures and to make use of wartime visitors, such as evacuated mothers, local civil servants and even members of the military who might be posted nearby.

Alphington WI members in Devon were much more determined than those ladies in East and West Hendred. On 20 September they announced a 'unanimous vote to keep going and form a working party to make garments for the Red Cross'. The following month was their 20th birthday, which they celebrated by knitting squares to be made up into blankets for evacuees. Their energy is apparent from their minute books: they invested in war savings certificates, they grew onions and outdoor tomatoes and made jam in the first few months of the war but in February 1940 their hall was commandeered by the Devon Education Authority and meetings were suspended. Fortunately they found another room to use for meetings and in March began again with renewed energy and continued for the rest of the war. On the evening of the fall of France the speaker, Miss Veitch, 'urged us not to give up the growing of flowers entirely during the war and to plan for the years ahead when we need not grow only carrots, onions and swedes'.

Herefordshire, being a large county with villages well spread out, was concerned primarily with the problem of getting speakers to monthly meetings. The Executive Committee recognised this was going to pose a major difficulty so they organised a lending library of popular lectures which could be borrowed from the county office and read out at meetings at a charge of 6d (£1.15 today), adding that the member selected as reader 'should study the lecture beforehand'.

Interestingly, Herefordshire was the only county to suggest in this first communication that the war might last for several years, and as a result their chairman, the Hon. Mrs Dunne, took a rather more measured view of gardening, suggesting that preparation of the ground was at least as important as planting. She also foresaw the probability of organised fruit canning and preservation being required for 1940 and so suggested that members of individual institutes should register an interest and ensure they were members of the Produce Guild.

The Herefordshire County Agricultural Organiser was on hand to advise institutes or members about preparing derelict land or neglected corners of gardens for potato growing. He advised members to buy day-old chicks in February and March, since they could happily survive on scraps of food and provide eggs in the future. He pointed out that it is only of 'comparatively late years that country people have become so dependent on shops for their food, and that in these ways our Mothers could teach us much'. This was a theme that was often revived during the war, both in propaganda and in advice dispensed at a local level in pamphlets and newsletters.

Mrs Dunne signed off her letter to her eighty-five presidents: 'We must remember that "The main purpose of WIs is to improve and develop conditions in rural life." To do this we must not neglect the education and social side of our movement. The war threatens civilisation, and we must do our best through the stress and turmoil to preserve all that is good and beautiful and true.'

Where halls were requisitioned it was necessary to find somewhere else to meet. Washington Station WI in Northumberland had their meeting place in the Glebe Welfare Hall commandeered for military purposes, so they moved first to Biddick Chapel, then to the Wesleyan School Room and later to the Youth Club. The inconvenience of constant moves meant that nothing could be stored in the meeting hall, so that china, books and other equipment had to be packed up and carted to the next hall by hand. There was a sigh of relief in February 1946 when they could return to the Glebe Welfare Hall. Barthomley Women's Institute in Cheshire lost the use of the hall as a meeting place but Mrs Brandon stepped in with an offer for the committee to use the kitchen in her house, the Cottage. This invitation was extended to the whole membership and in October 1939 they held their first meeting at 2 p.m., at which they appointed a tea-treasurer who would be responsible for looking after the 2lb of tea and a tin of biscuits which they agreed should form a basis for their 'larder cupboard'. By November things had picked up and they held their annual general meeting at the Cottage at which they resolved to arrange their 1940 programme month by month but, more importantly, to forgo their usual Christmas party and instead give a party for the local children and the evacuee children, of which there were a large number in the village.

Arnside Institute in Cumbria agreed a satisfactory deal with the local ARP. Formed in 1919, they were one of the oldest institutes in the county. In 1928 they had purchased land in the village and erected their own hall as a meeting place. The hall was initially commandeered at the outbreak of the war and the minute book records that the WI Badminton Club and WI Library (both held in the hall) had ceased to function 'due to the taking over of our Hall by the Westmorland County Council for A.R.P., Red Cross and other National Work, but we do appreciate their kindness in allowing us to use a small part of the Hall for our monthly meetings'. The hall was divided lengthways down the middle, the left-hand side being used for WI meetings while the right-hand side was used for all other activities. The 'partition' was made up of camouflage nets, waiting to be garnished, suspended from large hooks that were still screwed into the beams in 2011.

Some institutes, such as Bradfield in Berkshire, simply got on with business as usual, whilst acknowledging the war was going to make life more difficult for them and add to their workload. They made two concessions to the war. First, they gave over their September meetings to blackberry picking and secondly, from 1941 they had ten-minute sessions at each meeting set aside for 'kitchen front questions'. This was a popular slot, especially when increasing restrictions limited what was obtainable on their ration cards and points.

They met in Miss Connop's room, which was a corrugated construction donated by the daughter of a local landowner at the beginning of the twentieth century. Ann Tetlow, daughter of an active WI member, Mrs Sims, explained:

> It was a shack, really, with a tortoise stove and a corrugated tin roof and walls lined with pitch pine inside. The loo was an earth closet with no light. If you wanted to use the loo in the dark you had to go across the road and borrow a torch from Mr Trotman. There was another hall in the village called Johnson's hall, which had a wonderfully sprung floor which people loved to dance on. That was a superior building, not least because it had an indoor ladies, though the men still had to go outside to use their facilities.

In the first few weeks of the war the WI raised money for blackout material to cover the windows of the Connop room but in 1940 it was requisitioned by the Home Guard so that the WI had to find somewhere else to hold their meetings. And they had to leave their blackout material behind, which must have been an irritation since they had paid for it out of their own funds.

At the first meeting after the outbreak of hostilities, Bradfield's secretary, Miriam Ward, was preoccupied taking minutes on the election of a new president. On 21 September Mrs Hyde Baker, the outgoing president, proposed a new member, Mrs Howlett. By the end of the meeting an election had taken place and the new member had been voted in as the new president, in what must represent one of the fastest routes to power. The following month Mrs Ward noted that the election was neither in order nor valid since it had not been a general meeting, so Mrs Howlett was demoted to acting president until their November general meeting. However, after this official glitch, she remained in office for twenty years.

Mrs Ward was unusual as a minute-taker in that she allowed herself interjections and opinions, which throw a light onto village life in a way that other institute minute books do not.

Ann Tetlow offered additional colour by talking about her childhood memories of the village during the war. Unlike Mrs Ward, Ann's mother, Mrs Sims, had not been born in Berkshire. Her father's job had taken him all over the country and Bradfield was her first settled home. Her husband was from London and wrote novels. They chose Bradfield when they got married in 1934 because it was convenient for bus and rail services. As their family grew, Mr Sims got a job teaching at Cheam School, a prep school, in Headley in order to support his family, and used his writing skills in providing plays for the boys to perform. These were subsequently published. Meanwhile, Mrs Sims threw herself into village life. After Ann was born Mrs Sims would push the pram around the village and meet Mrs Ward, also with a pram, hers containing a baby girl named Dorcas. Ann and Dorcas grew up to become lifelong friends and their lives have woven in and out of each other's family narratives over the course of seven decades. Both girls have vivid memories of the ladies who made up the core of the Bradfield WI. In that delicious way that childhood memories are defined, many of their recollections of individual women are of characteristics such as shape, size or unusual use of words. The picture that emerges is one of a diverse group of women, some quiet, some outspoken, but all passionately involved in village life and energetic in their WI.

Dorcas's grandmother had been the founding president of Bradfield's institute in February 1920 and her mother had been the secretary, so that their association with the Women's Institute stretched back nearly twenty years before the Second World War. Dorcas remembered the committee meetings that used to take place at Copyhold Farm prior to the main WI monthly meeting.

> It was always in our sitting room which was a small room and quite a squash with twelve chairs, including my father's large armchair. And his desk was in the room too. It used to be shut as firmly as possible for the meeting so that there was enough space for everyone to squeeze in. My mother always wrote using an inkwell. She never took to using a fountain pen though later she liked to use biros. But my memory is of the inkwell standing on the little pie-crust-edged occasional table between my mother and Mrs Howlett.

There was an open log fire and a large, brown wood and Bakelite radio on a shelf behind Mrs Ward. 'My sister and I used to go to these meetings because the sitting room was the only warm room in the house. Mrs Howlett used to sit next to my mother. She did not know much about the business of the WI so my mother would guide her on those matters,' Dorcas explained. Mrs Ward was the secretary minute-taker throughout the war years and Dorcas said that despite her positive comments and observations she did sometimes get frustrated with the women on the committee, especially those who would sit through meeting after meeting without saying a word.

Ruth Toosey, in the village of Barrow, Cheshire, was also the secretary of her WI during the war. Her daughter, Caroline Dickinson, remembered that meetings took place in the evenings throughout the war as the farmers' wives would have found it impossible to get to afternoon meetings. Mrs Toosey would spend the following evening writing up the minutes. Caroline has a strong memory of her mother 'sitting at her desk, fountain pen in one hand, cigarette in the other, huffing and puffing over the minutes. Sometimes she would tell us stories about what had gone on at meetings and often these were very funny. One evening she came back giggling about an almost stand-up fight between two ladies over washing woollen items. She said it had been like a Punch and Judy show.'

For Caroline and her brother, John, living at the White House in the village, the war dominated their childhoods. Life in Barrow was similar to that of many other rural villages at the time. It lay some five miles from Chester, at the head of the Wirral. Liverpool was a little over twenty miles away and both of Caroline's grandmothers lived there so she grew up with memories of both peaceful Barrow and the bombed-out city.

The centre of the village had focused around the millhouse, which stopped working as a mill just before the war, but Caroline could remember the delicious smells that came from it. The majority of the villagers worked on the farms around Barrow but there were a number of larger houses owned by families with business interests elsewhere. These women were leading lights in the WI. Mrs Norman's family owned the department store Owen Owens in Liverpool and Mrs Synge, who was president, and Mrs Gamon, who was also on the committee, lived in two of the other large houses in the centre of the village.

Tiny though it was, Barrow had a post office, a shop and a pub. The shop was owed by Ada Hitchen, who was known by everyone as Ha'penny Ada as she put a halfpenny onto the price of everything she sold. The shop was an old-fashioned little store with big blue bags of sugar in the storeroom and jars of sweets on shelves for the children who would spend a long time trying to decide what to spend their 3d pocket money on. The pub was off limits. Caroline was told firmly by her mother that she and her brother were never to be seen in the pub, even when they were old enough to go into one. It was not proper, she said, to be seen going into your own village pub. 'My mother wasn't prudish about things, in saying this she simply reflected the era. The Red Lion was a spit and sawdust type of pub.' Although not far from Chester, Barrow had a butcher and a baker who came weekly in their vans. The baker, Mr Meakin, resorted to a bicycle during the war but he still made his rounds. Milk came from the farms in cans to individual households in the village so that even during the war they had plenty of milk and butter. 'I remember that when we went to see my grandmother we always took her some butter because that was rationed and difficult to come by in the city.' Coke and coal were delivered by horse and cart, although less frequently during the war than before it. The only warm rooms in the White House were the kitchen, which had a range, and the bathroom, which was heated by the hot water cylinder. During the winter the children used to dress in bed or make a dash for the bathroom.

When war broke out Ruth Toosey's sister came to stay at the White House. She lived in Camberley and her husband thought she would be safer in Cheshire, so she spent several years living in Barrow. They worked the vegetable patch together and grew cabbages and leeks, as well as apples and raspberries. The raspberry canes were magnificent and yielded wonderful fruit in the summer. Mrs Toosey's children and two boy cousins were quite convinced that if Hitler were to invade Britain he would certainly come to Barrow and steal their raspberries. So they dug Hitler traps to catch him. Caroline remembered: 'They kept us busy for hours. First we dug holes in the ground and then we covered them with sticks, leaves and finally a layer of soil. Fortunately Hitler did not come to Barrow but unfortunately we succeeded in trapping our mothers, which was not the plan.'

Like so many other WI members, Mrs Toosey took on a number of extra voluntary duties. She joined the WVS and was a registered ambulance driver, with an ID card to prove it, despite the fact that the WVS and the WI represented military was not threatened by bombs and life was able to carry on more or less as normal, albeit with additional responsibilities such as evacuees, the family staying and paying guests, constant WI drives for knitting wool, fundraising for troops and collections for the local hospitals. Yet there is in her diary a rumbling sense of the menace of the war, which occasionally she comments on. 'Bombs heard in distance', she wrote in March 1941. 'Planes overhead tonight', she wrote three days later. Then 'bombs fell at Chelmick [7 miles away] on Monday 7th. White washed the pantry.'

3

THE PIPER'S CALL

> The social needs of mother, teachers and children will make calls on the resourcefulness and ingenuity of every member.
>
> *Miss Farrer, 1939*

The mass evacuation of people from the cities to the countryside is, after the Blitz, probably the single most famous event in the lives of the civilians living in Britain during the Second World War. Today the shorthand for evacuation is the image of a tearful child clutching a suitcase and wearing a luggage label waiting with crowds of others for a train at a station. Yet that is far from the whole story. In addition to women, children, the disabled, the elderly and other groups considered vulnerable by the government, went businesses, hospitals, government departments and private firms. James Roffey, an eight-year-old boy who was evacuated to Pulborough in West Sussex, remembered that the Max Factor cosmetic company moved one of their factories to West Sussex. 'At Pulborough they took over a large house called Templemead to use as a packing factory. The young women who worked there . . . found the village too quiet for their liking and soon began to drift back to London.' Great Ormond Street Hospital was evacuated to Tadworth Court, their country branch in Surrey, and other temporary locations outside London; the National Gallery moved its collections to a quarry in North Wales; the Bank of England moved to Whitchurch near Overton in Hampshire and senior Post Office staff were relocated to Harrogate. Hundreds of military camps, anti-aircraft posts, airfields, depots and secret training units were set up throughout the country, often on the outskirts of small villages or hamlets, so that the population of some areas of the countryside almost doubled, putting pressure on everything from transport, policing and schools to local services, shops and the water and sanitation systems, where they existed. Rural Britain was in a state of almost permanent flux. The Post Office recorded over 38 million changes of address during the war. That is nearly one move per head of population.

Netherbury in Dorset was an example of how a small village was overrun with visitors during the early months. Their WI war record illustrates what happened:

> The first to arrive in September 1939 was a Roman Catholic School from Acton, which was evacuated to Slape House: the sisters living in the house, the Priest being billeted at the Inn, and the children in various homes. In September too, came a Company of the Lancashire Regiment, to occupy the village hall, and the Women's Institute ran a canteen in the old New Inn premises for the soldiers. These were followed by the Sussex Regiment. In February 1940 a further batch of mothers and children came from Southampton. On this occasion there was trouble, as the mothers sounded as though they would rather have stayed to be bombed in Southampton, than be

> buried alive in Netherbury. A vivid recollection is of one mother who refused to get out of the bus or to be parted from her cat which she had in a wooden box.[1]

By the middle of 1940 the village had almost twice the number of inhabitants as it had the previous year. The WI was affected by this mass movement of people on two levels: as an organisation and individually. Institutes played an important role in entertaining, catering for and helping out with any number of military camps and units, holding mending parties, dances and money-raising events for the forces. However, it was their work with the evacuees that affected the WI most deeply. In the first days and weeks they were wholly occupied with caring for children who ranged from the homesick five- or six-year-old to the truculent twelve- or thirteen-year-old. For some women this caring role lasted for the duration of the war and for many this developed on both sides into warm and loving relationships. However, at the outset everything was new and strange for both sides. Mrs Miles in Surrey was not sure about evacuation. She recorded her surprise at 'the attitude [to the news of evacuation] of my charwoman which was pure joy. "I'm having 2 girls, poor kiddies. Could I rest when I have a spare room and I thought of them wanting a shelter?"' Mrs Miles herself was more circumspect about the coming influx and was annoyed by the BBC's announcements: 'The evacuation notices are most inappropriately given out by BBC young men, who little know what despair enters the hearts of various women expecting the strangers and afraid to have them. Men just haven't the foggiest.'[2]

At the beginning of September 1939 over 1.5 million mothers and babies, unaccompanied schoolchildren, disabled and elderly were evacuated from Britain's major cities to the countryside. A further 2 million children were evacuated privately and over the next six years the movement of people back and forth between the cities and the countryside was unceasing. Planning for the removal of non-essential residents in the event of a major aerial attack had been under consideration since the mid-1920s and detailed planning had been carried out over the latter half of the 1930s. During the Munich crisis in September 1938 the Home Office was swamped with enquiries about evacuation and the WVS, by then only in its earliest stages, was unable to cope. Miss Farrer suggested that the WI should lend the Home Office a typist and a typewriter, which was accepted 'with deep gratitude'. Not only had the WI practical experience to offer at the national level but of course it had the unparalleled network of institutes throughout the country, which was of great value to the authorities.

Following the Munich crisis, when an emergency evacuation of a small number of children had been carried out prematurely, Miss Farrer commissioned a short report from one of the officials involved. Mr Draper was very critical of the existing plans and made several suggestions which Miss Farrer condensed in a letter to Sir John Anderson, the minister responsible for air raid precautions and evacuation, in November 1938. The letter contained many of Mr Draper's recommendations, the first being to suggest that every local authority should appoint an advisory committee representing voluntary organisations so that each society could be allocated particular duties, thus avoiding duplication or glaring gaps. He had been annoyed by the county council clerks' complete dismissal of the WVS: 'In one county which I visited, the Clerk refused to meet the representative of the Women's Voluntary Service or the Secretary of the County Federation of Women's Institutes or to give any information whatsoever about his proposed billeting arrangements.' The government knew that they would have to rely on the goodwill of country families, and in particular housewives, to make evacuation work and this

National Federation of Women's Institutes and asked them for their cooperation in carrying out a major survey of 16 million homes in the countryside in preparation for evacuation. Such a monumental piece of work could never have been undertaken without the help of voluntary bodies and in the event 100,000 volunteers, including a very large number of WI members, completed the survey in record time. The purpose of the survey was to establish a comprehensive picture of the housing situation in reception areas and to pin down the number of households who would be prepared to take in children and mothers. When the survey was submitted Miss Farrer and her colleagues were frustrated by the government's recommendation for billeting one child for every spare room, pointing out that larger houses not only had more rooms but also bigger rooms, which would be able to accommodate more people. This would put the onus on wealthier households to take responsibility.

The most significant problem about evacuation was that it was not compulsory and parents could wait until the last minute to decide whether their children would go or stay at home. However, the government gave the Ministry of Health power to make billeting, together with the feeding and care of evacuees, compulsory. A householder who refused to take evacuees could be fined £50 or given a three-month prison sentence. 'This is to apply not only to evacuated children but also adults who are given the right to share the kitchen and everything else in the house, and not only for a few months but for the duration of the war.'[5]

In 1940 a member wrote in puzzlement to the editor of *Home & Country*:

> I live in Road A of a reception area which contains some dozen houses each standing in a good half-acre of ground. The billeting officer came among us and we all with one consent began

> to make excuses. So she passed on to Road B, which contains about four times as many houses in a smaller space. Here she planted children thick and firm, softly murmuring a phrase about police powers when protests occurred. When asked later why Road A got away with it, she said, 'It's useless to dump children in big houses: it never works.' That I can well believe; but why were we not summonsed and fined for evading duties thrust upon our neighbours. Is the government afraid?

It was a knotty problem and one that was never properly addressed. Some very large houses – Blenheim Palace, Chatsworth and Buscot Park in Faringdon – were made available to evacuees and schools but it is true that the poorer households in the countryside took on far more evacuees proportionally than the wealthy.

A Divisional First Aid commandant from Merstham in Surrey posed an interesting question about compulsory billeting and one that directly related to women. How should a woman, trained for example as a first-aid worker, deal with the dilemma she would almost certainly face if there were an air raid? Would she go out and do her duty or remain behind to look after children who had been committed to her care? 'How can any woman leave a house of frightened children during an air raid to work with a first-aid unit? And furthermore, would she be doing her duty if she did?'[6] These and many other questions remained unresolved.

At 11.07 a.m. on Thursday, 31 August 1939 the Ministry of Health sent out a brief order: 'Evacuate Forthwith'. The enormous machine that had been prepared over the previous months and years cranked into motion. The transport arrangements ran efficiently and as Tom Harrisson of Mass Observation wrote later: 'Because a lot of trains took a lot of people in a little time, our leaders turned cart-wheels of self-satisfaction; uncritically, un-analytically they wallowed in Maths. There was a chorus of self-congratulation, and relevant ministers ladled out congratulations to every conceivable local authority: to the teachers and mothers, to the hosts and to the children of Britain.'[7]

James Roffey, who had been evacuated to Pulborough in that first wave, remembered first the excitement and then the anxiety of evacuation. At the end of a long day he just wanted to see his mother and father again. He wrote in his memoir: '"So this is evacuation!" I thought. "A long journey in a crowded train, followed by ages spent in the pens of a cattle market. The smell of disinfectant that has trickled down my neck. Now a feeling of anxiety as we all sit on the bare floorboards of a school in a place the name of which I still didn't know." I didn't like evacuation anymore; I just wanted to go home.'[8] Despite his distress he was able to register the trestle tables all down one side of the school room piled high with sandwiches, cakes and biscuits. 'There were jugs of lemonade and big teapots filled ready with hot tea, beside bowls filled with sugar, jugs of milk and rows of cups and saucers.'[9] He learned later that the local women, organised by the WI, had been working since the early morning to get the refreshments prepared for the incoming evacuees. Some of them had been baking cakes for several days previously, he recalled, though the children were too nervous to do justice to the spread.

Acts of kindness such as the feast laid on for James and his schoolmates were recorded in several memoirs. A group of mothers and infants in Bedfordshire were delighted to see marquees with teas laid out 'just like at a garden party' but all this was swiftly forgotten as the process of billeting began. Children were herded into halls, meeting rooms, schools, and scrutinised, picked or left by families who were prepared to take them in or leave them. Many were left unhoused and the hapless billeting officers spent hours traipsing around lanes, knocking on doors, urging unwilling householders to accept a child here, a pregnant mother there, a tearful brother and sister who would not be separated. The evacuees, exhausted, homesick and hungry, felt anxious at the prospect of who they might be sent to live with. The would-be foster parents felt the resentment, foreseen a year earlier by the WI, that they had no choice in the matter. Mary Marston's mother was a billeting officer in Cheadle Hume, near Manchester. Mary's early wartime memory is of hordes of children carrying gas masks being directed into the school hall. They were sorted and sent off to live with families all over the village. After all the billeting was over Mary's mother was left with the adults, who also needed housing: 'We had a headmistress from Wood's Lane School billeted with us. I remember being surprised that she called my mother and father by their Christian names. I never saw any children from her school but later on there were evacuees from Manchester High School at our school.'

Initially there were problems as children and mothers found it hard to settle down. Jean Ridgeway and her sister, Fran, went to live with Mrs Winter, who was a billeting officer and treasurer of her local WI near Barnstaple in Devon.

> At first we were terribly homesick and Mrs Winter was quite hostile towards us. At least that's how it appeared. She was very busy sorting out children who had gone to homes that didn't work out and I expect she thought we would get on at her house because we were sisters but we were homesick and everything was new and smelled strange. One afternoon she found me comforting Fran in the garden and I think it made her sad to think we were so unhappy. After that she paid us more attention

> and things worked out OK. I remember she was constantly going to 'the institute' to sort things out but she never talked about that. She was a good cook and a great cake maker, that I do remember. We were with her for about eight weeks, then Mum came to pick us up as the bombs had not come.

Long after the journalists had lost interest in the evacuees, and those families and children who were only briefly in the country had returned to the cities, WI members were left caring for children and young mothers who, uprooted from their homes, had no choice but to learn to settle in the countryside. For both sides there was unfamiliarity, some early hostility and much adjustment, but where it worked it worked well and whole communities changed and flourished as the incomers learned to adapt to a different way of life.

In common with most village families, the Simses in Bradfield had evacuees. They had two boys: Albert Mersh and his brother, Harry Boy. Albert was six and Harry Boy was a little older. Ann Tetlow recalled the shock she felt when she realised that the children had come from a tenement in Stepney with one lavatory for twenty-one people. The boys had two sisters who lived with Mrs Worthy down the road and there was another sibling who lived in the next village. Harry Boy stayed in Bradfield until he was fourteen, when he went back to live in London, but Albert was too young to leave so when the Simses moved to Burgess Hill for eighteen months, he moved in with the family's maid, Emily, where he was very happy. He eventually left and became a goldsmith but as far as Ann knows, he never made contact with either Emily or her parents again. However, Harry Boy did come back to Bradfield to visit her mother after the war. His had been one of the many happy experiences, which tend to go unrecorded in the histories of evacuation.

Like other villages around the country, Bradfield had been led to expect one sort of evacuee and received quite another. Mrs Ward wrote a description of the September 1939 evacuation in a little notebook that her daughter Dorcas found and transcribed many years later. It made for uncomfortable reading. As Dorcas explained in her accompanying notes: 'I have modernised the spelling, but have not edited the language or attitudes, believing them to be representative of the reaction of country people to the poverty and distress emerging from London sixty years ago, when the bombing was still only anticipated – a mixture of planning and chaos, good will and misunderstanding leading to exasperation.' Following the census of accommodation available in Bradfield carried out in early 1939 the Rural District Council told villagers that they should prepare to receive 300 evacuees in two consignments. Closer to the time they learned that they were to receive 270 children and 30 teachers, in effect increasing the size of the village population by over a quarter. 'The whole parish was re-canvassed, and a fine response was made by those prepared to take in children up to this number,' wrote Mrs Ward.

> On September 1st the blow was . . . that there were no blankets or mattresses. However everything else was ready. The billeting officer had every household's voucher ready filled in with details as to numbers of children and money due, only the names of the children remaining to be added, so that we reckoned the whole 300 could be disposed of in about one hour. This being so we decided that it would not be necessary to provide refreshments other than water (which had to be fetched from a farm nearby) and that the present sanitary arrangements would be sufficient.

The children were due to arrive on the Sunday but on Saturday evening the billeting officer received a telegram to say they would not be arriving until Monday.

> At 11 am on Monday another telegram arrived, 'expect children this afternoon'. At 3 pm a third telegram, 'arrangements cancelled'. The billeting officer disperses the helpers and goes out. At 5.30 a fourth telegram, 'children arriving 6 pm'. Billeting officer's small daughter cycles frantically round parish searching for her father. WVS committee hastily re-assemble. 6.30 billeting officer found. Large numbers of club members and children arrive on spot. 7.30 buses arrive. They unload their contents – 35 school children, 220 mothers and infants!

There was dismay on the part of the villagers, faced with this now completely new problem. The evacuated mothers were equally upset to find themselves being billeted to private homes in a village far from anything or anywhere familiar. Several spent the night in the club house and then returned to London. Others stayed but were difficult to house. Mothers with as many as six children were clearly a much bigger problem for the billeting officer than unaccompanied schoolchildren. Some spoke no English as they came from the Polish, Jewish or Chinese communities in Poplar, Limehouse or Stepney, and Mrs Ward was as shattered as any of the villagers by the extreme poverty and destitution of some of the families who arrived in the village:

> For the last two days we have laboured unceasingly to fix up the worse cases of hardship. The LCC [London County Council] helpers, both men and women, have been unfailingly tactful, hardworking and efficient. We appeal to the RDC [Rural District Council] for help. They tell us we must keep them all

> in the parish somehow, but can offer no helpful advice. We have fixed up a few empty cottages and sheds for some families. The school children and the sprinkling of respectable families are happily housed. But there is a residue so uncivilised as to completely defeat our efforts at solution.

Over the next few weeks the situation eased. Many women who could not bear the idea of life in the country returned to London. For them it was not just the lack of familiar surroundings and husbands but the enforced inactivity, which left many feeling uncomfortable. As the war progressed and bombs did not drop on the capital others returned, so that by Christmas 1939 only a very small percentage of mothers and children who had originally left the cities were still living in rural villages. Some of the women who came into the village as evacuees settled well and soon brought a breath of fresh air to village life and to the WI in particular.

Three stood out in Ann's mind and became members of Bradfield WI during the war: Mrs Clarke, Mrs Amor and Mrs Turner. Mrs Amor was a Londoner, despite her exotic surname. Ann recalled: 'I remember her well as a plump lady in a very tight purple dress and high heels and with a pompadour hair style (very different from our village ladies) but she was a first class blackberry picker and was very active in the WI.' Mrs Clarke turned out to be keen on amateur dramatics and took part in several wartime productions in Bradfield. Ann remembered her performances well and looked forward to them. Mrs Turner never returned to London. She and her family felt so comfortable in Bradfield that they stayed on after the war and Mrs Turner's daughter still lives in the same house.

In recent times much has been made in the evacuation history about the difficulties encountered by the Liverpudlian children who were sent to North Wales, where the clash of cultures between them and their chapel-going hosts was perhaps the most extreme. Trenchant views held by minorities led to unpleasant insults on both sides with Tom Harrisson remarking in a book published in 1940: 'Thousands of cases in our files, atrocity stories about our own people which exceed anything yet about our enemies. Is that a measure of the national unity so constantly trumpeted by King, Halifax, Chatfield, Stanhope and other lords?'[10]

A counter-view was offered by a Denbighshire village which helps to redress the balance and show how the story of evacuation was primarily a human story. The reception committee in the village had been working for several weeks in preparation for the arrival of schoolchildren with over thirty enthusiastic women canvassing their districts for billets for the evacuees from Merseyside. On 1 September the big red buses drew up outside the school gates and the long 'march in' began.

> Tired but smiling teachers thankfully surrendered their luggage to our local company of Girl Guides and our very willing male helpers, and the children entered the school in orderly ranks to be registered. When they had collected their bags of 'rations for forty-eight hours' they were ready to set out for their billets, each little party in charge of a woman committee member. No fashionable wedding ever had such a fleet of cars as that which waited outside our gate and car after car of happy youngsters, each with his gas-mask still slung safely over his shoulder, was cheered away by a crowd of people the police had difficulty in restraining.

Few of the children had been outside Liverpool and they were all fascinated by the village:

> Many had not seen a mountain before, many had not seen grass or flowers, and it was not long before several got lost. Georgie, aged six, found the river Dee with its deep, treacherous pools, flowing a few hundred yards away and had gone for a swim. Johnny had set out declaring he was 'going to climb that high mountain'. Tommy was found with one of the neighbour's prize hens under his arm. He had pulled out several feathers and he explained that he was 'only trying to put them back'. Mary was found gazing in awe at a huge pig in a field. 'Look at that lovely white pony!' she exclaimed.

The following day the village received another contingent, this time mothers and babies. There had been a mistake at the billeting centre and the wrong party of mothers turned up. 'Mothers, disappointed at not seeing their children, were in tears, babies were crying, until some of our helpers showed unmistakable signs of breaking down too. However, after a superhuman effort at the telephone and a sympathetic appeal to the women concerned, matters adjusted themselves and all were safely housed for the night.'

Sunday brought yet more children and the village had no more accommodation available so they commandeered empty cottages and cleaned them out for the mothers with young children. People lent what they could: 'A lorry was ready and soon came some furniture – a bedstead from one house, a mattress from another, a kettle from here, crockery from there; rugs, curtains, blankets, tables, chairs appeared as if by magic. Someone gave a little coal – "not much for we are poor"; someone found milk for the babies, lighted fires, boiled kettles and soon several families were settling down contentedly. The work is still going on "for *Home & Country*".'

This kind of improvisation was going on up and down the

country. Children were moved around if billets were found to be unsatisfactory and some women found they were happy to take on additional evacuees or siblings of children living with them. James Roffey's first billet had not turned out well so after six weeks he was sent to live with a couple and their daughter who ran a sweet shop. A more ideal billet for an eight-year-old boy can hardly be imagined and he enjoyed getting paid for the jobs he was asked to carry out in sweets rather than cash. He was keen to point out that adjustment had to be made on both sides: 'Some of the people who had willingly taken evacuees into their homes during the early days of the war became less amenable as the months turned to years. Also, evacuees were no angels: like all children they misbehaved and got into trouble, although all too often they were wrongly blamed for field gates being left open resulting in cattle straying, and other such mishaps.'[11]

The evacuation from the cities to the countryside came in three waves in Britain. The first, in 1939, was codenamed Operation Pied Piper and it was the mass movement that caught people's attention and has occupied historians over the ensuing decades. Of the 1.5 million people moved by bus, train or paddle steamer over the four days at the beginning of September, it was the unaccompanied schoolchildren, all 618,739 of them evacuated from English cities and 103,637 from Scottish cities, who one now thinks of in connection with this movement, and their situation has won the public's sympathy. However, that leaves almost the same number of 'others', comprising mothers with children under five, expectant mothers, teachers and helpers for the unaccompanied schoolchildren, the disabled and the elderly, all of whom had to be accommodated in rural towns and villages. In many ways the unaccompanied children were easier to accommodate and in turn found it less difficult to assimilate in their new surroundings than the young mothers with babies or young children, who often had to share a house and a kitchen with another family and for whom the countryside was more of a challenge than it was for children.

Mrs Street worked as a Mass Observer during the war and a friend of hers, Agnes, had been evacuated to Dunstable with her little boy. She wrote to Mrs Street a month later: 'I have left Dunstable and am at my sister's. I couldn't stick it any longer. We were treated like bits of dirt by the locals as though it wasn't bad enough going through what we did to get there.' Five changes of train and then hours waiting at a skating rink to be billeted had been her experience and that of many other families with children. She had been housed quickly as she had just the one child, but others were still at the rink the following afternoon. 'I admit some of them were a bit too much with their hair in curlers and overalls but we are not all the same. I was lucky, I was in a very nice house and spotlessly clean. It was a Warden's Post but I felt in the way as they were so busy.' Agnes's position was difficult as she had nothing to do. She missed her husband so decided it was safer to return. Her story illustrates the bias felt against the town mothers arriving in the country but also the problem of planting mothers and children with initially nothing to do into busy households.

The second wave of evacuation took place in the summer of 1940 and was in direct response to the threat of a German invasion. Children from Britain's coastal towns and villages were moved inland to safety. Some 212,000 children were moved over a very short space of time, sometimes with their schools, at other times individually. For women in coastal villages who had taken in and got used to their evacuee guests over the autumn and winter of 1939–40 this was a wrench. For women in villages in designated safe areas there was a new influx of children to get used to.

Peggy and Marjorie Sumner did not have evacuees billeted to them in the first wave. Their early war years were overshadowed by the tragedy of their mother's death in 1940 when Peggy was not yet twenty. Their father remarried in 1942 so the girls were on their own from then onwards, sharing the family home for the next seventy years. Peggy, who was a good driver, got a job with the Civil Defence as an ambulance driver. Not long after their mother died Marjorie offered to have evacuees to stay. Peggy said this was the best thing that happened to her during the war because it gave her a family. Two little boys from Salford called Peter and Geoffrey Richardson, aged eight and five respectively, came to live in Albert Road, Hale. It was a truly happy time for both the sisters and the little boys. They lived together for two years until the boys' father asked for them to be sent home as their mother had died. Peter, especially, was broken-hearted but there was nothing that Marjorie and Peggy could do. Peggy said:

> We had the odd letter over the years and we heard that Peter had gone into business and Geoffrey to university. Then on Boxing Day 1984 contact was finally properly re-established. Peter is almost my younger brother. He is just fourteen years younger than I am. I never married or had children so those boys were really my family and after 1984 we became close again. Peter and his family have me to stay every Christmas. Just think: if Marjorie had not taken those boys in as part of the war effort I should have missed all that.

Cheshire took a large number of children from Guernsey. Most came en masse with teachers, though some came with their mothers. Those families and children were far away from home and the life they had left behind was being trampled upon by the jackboots of Nazi invaders. Many ended up living in villages on the Wirral where the children enjoyed a great deal of freedom on farms and in little villages. Betty Moore was an evacuee from Guernsey. She described her memories of Barnston WI during the war.

> My foster mother, a lovely kind lady, Anne Prance, was also a member of the institute. She cheerfully cooked school dinners at the institute for our school and also pupils of Barnston School who used to walk down the road to join us at the institute. She managed to produce tasty, nourishing meals that we all enjoyed out of the wartime allocations. There was no shortage of helpers to take the saucepans in a little wooden truck back to Manor Farm where she lived, as there was usually a slice of her delicious cake for anyone who helped.

An aside about Barnston WI's hall is that during the 1960s it was used on a Friday night by Heswall Jazz Club. In 1962 the Beatles made three appearances at these Friday night sessions, and actually wore their new and distinctive collarless Beatle suits for the first time.

The third wave occurred four years later, in 1944. The evacuation was principally from London and the south-east. Over a million people fled from the much-feared V-bombs that rained down on London in the autumn of 1944 and throughout the spring of 1945. This last bitter effort on Hitler's part to bring Britain to its knees succeeded in inducing panic in some Londoners. Exhausted, bombed-out, frightened women took their children away from the city and fled to the countryside, often back to village homes they had spent weeks or months in years before. This wave of evacuation had no major impact on village life, for the shaking up of the old order had long since occurred and the feeling that town and country had nothing in common had broken down. Five long years of war had worn people down and there was more tolerance on both sides. Mrs Sims took in a young mother, Mrs Leyton, and her eighteen-month-old twins, Dick and Celia. It was a happy arrangement and Ann has no recollection of any difficulties between the families. The two women kept up correspondence after the war and had the occasional visit until Mrs Sims died in 1996 at the age of ninety-two.

The first mention of the incoming evacuees in the WI minute books is in early September 1939. There were few complaints about the state of the children, which was later to become a burning issue and the subject of a lot of heated debate about hygiene and the children's health. The main concern was the amount of time women had to devote to help the children get used to their new homes. Some WI members felt put upon by having evacuees billeted to them where others, for one reason or another, had none, but the reaction of the institutes was always to club together and help out, particularly with mending or making clothes. The town boys were the main cause of this extra work, ripping their trousers and shirts as they discovered the delights of climbing trees, clambering over walls and fences or running and tripping across fields and paths.

There were some funny stories linked with the schoolchildren from Acton who were evacuated to Dorset. A brother and sister were sent to live in a large house with a middle-aged couple who grew extremely attached to their charges. The woman of the house reported a conversation she had with the youngsters at one of her monthly institute meetings. The children were helping her to make her bed and spread the eiderdown over the blankets. One of them said: 'What a big bed, there would be room in it for our Mum and Dad <u>and</u> you.'

A lady in Sixpenny Handley, on the other side of the county, collected a little boy from the village hall and offered to carry his bag for him as it was clearly too heavy. 'No thank you, I have to be independent,' he replied. He must have been all of six years old, the woman said later. Winfrith Newburgh in Dorset was a village of 400 inhabitants. They were invaded by 80 children from East London with strong cockney accents who immediately fell in love with the beautiful Dorset countryside and could be heard running around the village and staring at everyday sights like fruit trees, shouting: 'Apples!! Not on barrers! But the real fing!!'

At Cuckfield in West Sussex an institute member had a hospital cook billeted to her. The cook, who had been evacuated to work at the newly formed Emergency Medical Service Hospital, had experienced the Zeppelin raids on London in 1917. She had a great fear of bombs and retired to the cellar and refused to come out. The member contacted the matron in charge of the hospital who sent a wire to London: 'Nurses starving, cook in cellar. Please send bomb-proof substitute.'

At a debate on the evacuation problems in the House of Lords in October, the Archbishop of Canterbury paid tribute to the role played by members of the WI in the evacuation scheme: 'Women's Institutes have been the means of seeking out hitherto unexpected proof of the resourcefulness, the capacity, the intelligence, and the initiative of our country women. Everywhere they have been ready to put themselves at the disposal of the communities in which they live.'[12]

Walter Elliot, the Minister of Health, wrote to Miss Farrer:

> I want to express my deep appreciation of the help Women's Institute members have given not only as householders looking after children, but also as willing helpers in that most difficult of all problems, 'settling in'. Institute members have done much more than help to organize the movement of mothers and

> children into the reception areas. They have taken their guests into the life of the countryside, worked in the sweat of their brows on community tasks, and made the city 'at home' by the village firesides. The WIs have earned the warm thanks of the government and the gratitude of the mothers of Britain.[13]

The greatest service WI members could contribute, above offering children billets and inviting mothers to join their institutes, was to entertain the children out of school hours and at weekends. In minute books all over the country there are descriptions of plans for keeping the children busy, ranging from tea parties and film showings, to country walks and helping farmers in the fields and gardeners on the allotments. As the glorious weather of September broke, the need to provide varied indoor entertainment grew. Some householders, understandably, wanted the children out of the house for a time at weekends, whereas others were happy to involve the children in all their family activities.

The unaccompanied schoolchildren were not wholly abandoned to their foster families in the countryside. They were accompanied by a whole raft of teachers and support staff. The latter group left quickly but the teachers remained as long as sufficient children from their schools stayed in the countryside. Some of these teachers were men who had been called out of retirement as younger teachers joined up. Others were women who had had to resign from teaching when they married. Many of them could see the benefits offered by evacuation.

A teacher wrote with regret: 'When we are not in school pegging away at the 3 Rs, we become the Evacuee Hikers. This exercise in the beautiful fresh air has made a difference to the health and well-being of these children. It has been of great interest and disappointment to record daily the absence of children who were evacuated with us. May I say that most of the children have returned to the vulnerable areas not because they wanted to but because the parents so desired.' Nearly half the unaccompanied school-aged children who had been evacuated from the cities in September were home by the end of the year. The teacher foresaw problems when the children returned: 'Having tasted of the fruits of such a good life, they will be very loath to settle down again to the routine of home.' This is so very different from the portrait painted in the press that autumn, where stories of badly behaved children running amok in villages are countered by tales of intolerant housewives who fed their guests on bread and dripping while feeding their own children on the townies' rations. Reports of boys asking for chips and beer for tea, eating soup with a knife and refusing to sleep in a bed 'because that's for dead people' flooded the letters pages of the national newspapers.

In December 1939 the WI conducted a survey into evacuation, which was published in 1940. The object of the survey was 'to provide the authorities with the comments of Women's Institute members on the condition and habits of the evacuees whom they received into their homes in September 1940'.[14] The authors felt the WI was uniquely placed to compile such a report because of its spread throughout England and Wales. They hoped the material would throw light not only on the 1939 evacuation but also on 'the long term social problems which have been so strikingly laid bare by recent events'.[15]

Questionnaires were sent to all institutes and members were asked to answer honestly and constructively, not in a spirit of grievance. Members were used to being canvassed for opinions and over the past twenty-four years they had contributed to numerous reports, so that those who took part saw this as an opportunity to make their comment on the state, as they saw it, of children's health and education, which was something they were concerned about. The National Federation received replies from just over a quarter of institutes, representing a wide band of the rural reception areas. The report pointed out that only a proportion of the children were sent to rural areas. Many had been sent to towns in safe areas, such as St Albans or Ware in Hertfordshire, Horncastle in Lincolnshire or Taunton in Somerset. The details of their findings were sent first to the health and education officials in the areas where the children had come from and the authors were delighted with the reaction: 'It would be difficult to overstate the value of this survey, so obviously unbiased and full of acute observations,' wrote one official, while another thanked the WI warmly for conducting the survey 'which I found intensely interesting and of great value to Public Health. Can you not make it more public, for these conditions should be ventilated and corrected. In spite of all that the Public Health Authorities have done and are doing, the neglect of the parents is astonishing.'[16]

In the introduction the authors wrote: 'When evacuation took place, our members did their very best to make their town visitors comfortable and happy, and made great sacrifices to this end. It was a real shock to them to find that many of the guests arrived in a condition and with modes of life or habits which were startlingly less civilized than those they had accepted for a lifetime. It is therefore all the more satisfactory that very few indeed of the reports sent in by the institutes were written in anything but a generous spirit.'[17] The main thrust of their concern, the authors concluded, was that people in authority should take notice of the findings in the report and tackle 'the weaknesses in our social system of which they have had first-hand experience of such a distressing kind'.[18]

The WI's Evacuation Survey, like Mrs Ward's report of the

evacuee mother arriving in Bradfield in early September, reflects the era in which it was written. It was an age when class distinctions were clearly defined and the gap between town and country was felt to be a gulf, which led to a great deal of misunderstanding. The report shows up some of the prejudices held by rural women about their town counterparts and the women they classed as slum-dwellers. The first and overriding concern of the women who took children into their homes was hygiene. The report suggested that almost every batch of children contained some with head lice or skin conditions, such as impetigo, while others were bed-wetters. Early press stories spoke about lice-ridden children arriving in the villages in their hundreds and it was this, almost more than anything else, that came to symbolise the state of the children arriving from the cities.

The subject of bed-wetting was a distressing one and several institute minute books refer to the purchase of plastic sheets for village homes, but individuals who contributed to the report suggest that bed-wetting was usually a short-term problem that went away once the child settled down and felt comfortable in the home. They also conceded that many had not been used to outside lavatories or chamber pots for night-time use, but above all it was children's distress at being away from home and in a strange situation which was the trigger for most damp sheets.

Skin diseases upset host mothers particularly and they found themselves feeling very sorry for children who had sores. An extract about children who came from Liverpool read: 'It appeared they were unbathed for months. One child was suffering from scabies and the majority had it in their hair and others had dirty, septic sores all over their bodies.'[19]

One advantage of evacuation for children who stayed on with their host families and who were well treated was that they had plenty of fresh food. The authors wrote:

> it is frequently remarked that the children 'looked at the country food at first with dark suspicion' but soon became accustomed to it. In many areas it is apparently the custom to give the child some pennies and for it to buy biscuits or fish and chips to eat in the street. There are frequent reports of children being quite unaccustomed to having to sit down to meals and using knives and forks; when they are hungry they are given hunks of bread and margarine which they eat sitting on the doorsteps or elsewhere. Some children said they had never seen their mother cook anything and had no hot meals at home.[20]

The Women's Institute members were nothing if not persistent. One wrote in triumph that children from Southampton evacuated to her village in Dorset were doing really well: 'Children gained in height and weight and it is remarkable how many things such as soup, green vegetables, milk puddings the children now enjoy which they would not touch four months ago.'[21]

By and large, where children stayed on, rather than going home after a few days or weeks, there grew genuine affection on both sides. One evacuee child remembers settling so well into his village school that by the time the next wave of evacuees came from London in May 1940 he saw himself as 'a proper little village urchin' and teased and tormented the 'townies' as he called them. 'I had the accent an' all,' he said. A foster mother in the North East wrote in her report: 'The children, after a few weeks' kindness, showed us what lovely natures they had, had they been helped and treated properly.' Another said that the children from Newcastle 'have joined in the village life and have become part of the community, helping the housewife and doing jobs on the farm'.[22] But the implicit criticism of these children's home lives is never far from the surface. The authors comment:

> Such children have to fend for themselves from an early age onwards as their parents go out to work all day and then go to the pictures in the evening. Certain cases are reported of where the art of stealing had apparently been taught the children by their parents as part of their outfit for life. One boy returned to his billet in Dorset with a live hen under his arms and informed his landlady that he could 'get plenty more for her'.[23]

The group who came in for the highest praise by the WI survey were the teachers. Unsung heroes of the evacuation scheme and without which it could not have functioned, many of them were uprooted from their homes and sent to live with strange people in the country and shoulder responsibility for their pupils twelve or fourteen hours a day, six or even seven days a week: 'Much of the success here [is] due to excellent relations existing between head teacher and staff and parents, boys and billets,' wrote one institute member. 'The school staff have gone out of their way to express to the villagers their gratitude for what is being done for the children,' wrote another and finally, for children and their teachers from Fulham: 'The children have settled in well and behaved well; a state of affairs assisted by the splendid staff of teachers.'[24]

Teachers were on call seven days a week, dashing in and out of houses where children were billeted, explaining habits and characteristics of seemingly difficult youngsters, moving boys and girls from unsuitable to more welcoming billets, teaching half days in school rooms and the other half days out of doors, never knowing how many children would be in their class on a Monday morning after parents swooped down from the cities to pick up their offspring they were missing so badly. Theirs was a huge and often thankless task but by and large they were praised by women, families and their charges alike.

One wrote a breathless account of her first two days in the country with her charges from Walthamstow:

> The next and following days proved to be full of district visiting, interviewing foster-parents, explaining the whys and wherefores of difficult children – various purchases (chiefly mackintosh sheets!) – correspondence with Walthamstow parents . . . During the day many tasks have been the teacher's lot. We, as a school party, did not take any helpers with us so we have had such duties as: taking children (and sitting for 2 hours) to the clinic, being very tactful and tolerant with foster-parents, washing children who come to school a little the worse for wear, and attending to their education. In spite of this, some of us found time to do a little voluntary clerical work at the local Food Control Office so 'Life has been full of a number of things, that I'm sure we have [all] been as happy as Kings.'[25]

The main problem for the teachers was that evacuation had been planned under their own local education authority and carried out under the same but as soon as they arrived in their town or village they were under a different authority. Many of them, having grown heartily sick of plans for evacuation that had occupied them over the summer and into early September, now found themselves taken aback by the singular lack of preparation for their arrival in the reception areas. No contact had been made between the reception and evacuation schools and this led to weeks and sometimes months of confusion for teachers and pupils alike. The most common outcome was that village schools and incoming schools had to share premises with one school having mornings one week and the afternoons the following week. 'I think that if the home council of all evacuated schools had set up an office and medical staff in each reception area so that we had had our own officers to represent us, the organisation might have been considerably simplified. We have with us *one* of Walthamstow's nurses who has the colossal job of visiting all the schools evacuated in this area,'[26] the same teacher wrote.

Edith Jones had schoolteachers staying with her at Red House Farm in Smethcote from the middle of September. She mentions their comings and goings in her diaries in her matter-of-fact manner: 'Miss Loughran, evacuee teacher, comes to lodge with us for a fortnight. I go to Shrewsbury, buy a new hat and shoes and slippers and wellingtons etc.' Over the next six years she had a series of private evacuees from Middlesex, an evacuee called Billy Murphy from Liverpool and paying guests from Northampton and Rugby. The latter came four times between 1942 and 1945. When they returned home after their first visit Edith wrote in her diary that she had given them nine hens as a present. As she was practical and good with her hands, Edith was constantly being asked to make and mend things for the children billeted in and around Smethcote. One evacuee mother, on hearing that Edith was practical, brought her a pram for repair.

Where the report was uniformly negative was in its criticism of the evacuee mothers.

> Warm tribute was paid by the Institute hostesses to those who showed themselves competent mothers, but they found it hard to be sympathetic to women who could neither cook, sew nor conform to the ordinary standards of human decency and whose one idea of enjoyment was to visit the public-house or cinema. They were frankly horrified and disgusted at the state of filth in which some of the mothers left their billets and many reports reflect the conviction that this state of affairs is a serious slur on our educational system.[27]

Never had the gulf between town and country life been laid so bare. Although the survey does admit that some young women were simply bewildered by the country and longed to get home to their husbands and the familiarity of their city lives. 'Unlike the children they could not quickly adapt themselves and it was a surprise to nobody that within a week or two of the evacuation a large proportion of them had left the villages.'[28]

One WI wrote a long piece that was quoted in full in the report:

> I know of four cases . . . where the mothers seemed to have no idea of how to train a baby in good habits. Something will have to be done to give girls before leaving school, practical knowledge of how to keep a baby dry, and that it is far less trouble in the end than washing napkins and blankets as well as essential for the child – not just telling them, but doing it themselves in a crèche. I don't want to underrate what has already been done in this matter, but the problem of child training has been brought home to us by this evacuation, and we have seen the need for ourselves, and it is up to us to see that the next generation are given a better start.[29]

The focus of their ire was against the education system that allowed situations to arise where young mothers had no help in learning how to run a home and family. This went right to the core of what Mrs Hoodless in Canada had been anxious to address when she first set up the WI at Stoney Creek forty years earlier, namely recognition of the importance of domestic science. A final remark on the mothers concluded: 'The best evacuee of all was an elderly woman who had not had the benefit of a modern and expensive L.C.C. [London County Council] education. After this experience I think England ought to be proud of her country women for their cleanliness, good housewifery and decent standards.'[30]

Today it is difficult to read criticisms of evacuee mothers and not feel that the authors were being harsh on them given the fact they had been uprooted from their homes, often unwillingly, and sent to the countryside to live with households who did not want them and with whom they had nothing in common. However, given the response to the report and the fact that these criticisms were taken up by Margaret Bondfield in her full report published eighteen months later in October 1941, it is clear that expressing what might seem to us judgemental views and opinions was acceptable at the time.

By early 1940 evacuation was less of a theme for village institutes. The vast majority of mothers and children, over a million, had returned to the cities. The only group that remained in force in the countryside were the unaccompanied schoolchildren. The government continued to lobby parents who wanted to bring their children back to the cities and urged them to leave them in the countryside, where they would be safe. An appeal went out from Miss Farrer in late 1940 for homes to accommodate bombed-out refugees from the cities. 'In spite of all the hospitality already offered, more billets are still needed; and there is no greater service we can do than to offer room in our houses when we have it.'[31] For the majority of village women, however, the great influx of September 1939 was not repeated and other waves of evacuation had a less dislocating effect on life in the countryside, although individual stories both good and bad continued to appear in the press.

Rationing had been introduced early in 1940 and the focus for the WI was now on food production. In February Mrs Milburn was tussling with what this would mean for her WI: 'We went to Coventry this morning and I spent 20 minutes in the Food

Controller's Office getting a permit for butter and sugar for the Women's Institute teas.' The Phoney War was coming to an end and life would soon change for everyone in Britain. In June she was in contemplative mood: 'How curious this life is. A sort of deep stillness comes over everything from time to time. There is not much traffic on the roads during the week and the village seems empty in the evenings. One misses the young life everywhere, particularly Alan coming in in the early evening.'

4

COUPON CULTURE

> Now is the time to show what we are worth and it is up to us to try and smile through these worrying times. We must not sit down and think, but get going and do something to prove our worth as women!
>
> *Mrs Diggle, President, Barnston WI, 1940*

Mrs Clara Milburn had begun her diary in February 1940. The first few pages were a summary of the previous five months giving a perspective of the way life returned to normal after the first three weeks of paralysis in September. 'By Christmas the expected air raids had not occurred. Threats from Hitler about a "secret weapon" put the wind up a few people and the word "jitters" came into vogue. But the great bulk of the people refused to be "jittery" and got to work: air raid precaution exercises took definite shape, knitting got well under way, Red Cross sewing meetings flourished, plots of new land were turned over and people prepared for the coming year.'

On Friday 5 January she heard her son Alan's voice on the phone for the last time in what would turn out to be five years and four months. That morning she and her husband invited two friends round for a glass of sherry 'because the blackout makes afternoons difficult. We all drank "to Alan" . . . and then "Oh my goodness! Cough! Splutter! Good heavens! We're drinking neat whisky!" And so we were – it was the wrong decanter!'

In January the snow fell thickly and for weeks there was no traffic in Balsall Common near Coventry. In early February she wrote: 'Along the road I hear a pleasing sound – the clip-clop of horses' feet. After the dull quiet of snowstricken days it is good to feel that traffic is rapidly becoming normal again.' That day the butcher's boy delivered a small joint: 'Such *little* joints, too, these days, conforming to the imposed rationing in a few weeks' time. It is a good thing to get down to hard facts, though, and make everyone come under the same rule and help to win the war.'

After the evacuation it was the introduction of rationing that made the largest difference to women's lives. Control of food had been foreseen by the WI at the beginning of the war and many column inches had been devoted to increasing food production. It had also, of course, been on the government's mind and 50 million ration books were printed by the summer of 1939 in preparation. The Subcommittee on Food Supplies in Time of War, appointed in 1936, had heeded the advice given by Sir William Beveridge, who was the Permanent Secretary to the Ministry of Food during the First World War. He urged them 'to think out in advance *and as a whole*, the civilian side of the next war is as important as to design measures of military attack and defence'.[1]

Rationing began on 8 January 1940 and became increasingly severe as the war progressed. Although only a limited range of foodstuffs, clothing and petrol were actually rationed, emergency legislation meant that all consumer goods were subject to comprehensive regulation. Ina Zweiniger-Bargielowska, in her book *Austerity in Britain,* wrote:

> As a result of rationing and controls, consumption of food, clothing, household goods, and private motoring were reduced dramatically as economic resources were channelled into the war effort . . . During the Second World War, Britain was transformed from an essentially free market economy into an economy distinguished by centralised control and economic planning. The reduction of civilian consumption played a critical part in this conversion of the economy to the war effort by facilitating the reallocation of resources necessary for mobilization in a total war.[2]

The rationing system developed by Britain was intended by the government to be conspicuously egalitarian. In *The Taste of War* historian Lizzie Collingham described the thinking behind the government's scheme: 'The British food rationing system was designed to avoid deepening social rifts, and instead to foster social consensus . . . By allocating everyone the same amount of food it emphasized its purpose as the equitable distribution of food and scarce goods across the entire population. This distribution of food resources, which apparently privileged no section of civilian society, is one of the characteristics of government wartime policy which earned it the title of "war socialism".'[3] All adults, regardless of occupation, had the same rations, with variations only for nursing mothers and those with babies, and children. This applied also to men and women in the forces living and working in Britain. This was at odds with systems in other countries that introduced a rationing hierarchy, and surprisingly the exact opposite of Russia, which allowed a free market to develop. Churchill had always been concerned about rationing. Even before he became prime minister he expressed his reluctance to limit people's food and when it became clear that workers in heavy industry needed additional food and 'communal feeding centres' were introduced, he baulked at the term which to him smacked of socialism. He suggested they were called 'British restaurants', not least because it sounded more patriotic.

At the outbreak of war, Germany had introduced rationing and the British government wanted to know whether this was having an effect on the German people. To that end a study was made in Cambridge on six men and women who were subjected to a very limited but carefully calculated diet. The scientists concluded that provided the diet was sufficiently bulky and that the staple, bread, comprised at least 92 per cent extracted flour, that is to say nearly wholemeal, then the physical and mental work which those living on rations could achieve proved that 'the present German ration, provided it is in fact reaching the individual, is fully adequate for the vital needs of her population'.[4] The key fact they had established was the need for carbohydrates, which would be provided in potatoes and cereals.

Anyone who lived through the war and remembers rationing will recall how potatoes became an ever-greater staple in the diet. 'Potatoes were used at every meal as far as I can remember. And not just as a side dish – boiled, baked, mashed or fried. They were used in baking, in bread making, in filling out pies,' my mother recalled. East Hendred WI had a potato demonstration on 17 March 1942. The minute book reads: 'Miss Cummings spoke of many ways of cooking potatoes & demonstrated them steamed in muslin tied on lid of saucepan; potato pastry on vegetable pie; potato scones; potatoes cooked and stuffed. She was rather hurried owing to Warship Whist Drive taking place immediately after.'[5]

In 1943 Lord Woolton, the Minister for Food, appealed directly to the WI asking them for help and ideas about how to make potato dishes more popular. Every county responded by suggesting that institutes hold a competition for recipes. The winning recipe would be put forward to a county competition and the winner of that sent to London, where recipes from all fifty-eight counties were gathered together into a potato cookbook. East Hendred rose to the occasion with a further cooking demonstration. This time there was vegetable flan with potato pastry and cheese sauce on offer. Then they had a potato omelette followed by potato Yorkshire pudding. They held a competition and the winning recipe, the vegetable flan with potato pastry, was sent to the Berkshire Federation for further judging. The overall winner was Mrs Biggs from Essex, whose recipe for potato suet was read out on the radio.

People recall the monotony of the wartime diet and the pressure on cooks to try to liven up dishes. WI recipe books and leaflets encouraged the use of spices but also offered practical advice such as cutting off bacon rinds to be used for flavouring soup or using Lea & Perrins to spice up a pasty. Minute books constantly refer to wartime cookery demonstrations, tips on how to make rationed food stretch and above all on how to make dreary food taste better.

As Lizzie Collingham explained in her survey of the economics of food in wartime, the change in the quantity of fat in the diet had a very great impact on taste: 'The British were used to a pre-war nutritional balance where fat made up 38 per cent of calorie intake. Although this dropped by only a small percentage during the war, combined with a shift from meat to wholemeal bread and potatoes as the basis of the diet, the less fatty meals became monotonous and tasted insipid.'[6] Mrs Ward in Bradfield reported on a fascinating talk by one of their members, Mrs Maddock, who was a vegetarian. 'She told us how she fed a family of five children without any meat, suet etc and brought some appetising looking examples of lentil cutlets.' At that same meeting members were told that they need not worry about the shortage of onions for flavouring as there were ample quantities of wild chives growing in the hedgerows.

Before the war broke out, Britain imported some 20 million tons of food annually. Over half its meat, nearly three quarters of its cheese and sugar, nearly 80 per cent of fruit and 70 per cent of cereals and fats came from overseas. The outbreak of war saw an immediate drop off in food supplies coming into the UK. A newspaper reported on 4 October 1939 that: 'Although Danish food exports to England stopped, because of German interference with shipping, I understand that Denmark believes that she can maintain in future an even flow of bacon and dairy produce. She is anxious to do so for economic and other reasons.' Shipments of bacon, eggs and butter from Holland were affected and the UK missed a shipment of 12 million eggs the week before the article was published. When formal rationing began, the first things to be put on the cards were bacon, butter and sugar. This was followed by meat in March 1940, tea, margarine and cooking fats in July of that year and preserves and cheese were added in 1941. Bread was never rationed during the war, though it was in 1946. Elsie Bainbridge from Cumbria recalled how her parents used to complain that bread was no longer white: 'Flour had been refined before the war but now it was grey and although I think we understood it was better for us it just looked so unappetising.'

Initially meat continued to be imported into Britain, including bacon and pork, from Ireland, Canada and the United States, with little trouble other than minor delays. What happened, however, was that prices rocketed, because of a doubling in the cost of shipping in October 1939. This also had the effect of increasing the price of animal feed, which was a large part of the import market. Food and rationing occupied the government and the population for the rest of the war and beyond. Rationing did not end completely until 1954. The restrictions dominated the lives of everyone living in Britain. Even feeding sparrows was declared illegal. Animals were not supposed to eat anything deemed fit for human consumption. Mrs Milburn, like many others, ignored that particular law: '. . . the poor birds, with feathers fluffed out, looked on from shrub and tree. From time to time I opened the window and put out a crushed biscuit or any little scraps, and how gladly they were received and devoured by sparrows, blackbirds, chaffinches, hedge-sparrows, robins, tits and the greedy gobbling starlings.'[7]

Propaganda about food rationing was aimed principally at women, and above all at housewives, who were responsible for managing their households, doing the shopping and feeding the family. Photographs of people queuing for food are so common as to be unremarkable but it is obvious to anyone who looks at them that the majority of people in those queues are women. Not necessarily young women, for they were often working or in the forces, but mothers and housewives who represented the majority of the female population at home. Before the war all but the most rural villages had received food deliveries of one sort or another but with petrol rationing this was no longer possible and women now had to go to larger villages or towns to queue for everything they could not grow themselves. One reason for the queues was that each individual could only obtain his or her full ration by registering with a retailer. This was meant to ensure sufficient supplies and complete control over the rationed food. In practice it was chaotic, particularly in the early months of rationing when people were evacuated all over the country and then returned again. For the women living in the towns and villages sorting out ration books for evacuees and visitors was a major issue and it led to some bad feelings, especially when parents came to visit their evacuee children and expected to be fed on foster parents' rations. Ann Tetlow and her brother, John, were often invited round to Copyhold Farm to see Dorcas Ward and her sister. Even though the Wards had cattle Ann and John would take their milk and butter rations with them if they were going to tea.

Elsie Bainbridge remembered queuing to get the family's ration books from Morland in Cumbria.

> There was one book for each member of the family. One for clothing and one for food. There were no vans coming round – we had to do our own catering and what we could not grow or trap we had to get from the shops and there would be queues. Sometimes people would just join a queue without knowing what they were standing in line for. I remember that once there was a queue for what turned out to be caraway seeds, which my mother didn't even like.

Elsie's father kept pigs and he would slaughter one, on licence. She said:

> I now think what a boon it would have been to have a deep freeze in those days. We had a few farmers round about and we used to give them a few sausages, spare ribs, liver and things and then when they had a butchering day they'd share it out. Otherwise you'd get sick of it. You'd have black pudding for breakfast, lunch and dinner. I can remember my mother cleaning the intestines for black pudding and sausage. When they were clean they were beautiful, not like the tough sausage skins we get nowadays. They were very delicate and mother used to blow them up to check they had no holes in them before she used them to make the black puddings, otherwise the blood would ooze out. Even the bladder got used. My dad

blew one up for us as a ball and we used to kick it around the garden.

Like everything else, the slaughter of animals in wartime was carefully regulated. Farmers were allowed to rear pigs but they had to obtain a licence if they wanted to kill one for the family's consumption. Slaughter licences usually had to be applied for in person and would then be sent out by post a few days later. Edith Jones always made a note in her diaries of the days that Jack applied for pig licences. When a pig was killed she had at least three days of work to preserve and make use of every bit of the animal.

In February 1941 Len Downes from the next-door village killed their pig, under licence. The following morning it was cut up: 'weighs very well. 15st 10lb gained from 6st 17lbs since Oct 23. Salt bacon and make black pudding. Have pork for dinner. Such a treat being home grown.' The next day Edith cut the fat and made lard, she cut up the pork meat and made black puddings and on the final day she wrote: 'make 23 pork pies, bake them in brick oven, also bread. Made sausage tonight.' Such industry and yet it had to be fitted in alongside all the other jobs that life on the farm required. On Fridays she would prepare the fruit, vegetables and eggs that she would then take to Shrewsbury market for sale on Saturday. She travelled by early bus and sometimes, if sales were brisk, allowed herself tea at the Empire Rooms or went to the cinema. She also used the Saturday visits to buy Jack his shirts or herself a blouse or dress. Money was always tight but the extra shillings Edith could make at the market with her home-grown produce meant that she had a little spending money for luxuries.

One farmer who was perhaps not quite as assiduous in sticking to the rules was Mr Shacklady. His daughter, Sybil Norcott, remembers that her father had added pigs to the farm for the duration of the war. This way the family could have meat and lard from the pigs, cream and butter from the cows, eggs from the hens and ducks, flesh from the turkeys and of course vegetables from the garden. Sybil's father once swapped a ham for a hundredweight bag of sugar and both parties were delighted.

Sybil explained about slaughtering the pigs:

> You had to get a licence to kill a pig and under this licence you could kill two a year. But it was a little more complicated than that. If you killed a hog then you only had one day to kill it. If you killed a gilt then you were allowed five days, which gave you more opportunity. What many farmers did was to get a licence to kill a gilt and then kill one pig a day for five days. If the Ministry men didn't come to inspect you were OK doing this, though it was risky. In the normal run of events you would check whether your neighbour was planning to kill his pig and then you would offer to share offal, sausages and the like. It worked very well.

Sybil remembered her father nearly getting caught when a ministry official made an unannounced visit to their farm. On this occasion he had six large hams hanging up in the house in pillowcases, cured and ready to be eaten. That was the day an inspector from the Ministry of Food came to call. With only the briefest of warnings from one of their neighbours, Sybil's father had to think on his feet. He told Sybil to keep the inspector talking downstairs for a few minutes while he hid the evidence. When the inspector finally met Mr Shacklady he learned that his wife was lying ill in bed upstairs so he had been delayed attending to her. In fact she was perfectly well but was tucked up under her large eiderdown with the hams stuffed down either side of her. The story was quickly adopted in family lore and the ham-hiding operation was widely retold after the war.

One restricted foodstuff was lard. Sybil's mother stored lard in the pantry and had to be careful that nobody discovered how much she was storing, so it was kept in jars on the top shelf and labelled 'apples' or 'pears'. That was code for reminding her which jar was to be used first. Winter apples kept longer than pears so that was the jar to be used last. It was a little industry that sustained not only their household but also others, including their neighbours, in the community. Sometimes they even had visiting children from a city school who would delight in seeing all the different animals on the farm. Sybil remembered one little girl saying to her: 'Now I know what chicks look like. They have two legs and I always draw them with four.'

As the first winter of the war drew to a close and the warm weather returned, bringing with it new growth, Hitler launched the Blitzkrieg. 'The most eventful day of the war! This morning Holland and Belgium were invaded by Germany and very soon afterwards they both appeal to the Allies for help,' wrote Mrs Milburn on 10 May 1940. Her entry concluded: 'Mr Chamberlain has resigned the Premiership and Mr Churchill has taken his place.'

The speed and ferocity of the Blitzkrieg shocked the nation. Regular news bulletins, eagerly listened to by individuals and groups crowded round wirelesses, gave out sombre announcements of horrors and atrocities being perpetrated not only on the armed forces but on women and children. Mrs Milburn was as distressed as anyone: 'There is so much one could write. Each day there is so much news that one is appalled at all the happenings and the terrible loss of life, given out so calmly on the wireless. Thousands of Germans in troop-ships, armoured trains, aeroplanes. Over a hundred enemy aeroplanes brought down by the Dutch in one day! And much nearer 200, counting their losses elsewhere. All this for a few madmen out for world-domination!' A fortnight later she wrote: 'Oh the horror and bitterness of war!'

As the German war-machine crashed its way westwards so the minds of everyone became focused on the threat of what would happen next. With British, French and Belgian troops cut off by the German Army there was no option but to order an evacuation. Churchill called the events in France 'a colossal military disaster'. With the capitulation of Belgium on 28 May the British Expeditionary Force, including Mrs Milburn's son, Alan, was in ever-greater danger. The evacuation – in total over 338,000 British and French soldiers – continued until 3 June. Men were picked up from the beaches in the now famous 'little boats' and brought to larger vessels lying at a distance from the shore. Some 580 boats took part in the evacuation and the miracle of the little ships is one of the most evocative stories of bravery from the early years of the Second World War. For mothers and wives waiting to hear news of their men the days, weeks and months following the evacuation of Dunkirk were agonising. On 1 June Mrs Milburn heard that two young men from their district had been killed. 'These are the first of the men we really know and my heart aches for the Winsers; Philip was so cheery and such a good fellow.'

Alan Milburn had been captured at Dunkirk and his mother still had no news. On 1 July she wrote: 'Always one is thinking of him, wondering whether he still lives and if so, whether he is well, where he is, what he does all day, what discomforts he is suffering. If . . . if . . . And so the days go by.' On the same day, the Germans landed on the Channel Islands following several days of raids and in August the Battle of Britain began.

Mrs Milburn wrote in her diary on 6 July:

> Twink and I took our little walk in the peaceful fields . . . No one to be seen there – just trees and hedges and the great blue

> arch of heaven. In the evening the village is quiet, with scarcely a soul to be seen walking about. But it is not a happy tranquility. It is unnatural and eerie, and tense at times. Behind it lies the unhappiness and anxiety of war and the not knowing what will happen to our dear, dear land in the next few months.

Two weeks later, in a bid to keep going, Mrs Milburn had been to her institute where a produce exhibition was being held, to see how the judges were getting on. She found them 'in the thick of things, tasting and judging the merits of jams, jellies, chutneys, salad cream and bottled fruit. Mrs Ford was sipping each bottle of wine and looking flushed by the time she had got to the eleventh!'

Mrs Sims and Mrs Ward in Berkshire were as busy as Mrs Milburn ensuring that life in their institute carried on alongside all the other responsibilities that fell on their shoulders. Theirs was a smaller village than Balsall Common. By the middle of the twentieth century Bradfield had a population of around a thousand and was divided into two parts: Southend and the old village round Bradfield College, a public school that had been founded by Dorcas Ward's grandfather. To give some idea of the character of the village in wartime, Ann and Dorcas listed all the different businesses, farms and shops that ran in Bradfield. There were seventeen farms, four milk-rounds, three post-offices, a garage, a village school and sixteen shops. There was also a clock and watch repairer, a radio repairer, a cobbler, a blacksmith, two garages, two dressmakers and a hairdresser. Bradfield also had its own policeman and a district nurse.

Life in Bradfield became ever busier for the womenfolk. First, many of the men were called up, so that women had to take over roles hitherto done by their husbands, sons or other men, and secondly, the amount of paperwork escalated. Ration books, savings books, identity cards, clothing coupons all had to be processed and dealt with by the shopkeepers. Ann remembers her own mother doing seemingly endless paperwork as she juggled a large number of voluntary jobs during the war and for years afterwards. In addition to serving on the WI committee for forty years at various times as president, secretary and treasurer, Mrs Sims also ran the National Savings Scheme in the village.

In January 1940 R. M. Kindersley, president of the National Savings Committee, appealed directly to the WI for help in raising the profile of the National Savings campaign. He told them it was essential 'that for the duration of the war a large part of the purchasing power of individuals should as far as possible be transferred to the State though the purchase of Government Securities'. He invited the NFWI to help by cooperating with organising the campaign alongside the National Savings local committees; by displaying posters and distributing leaflets and by setting up in each WI a branch of the National Savings Scheme. This was something that the WI agreed they were able to do and actively supported the Treasury in its aim to raise substantial sums of money for the war effort. By December 1940 the war was costing £10 million (£426 million today) a day and the government needed to borrow over half the amount from the public. The scheme had started in 1916 to help pay for the First World War and the legacy had been a strong organisation of local and regional committees. When the government launched the new campaign it was able to tap into that network. 'Running a Savings Group appealed to many people unable to take a more active part in the war, and group secretaries included people in their seventies and at least one blind woman, but most were housewives, often those same "willing horses" who were the backbone of every form of service, from ARP to collecting salvage.'[8] Ann particularly remembered Mrs Adams who, in addition to her WI work, sold savings stamps every week. She would come over to the house to do the 'sistifficates' as she called them. Once the money was counted and the fifteen-shilling certificates had been made out she would regale Mrs Sims with all the village gossip she had gathered as she rode around the village on her bicycle.

Raising money is a running theme in war diaries and institute minute books. Although the WI was not supposed to raise funds directly for war work, this was often ignored at an institute level. Some institutes regarded requests as a challenge and succeeded, over the years, in raising impressive sums of money, mainly through the purchase of savings stamps but often for a specific cause, such as the Spitfire Fund or Wings for Victory week. Stotfold in Bedfordshire had topped the WI 'Savings Ladder' in 1943 with a sum of £8,190 (£283,000 today) raised in just two years and of that total £3,446 (£119,000) was raised for Warship Week in 1942. As the village had a population of less than 5,000 this was remarkable.

Over the course of her life Mrs Sims served as a trustee for the Almshouses, was a parish councillor, a school manager, sat on the Parochial Church Council, ran the Brownies and Girl Guides, where she was respectively Brown Owl and Captain, she organised Christian Aid week for twelve years and took part in Meals on Wheels. This in addition to bringing up a family, managing a house on a wartime budget and with rations as well as helping to keep village spirits up during the six years of war.

She was not the only busy lady. Mrs Elsie Young, who lived until she was ninety-eight, was a stalwart of Bradfield village. She joined the WI the same year as Mrs Sims and helped out with the National Savings Scheme. When her husband was called up she took over his work at Bradfield College, which meant that she cleaned two classrooms before breakfast, washed up for 240 after breakfast, the same after lunch, collected the post from the various letter boxes and put the post on the bus for Reading. Then her daughter, Pam, came home from school and after their meal they returned to the college to wash up after supper. At this meal ten boys helped, so Mrs Young enjoyed the evening wash-up.

After the fall of France at the end of June the fear of a Nazi invasion grew. Mrs Ward wrote the minutes for their June committee meeting. There had been an announcement that the children's party would be held at Horseleas, Mrs Howlett's house, on 11 July. This suddenly seemed optimistic: 'I think when this announcement was made each of us wondered in our hearts whether by that date any children's party would be possible or whether our lovely countryside would be suffering as that of France is suffering today.' The reaction of parents was once again to evacuate their children, first from the vulnerable coastal towns and then overseas. Tens of thousands of children were sent on private and government schemes to America, Canada, Australia, New Zealand and South Africa. These children faced a new and unseen horror as they made their journeys by ship: German submarines lying in wait that caused immense losses amongst merchant shipping bringing food and supplies to Britain.

Although food from the continent to the UK was disrupted during the autumn of 1939, it was not until the fall of Holland and Belgium and the capitulation of France that food exports from the continent ceased completely. Apart from bacon, eggs and butter, the single most sorely missed item in the kitchens of Britain was the common onion. Until 1940 the majority of Britain's supply of onions had been shipped from the warm fields of France and Spain, where crops produced large yields. The end of onion imports led to a great surge in the desire to grow onions. It was successful only in certain counties where the growing conditions were favourable and there was, for the rest of the war, a shortage of onions. This had a big impact on the taste of food and Elsie Bainbridge remembered how dull their food was

diary, in July 1941: 'We have worked so hard in the garden and a lot of it is in vain, it seems. I am particularly vexed with the onions, which have onion fly badly, and my own seedlings are dying off one by one.'[10] The following year she gave up completely, miserable that her beautiful bed of onions had been attacked by the onion fly grub. 'It was no use to leave them to be eaten off one by one, Hitler fashion, and I shall not grow them again. They were a back-aching job to plant out, and I have spent many hours on their culture – all for nothing.'[11]

While onions thwarted many gardeners, other vegetables were easier to grow and were used successfully to supplement the monotonous wartime diet. The Ministry of Food encouraged cultivation of potatoes, carrots and tomatoes and the National Federation distributed tomato seeds and bags of seed potatoes in great numbers each year, as well as thousands of packets of Suttons' seeds that they obtained at special rates ahead of the planting season. Minute books and county agricultural subcommittee notes list all the different varieties of seed that were available through the National Federation. In 1940 Suttons provided 10,000 collections of vegetable seeds, the price to members being 2s 6d (£5.74 today), which contained peas, broad beans, beetroot, Brussels sprouts, broccoli, cabbage, leeks, lettuce, spinach *or* parsnip (members had to choose one or the other), onions and turnips. The quantities were sufficient to sow in a large vegetable garden or allotment, giving about eight rows of 25 feet and 200 plants of broccoli, Brussels, spinach, cabbage, etc. Were everything to grow from the seeds, this would have been enough to feed a family and supply a surplus, which could be sold at a local WI market. The government set high targets for WIs. In February 1940 East and West Hendred's minutes secretary wrote: 'The meeting was informed that the Government wishes each Institute to contribute by sale 2 cwt onions and 3 cwt tomatoes above what members need for themselves.' They decided to join with Harwell and work as a fruit-preserving centre so that they could get a sugar allowance. 'Major Borwick has kindly offered to take market produce to the WI stall at Didcot therefore members should sow a surplus of vegetables.'

Edith Jones was a regular visitor to the Saturday market in Shrewsbury. She sold surplus produce that was not needed by the household or her neighbours and at times made a small profit. She grew peas, beans, broad beans and soft fruit in the summer. She planted cabbages, winter beans and onions and had an orchard outside the kitchen from which she harvested apples and pears. 'It is late for planting cabbage but rabbits have been troublesome. Autumn sowing of beans is a new venture,' she wrote in November. What they did not eat fresh or sell at the market she bottled, jammed, canned or pickled. Everything that she grew in the kitchen garden and orchard was used and from her diary it is clear that she was enormously industrious. Chris Downes remembered her larder with its stacked shelves: 'there were salted kidney beans in jars, jams, cooked and uncooked meat, bottles of plums, damsons and pears. That was the only way that fruit and vegetables could be preserved and used throughout the rest of the year.' With no electricity at the farm until the late 1950s there was no cold storage. Edith also kept hens. She was very interested in her poultry and made frequent mention of them in her diaries. In November 1939 she was delighted with a new trapdoor that Mr Tomkins had made in the fowl house 'easier cleaning. 1/1.', she wrote, presumably referring to the cost of the door.

As we have seen, the government made the decision to issue the same rations for every adult, deeming it iniquitous to differentiate between types of work carried out by members of the population. They believed it would make rationing more acceptable to the British public and generally it worked. However it was acknowledged that certain types of manual work meant that people needed more food in order to be able to work efficiently. For men and women working in factories in the towns and cities this could be provided by the use of canteens where food could be purchased over and above rations. There was a dramatic increase in the numbers of canteens for miners and factory workers from 1,500 in 1939 to 18,486 in 1944.[12] In addition there were the British restaurants which had been started during the Blitz and served up to 600,000 subsidised meals a day to urban workers in over 2,000 restaurants by 1943.

This did not help the farm labourers and other workers in the countryside. These people usually took their midday meal with them from home, using their weekly cheese or bacon ration. In 1942, Lord Woolton, the Minister of Food, enlisted the help of the WVS, who developed the Rural District Pie Scheme, through which they took meat pies to the workers in outlying villages and farms on certain days of the week. As the Denbighshire County Secretary explained to the president of Trefnant WI, it was designed to provide 'country workers with meals outside their rations, thus bringing them into line with industrial workers who have access to work canteens etc. Moreover the Ministry of Food realises that the provision of carried meals for men and women working long hours in the fields has become a very real difficulty for the house wife, and hope that the pie scheme will help to overcome this.'[13] The WVS was active in small towns but not in remote rural villages so that the WI's help was needed to make the scheme work as the government had intended.

The plan was to find a local baker who would agree to bake the pies, which would be made by volunteers. Distribution would be the responsibility either of the baker or of volunteers who would be prepared to drive, cycle or walk around the villages taking pies to agreed drop-off points where they would be sold to local workers. The scheme would only work, the Denbighshire committee told the WIs and other bodies, if farmers, farmers' wives and farm labourers bought in to the idea of the pie scheme from the outset, so the presidents were encouraged to ensure as many people as possible were aware of it. Almost all counties were involved in the pie scheme and the profits from the sale of pies made a tidy sum for individual institutes, which they were free to dispose of as they wished.

Betty Houghton in Chiddingly in Sussex was a young WI member in the war, joining her institute at sixteen. One of her duties was to distribute pies. There was a beautiful oast house in the village with an empty ground floor. 'Every Thursday we would meet up to take delivery of the pies, which came from the baker's. They looked a bit like Cornish pasties and we would sell these to anyone who came to buy them. The art was deciding how many to order each week so that you did not run out too quickly but so that you did not have a large number left over either. They were very popular as I remember,' Betty said.

Margaret Wright, like Betty, remembered the pie scheme. Her mother was an active member of the WI in Mobberley, Cheshire, and many of Margaret's wartime memories revolve around the activities of the institute: 'I remember the pie-making machine that squashed the pastry into pie shapes and made a lid for them. They were very popular.'

Cheshire records show that one million pies were sold by their institutes in 1944 but the bureaucracy was enormous. Burton and Puddington's annual report for 1943 complained: 'The Pie Scheme admirably illustrates the Love of Forms that seems bred into the bones of all Ministries, since the Pie Returns have to be made out on 6 different forms and sent to 5 different places every 8 weeks! If returns are late, back comes another form. Sometimes they even decide they want something quite different . . .' Hilary Morris of Burton WI did some research in 1995 into the pie scheme on the Wirral:

> Pies had to be ordered in advance, and were distributed in Willaston from the Institute or the War Memorial Hut twice a week. The prices were 4d for small pies and pasties, and 1s 4d for large pies. The prices went up by 1d and 4d respectively in 1947, and the scheme continued in Burton until 1947, and in Willaston until 1949.
>
> Huge numbers of pies were sold. In May 1943, 545 were being distributed weekly in Burton and Puddington, and in June the grand total was 2,914. Willaston was a little behind, selling 2,421 in June, but by August nearly 1,000 were being sold each week. By the end of the war, Willaston had sold 128,000 pies, and by the end of the scheme another 62,000. In Cheshire, in 1944 alone, nearly a million pies were sold.

And what was in these pies? The meat ration for cafes, canteens and restaurants was one pennyworth per person per meal or about an ounce in each pie. The rest of the filling would have been vegetables and potatoes. 'Perhaps they resembled the famous "Woolton Pie", which was described by the Lord Mayor of Liverpool, Sir Sydney Jones, as looking on the outside exactly like a steak and kidney pie, on the inside it looked just like a steak and kidney pie – without the steak and kidney. I have enquired from people who were in Willaston at that time, and although they remember that pies were sold, no one has admitted to actually eating one,' wrote Hilary Morris.

Some WIs made so much money from the pie scheme they were able to fund their jam-making centres as well as making donations to war charities and hospitals. At the end of the war Willaston bought a new clock for the church hall and a banner for the Scouts with the remaining money from the pie scheme.

It was always clear that in the event of a major war there would have to be petrol rationing and by the time of the Munich Crisis in September 1938 a coupon replacement scheme was in operation. Five months before the outbreak of war Miss Farrer had written to the Assistant Secretary for Defence asking for key workers within the National Federation of Women's Institutes to be considered in the event of an emergency. She pointed out that the 'Federation has a membership of over 300,000 and it has applied to the Lord Privy Seal for recognition that its work will be of national importance in time of emergency in order that its "key workers" may be included in the list of reserved occupations. Petrol will be required more particularly for the Federation's full time organisers and for the Secretaries of the County Federations in England and Wales of which there are 58.'[14]

One of the biggest headaches for national and county federations was the issue of petrol rationing. Although the WI was requested formally by the government to assist with food production, they were not entitled to extra petrol rations since the WI was a social organisation. It was a source of tremendous frustration to Miss Farrer, whose correspondence with the relevant people at the Ministry of Food became ever terser as the pressure on fuel increased. It was particularly galling since the Women's Land Army and the Women's Voluntary Service, as military organisations, were each entitled to bulk supplies and this led to friction.

The government had two departments dealing with the rationing of petrol. The Ministry of Transport dealt with commercial vehicles and road haulage while the Board of Trade and then later the Ministry of Supply dealt with private motoring, which had three categories: essential users which included doctors, semi-essential users such as commercial travellers, and non-essential users which comprised the bulk of people and into which category the WI was placed. This was one of the reasons why they ended up by having to do such battle with the Ministry. By the outbreak of war there were almost 2 million private cars in Britain and motoring had become a way of life and not just a hobby. The government did not feel sufficiently confident to deny civilian motorists petrol completely but they limited the supply to sufficient fuel for 1,800 miles a year. By the end of the war the number of civilian cars on the roads was just 11 per cent of its pre-war high. Peggy Sumner put her beloved Morris 10 on blocks and the only vehicle she drove during the war was a civilian ambulance. Sybil Norcott was more fortunate. Her father was a farmer so had a larger petrol ration, which meant he could keep a car on the road. Although there was a brisk black market in petrol, as there was in so many goods, the WI could not be seen to be taking advantage of this source. My grandmother, however, did. She would receive a phone call from the garage who would tell her that 'the bicycle is repaired' and that would be a cue for her to drive down and fill up her car. Her sister-in-law, Ruth Toosey in Barrow, seldom drove her family car and used her bicycle during the war. It was an upright model with a skirt guard which the children nicknamed the 'potato peeler' because it rattled and clanked.

As a method for savings stocks of petrol rationing worked. In fact it was so successful that in July 1940 all motorists were granted a concession of 300 miles for servicemen on home leave. This lasted for the remainder of the war. The grey area as far as voluntary organisations were concerned was the definition of semi-essential users. The National Executive of the WI considered that the work their members performed, particularly with reference to fruit preserving, was war work set for them by the government. Thus they ought to be entitled to extra petrol in order to be able to carry out this essential work. At the beginning of the war Miss Farrer was able to report with satisfaction to county secretaries that the Petroleum Department of the Board of Trade had agreed that key workers would be entitled to normal fuel allowances and that Voluntary County Organisers and county workers should apply directly to the Board of Trade. It was particularly for those women running the WI market stalls, as it was often their responsibility to drive round villages collecting the produce to be sold.

In late January 1940 the Ministry of Agriculture confirmed that WI national and county organisers would be entitled to supplementary petrol rations in view of the valuable work they were doing, especially in their efforts to 'stimulate local education authorities to provide further facilities for instruction in rural domestic economy'.

However, by June 1940 the attitude of the civil servants at the Ministry and the quantity of petrol available for domestic use meant that the WI would not receive special treatment. Mr Squance in the Petroleum Department, formerly the Department of Mines, locked horns with Miss Walker at the national headquarters. She wrote testy letters to him explaining that the Ministry of Agriculture had formally asked the WI to be involved in the fruit preservation scheme and that this was not possible if organisers could not move around their counties. Mr Squance wrote back: 'I should emphasise that the 300 miles is a maximum [per county] and the allowances on that basis will only be granted in special cases where it is considered the circumstances demand this mileage.'[15] The atmosphere between the two bodies deteriorated and Miss Farrer took over the correspondence from Miss Walker. She wrote, in early 1941, to complain that the Women's Land Army and the Women's Voluntary Service were both entitled to bulk supplies of petrol so why could the Women's Institutes not be treated in the same manner? The battle for petrol rations continued throughout the war and at times the arguments became acrimonious. On one occasion, when Miss Farrer tried to force the point that the WI was a voluntary organisation tasked with doing work for the country for which the vast majority of the contributors got neither pay nor petrol nor even a free pot of jam, Mr Mackay wrote back explaining that WIs would have to 'take their place with the many peace-time social and cultural organizations whose use of petrol must be severely restricted in war-time'.[16]

The problem of transport affected the WI at all levels. The institutes were particularly resourceful when it came to organising alternative transport, especially when getting food to the WI market stalls. Some food was boxed up and sent with the local grocer if he was going in the same direction, other women took fruit and vegetables into markets by bus, the pony and trap saw a resurgence of use and others still cycled with heavily laden baskets back and front on their bicycles. Where a cycle was not available and the distance was not too great, some women resorted to pushing their wares in babies' prams or carts. Such was the determination not to waste produce and miss the market sales that any method was acceptable provided the fruit and vegetables arrived in good condition. Grocers would sometimes help by offering a corner of their trailers and the market controller would collect from homes if she had a car and petrol. 'One controller broke her gear lever as she was driving along with a heavy load of produce. There was no way of changing gear, no time to get it mended, so she drove on in the same gear, past traffic lights, past startled policemen, called out blithely, "Can't stop. Must get to market." And she did.'[17]

The Voluntary County Organisers (VCOs) and other officers responsible for lectures, demonstrations and checking produce stalls and preservation centres often had to do without their cars and make journeys by bus or cycle. One VCO in Warwickshire cycled 1,258 miles in a year to fulfil her commitments, a feat that impressed the National Executive Committee who recorded it in 'What the WIs Did in 1944'.[18] A Denbighshire VCO had a motorised bicycle called 'James' that she used to reach hamlets tucked away in the hills. Miss McCall calculated that a minimum of 30,000 visits were made by these county volunteers annually and that the true figure was quite possibly double that, even in wartime when travel was so difficult. Mrs Herschell, head of the Pie Committee at Willaston, had to cycle to Ellesmere Port one week as the baker had failed to deliver. The distance was only six miles but the problem was that she had to carry 600 pies on her bicycle.

By the middle of the war the WI market stall had become a valuable addition to county towns and villages. Surplus fruit, vegetables and flowers were sold on a regular weekly basis in 300 locations throughout the country. The market stall had humble beginnings and was slow to grow. The first market was opened on 14 December 1919 in Lewes, East Sussex. It was a collaboration between several WIs and at its height sold produce from twenty-three institutes. At first it was intended to sell produce from members only but it soon expanded to include goods from smallholders, allotment-holders, owners of cottage gardens and ex-servicemen. This last was helpful for men who, on their return from the Great War and during the years of the Great Depression, found themselves without jobs and a prospect of work and an income in the future. Cooperative markets meant they could grow vegetables and sell them, bringing in a small amount of income. For some it proved to be a turning point in their lives and led to more ambitious business ventures. The markets also filled a gap since the quantities of fruit, vegetables and other goods sold were too small for any commercial business to handle.

From the outset the markets were registered as cooperatives under the Industrial and Provident Friendly Societies Act. Producers became shareholders by buying a share for one shilling. They then elected a committee of management to run the markets, often a mixture of men and women, with a number of WI members included. The Ministry of Information, which commissioned a short report on the markets, deemed them to be 'business-like and practical examples of cooperative rural enterprise'.

Miss Vera Cox, the marketing organiser of the WI, was a spirited lady and tireless. She claimed to have been born in London by mistake and was brought up to dislike towns. After leaving school she worked as a farm labourer in Devon and Surrey from 1916 to 1920: 'four years of spreading dung, standing knee deep in water ditching, patching sheep folds in the icy cold and singling roots in extreme heat'.[19] After those challenging early experiences she obtained a war bursary to Seale-Hays Agricultural College in Devon and then attended the West of Scotland Dairying School in Kilmarnock, so that by the time she gained her national diploma in dairying she could say with confidence that she knew a great deal about farming in different areas of the country. Once qualified she went to work on a mixed farm in North Lincolnshire, where she ran the accounts. She also 'acted as unofficial bailiff and helped to settle lock-outs and labour disputes and gave advice on everything – from the choice of wallpapers to the choice of wives'.[20] After she moved to Hampshire to run a small grass farm she joined the local WI as secretary and served on the Hampshire County Federation Agricultural Subcommittee. She was also keen on drama and helped to produce plays in the village. When she became the marketing organiser in September 1932 she beat fifty other candidates to the post.

Miss Cox advised WIs on setting up new markets, on running

them and how to manage their registration as provident societies. She helped to draft a set of model rules by which markets should operate and these were published in a handbook. The Carnegie UK Trust, who had been supporting the WI market project financially by paying for the marketing organiser's salary, continued to fund the role until 1941, after which the post had to be funded by the markets themselves. The commission charged to the market stalls rose from 0.5 per cent to 1 per cent of turnover. This was altered in March 1943 to exclude market stalls that had a turnover of less than £500 from then onwards until six months after the end of the war. It was clearly a policy to ensure that the markets carried on, if subsidised by the National Federation, rather than closing for want of being able to pay the commission. Even by this time there were still counties that had resisted, for one reason or another, the call to set up and run markets. At the same meeting in March Miss Cox reported that she had had success in Middlesex, Somerset, Devon and Huntingdonshire and that she was planning to visit Northumberland and Anglesey, neither county having developed markets. Cambridgeshire, she noted in her report, had refused to cooperate.

Until 1939 WI markets were held mainly in local market towns with the produce being supplied from the surrounding villages. The stalls ranged from the larger markets with a turnover of £2,000 a year to the small trestle-table type of stall with a turnover of about £200. 'Every kind of home produce was sold, home-made brawns, cakes, cream, butter, eggs, poultry, vegetables, flowers and all kinds of preserves.'[21] This of course changed as the war progressed and rationing became more restrictive. In the autumn of 1939 it was still possible for stallholders to sell cakes and biscuits, which were popular and always sold first. They could also sell the jam produced by WI members with sugar ordered from the National Federation but this too was stopped after sugar rationing was introduced and the goods on sale gradually became fewer and fewer. The book on the history of WI markets reported in 1944:

> Since 1939 the markets have increased to over 300 but changed somewhat in character. Rationing has limited their sales mainly to vegetables and fruit. It is no longer possible to sell dairy produce or jam, poultry is very limited and only markets in existence before the outbreak of war are allowed an allocation of fat and sugar for the manufacture of cakes and cooked foods; transport is also very difficult. In spite of this individual market turnovers have increased, sometimes as much as £500 in a year.[22]

There was pressure from government for the WI to take over responsibility for the collection and distribution of surplus produce around the country. Although they were ideally placed to do this, the Marketing Subcommittee refused, feeling that the WI should take part in rather than initiate any scheme of that kind. They were right to do so since the problem of distribution would have become insurmountable because of petrol rationing. It is clear from correspondence between goods vehicle organisations and the Ministry of Petroleum that no concession was made as petrol rationing got worse and many small producers and distributors found themselves in great difficulty.

Despite the lack of willingness to run collection and distribution, the Marketing Subcommittee was keen to promote market stalls and to encourage more WIs to set them up. Oxfordshire already had two large markets prior to the war in Oxford and Banbury. In 1942 they set up a market at Henley which, after a somewhat slow start, became profitable and recorded good sales figures, though was never in the same league as Oxford. 'Both Oxford and Banbury Stalls had record turnovers during the summer in spite of so many of the most paying goods being cut off by rationing, and many regulations controlling the sale of practically all produce. Fruit from small gardens, at a time when all the large growers had to send to the factories, was especially welcome in the towns, and fresh vegetables and rabbits also found a ready sale.'[23]

The feeling amongst the Marketing Subcommittee was that country people had a duty in wartime to make sure they were self-supporting. Members were discouraged from buying food in a town if it could be produced in their own village or, better still, by themselves. The success of the local market stall in selling surplus food depended on the running of the stall being as simple and free of red-tape as possible. This was a great deal easier in peacetime than in wartime, when the only major concerns were the formation of a small committee and the opening of a bank or post-office account. During the war the government introduced restrictions on a monthly basis so that one of Miss Cox's main tasks was to keep market stall coordinators up to date with the latest maximum prices for food and the restrictions on what could or could not be sold.

The market stalls were run by committee and each appointed a volunteer to be the controller. She was a member of the WI but not necessarily the chairman of the organising committee. Her role was to ensure that the produce to be sold was up to standard and she had the authority of her committee to refuse produce that she decided was below par. She also organised the layout of the stall, keep abreast of government regulations relating to rationing and the sale of food and was present on market day come rain or shine. Most markets paid their controller a small honorarium and took care of her out-of-pocket expenses but for many of them it is clear that they undertook the work for love and not money. A description of a market stall run from a street in Norfolk gives a picture:

> The stall had an awning which sheltered the produce and conducted rain-water in a penetrating, well-directed stream straight down the backs of the helpers. They stuffed newspaper between their necks and the collars of their mackintoshes and resolutely refused all suggestions from headquarters that a stall under cover might have advantages. It would be so dull, they said. Out in the street you could talk to all the passers-by and to your neighbouring stall-keepers. Shut away in a shop you might be dry, but how could you see what was going on? And with delighted smiles they offered a wad of dry newspaper to the head-quarters organizer if she cared to stay for a bit and share the fun. Often it was impossible to rent accommodation under cover, and hundreds of people owe a deep debt of gratitude to market controllers and helpers who day in and day out in snow, rain, or east wind, not to mention bombs, shells, and doodles, carried on cheerfully and efficiently.[24]

One of the most difficult areas for all WI market stall controllers was the subject of eggs. They were rationed and the sale of eggs highly restricted. But there was also a thriving black market in fresh eggs, especially when the much-loathed dried egg powder became a staple. Adults today still speak with intense dislike at the memory of grey, watery scrambled eggs made with the powdered variety. In 1941 the Ministry of Food agreed to meet Miss Cox to talk through current thinking and the new policy on sales. She met with Mr Flatt of the Eggs Branch of the Ministry who explained that: 'Under the present order, owners of 50 or less hens may sell direct to consumers, but they are not allowed to supply eggs for sale on WI market stalls.'[25] The subcommittee decided 'to recommend that an interview be sought if possible with Sir Henry French of the Ministry of Food asking that owners of 50 or less hens should be allowed to supply eggs to WI market stalls for sale to registered customers under the ration scheme. The subcommittee felt that such an arrangement would bring into the ration supply eggs which would otherwise be kept for distribution in the village in which they are produced.'[26]

Oxford market misunderstood the Ministry of Food's regulation on the sale of eggs in early 1941. Miss Saunders submitted a report to the county federation saying: 'It is deplorable to have to report that the Oxford Stall is likely soon to be prosecuted for two offences, (i) selling more than 5 doz eggs to one consumer at retail prices, which was done in ignorance of a new regulation, and (ii) selling ungraded eggs at more than the legal minimum price. The Oxford Controller has seen a solicitor and we are now waiting to see what happens as so far no steps have been taken against us.'[27] The following month the committee heard that the case had been heard in court and that Oxford had been fined £5.00 which the market controller, Miss Bartlett, had paid out of her own money in a bid to keep the WI's name out of the proceedings. The committee immediately reimbursed her as the offence had been committed 'in genuine ignorance'. The minutes noted that 'Worcester College was fined considerably more for buying the eggs'.[28]

Oxfordshire was not the only county to be fined for failing to operate within the ever-changing rules. In 1943 the Marketing Subcommittee learned that Tunbridge Wells had got into trouble for overcharging for onions. This was regarded as such a serious issue that the secretary of the subcommittee was 'instructed to make further enquiries concerning the possibility of the NFWI becoming affiliated with the Retail Fruit and Vegetable Association and to make similar enquiries from the Retail Distributors Association'.[29]

The WI saw the markets as an excellent educational opportunity. Emphasis was laid on the need for members to learn about the right kind of produce to grow for markets, and on the necessity for proper grading and packing (the market controller was given authority to refuse produce not up to the required standard). It was also a good way for women to get to grips with running a business and earning a small amount of money for themselves from the profits on sales. If WIs had learned one thing about food production in 1940 it was the need to grow fewer perishable vegetables and more root vegetables. Nothing was more dispiriting, one member wrote, than having a surplus of perishables at the same time as everyone else and thus witnessing waste.

As food rationing and other restrictions were introduced, pressure on women to be the leaders on all aspects of home and family life increased. *Good Housekeeping* published an editorial in August 1941 that summed up expectations:

> Yours is a full-time job, but not a spectacular one. You wear no uniform, much of your work is taken for granted and goes unheralded and unsung, yet on you depends so much. Not only must you bring up your children to be healthy and strong, look after your husband or other war-workers so they may be fit and alert, but you must contrive to do so with less help, less money, and less ingredients than ever before. In the way you tend your family, especially, your skill – and your good citizenship – are tested. Thoughtlessness, waste, a minor extravagance on your part may mean lives lost at sea, or a cargo of vitally-needed bombers sacrificed for one of food that should have been unnecessary . . . We leave it to you, the Good Housekeepers of Britain, with complete confidence.[30]

5

DIGGING FOR VICTORY

> These are critical times, but we shall get through them, and the harder we dig for victory the sooner will the roses be with us.
>
> *C. H. Middleton, 1940*

'Dig for Victory' as a slogan for a campaign to produce more food from gardens and allotments was adopted by the government at the beginning of the war but a renewed push came in the summer of 1940. It was a time of great anxiety but there was a determination not to be defeatist. The message came through that 'the government expects the Women's Institutes to play an important part in replacing those lost supplies'. They were encouraged to plant root crops for the winter and to harvest whatever they could in their own gardens but also in the orchards, hedgerows and woods. 'With the help of sugar and without it, our members are going to be instrumental in saving for future use hundreds of tons of fruits of the earth from our home gardens and orchard.'[1] The war had entered a new phase, as we have seen, and the two threats that concentrated people's minds at that time were the potential invasion of Britain by the Germans and potential food shortages.

Mrs Milburn wrote in her diary on 6 July:

> Twink and I took our little walk in the peaceful fields . . . No one to be seen there – just trees and hedges and the great blue arch of Heaven. In the evening the village is quiet, with scarcely a soul to be seen walking about. But it is not a happy tranquility. It is unnatural and eerie, and tense at times. Behind it lies the unhappiness and anxiety of war and the not knowing what will happen to our dear, dear land in the next few months.

Lord Woolton's call to arms was directed at the housewives of the country and his familiar, friendly manner through radio broadcasts encouraged them to do their bit. None more so than members of the WI who were reminded of their role in feeding the nation during the First World War. It was the affirmation of the WI's nurturing role. Talks aimed at inspiring women at institute level to reach for their spades and dig up their borders were successful and popular. Within two weeks of the outbreak of the war Ningwood and Shalfleet's WI on the Isle of Wight had invited members to a meeting to learn about various soils and their treatments. The afternoon was a practical exercise working in the garden of a large house planting roses and fruit bushes. All members were cordially invited and told to bring gumboots, a spade and a packed lunch. The county federation suggested to institutes that there should be a campaign to use the gardens of holiday homes and derelict cottages for cultivation, provided permission was sought from the owner of the property.

In addition to talks, demonstrations and letters to county chairmen the WI had *Home & Country* as a way to reach its members. At the beginning of the war, Miss Moore, the editor of *Home & Country*, decided to reduce the size of the magazine from thirty-six to twenty-two pages and to suspend the monthly supplements but to continue to publish once a month. The size was further reduced in 1945 to fourteen pages as paper became even more scarce. The magazine was full of advice on coping with wartime conditions: how to preserve fruit without sugar, how to deal with 'strangers in our village', knitting for winter warmth, the produce guild and so forth. But there was always space for a diverting story or a humorous column to entertain hard-pressed women and there was, for the first two years of the war, Booy's calendar, the picture story of a black Scotty dog who got into all sorts of funny situations. Sales of *Home & Country* fell during the war-reflecting a drop in membership, but rose gradually almost to pre-war levels by 1943. The letters pages are clear evidence that the magazine was popular not only with women, as there are monthly communications from men, not just husbands, commenting on one or another matter brought up in a previous issue.

Miss Moore encouraged her readership to send in success stories and one was published by a Mrs Wilkinson from the West Country in September of that year. Mrs Wilkinson had attended a meeting of her local Produce Guild and listened with increasing fervour to 'an earnest and impassioned speaker, who implored us to organize our WI members and cultivate that waste ground in our village, urging us on to this praiseworthy objective like some great reformer of old. Digging was good for us, the most perfect of all physical exercises, he said, holding us with a basilisk-like intensely patriotic eye.'[2]

Mrs Wilkinson confessed that at the start of the war she was not a keen gardener and had become an early convert. She wrote: 'I sat through it all in a rosy haze of patriotism, and then, still fired by patriotic zeal, I attended our next WI monthly meeting.

When I told them all I had heard, the members became as enthusiastic as I was.'[3] One of them immediately volunteered to go and ask an elderly member of the village whether they might take over her derelict allotment and when the answer came back yes, they all grabbed their spades and set off to dig.

When they arrived they were almost overwhelmed. The entire allotment, all fifty square yards of it, was completely overgrown and the ground was hard and rough. They decided they needed to employ a man to break it up. 'Deploring our weakness, we shamefacedly asked many able-bodied men to undertake the task. One agreed to do it, but on seeing the ground said he would not do it for £5.00. Another said he had once had that piece of land, and wouldn't give us 5s for any crop we could grow on it. We even went outside our own village; but no man would touch it.'[4]

The women decided they would have to tackle the job of breaking up the ground and preparing it for sowing themselves. After several serious setbacks, including a conflagration that nearly consumed the neighbouring hedge as well as the scrub on the allotment, they succeeded in clearing their plot of tins, bottles, bricks, stones, foxgloves, dandelions, twitch, blackberry brambles, wild horseradish and an odd assortment of junk. They met whenever the weather was fine and continued to work on their project, sowing and thinning the vegetables. Mrs Wilkinson observed the men on the neighbouring allotments looking down their noses at the WI handiwork. 'Some remarked that it looked as though a lot of old hens had been scratching about, and others said, "more like swine rooting". But we were convinced they were merely jealous.'

In September 1940 Mrs Wilkinson was delighted to report to *Home & Country* that they had lifted their early crop of potatoes and sold the lot, re-sowing the ground with cabbages, carrots, parsnips and swedes. 'Our main crop we have not yet lifted, but we have many orders for it – one of 2 cwts. The early potatoes are amazingly good. Our bill for the seed was £1, and our first few rows made £1.5s. We shall certainly have a good profit.' She was pleased to note that the men who had jeered at the women were 'struggling to keep their minds on their work and their eyes from straying to our superior and very healthy plants'.[5]

Urchfont WI members in Wiltshire were equally triumphant about the half-acre plot of land they managed to acquire for WI use from the local manor house. It had been very hard work digging the ground but, to their delight, the crops they produced were magnificent. The secretary of the WI suspected it might have something to do with the fact that the land had been a pig pen for the past ten years. 'The best sprouts in the district were the envy of all men growers. Our cabbages were weighty: we very soon sold every ten shillingsworth to the Pewsey Vale Association for resale to HM Forces. The carrots, parsnips, artichokes, leeks and onions are looking fine, and we intend to give the local hospital a good crop of potatoes.'

These gardens were no exception. Institutes took over deserted gardens all round the country, with the work being shared between members and willing helpers, such as schoolboys and evacuees. Sulgrave in Northamptonshire was running two cooperative patches side by side, one dug by their members and the other by local schoolchildren. Although WI members who sold produce were entitled to keep the profits it is striking how often these were sent off to help the war effort or to charitable organisations to help people who needed support. Baggrow and Blennerhasset in Cumbria donated the profits from their produce shows to mobile canteens while Sharnbrook WI in Bedfordshire gave their surplus funds to the WI Ambulance Fund. Members of Old Warden in Bedfordshire regularly sent vegetables to the communal dinner canteen for evacuees and troops.

Thornthwaite-cum-Braithwaite in Cumbria announced that many new gardens had been created by the summer of 1940 and that most of their local waste land that could be cultivated was now under WI control and expected to yield a good harvest of vegetables. Allotments run by local institutes became a valuable addition to gardens and were often sown with a single crop, such as carrots or potatoes, so that the yield could be shared out between members and any surplus sold. Mrs Sims dug up part of her garden in order to grow more vegetables. 'Part of the tennis lawn was sacrificed for potatoes and a plot in the orchard was known as the Victory Bed. My parents grew all our own vegetables and fruit. We had raspberries, gooseberries, red- and blackcurrants as well as apples, plums and pears. I also remember my mother planting leeks and my brother John once pulling them all up in a fit of pique,' Ann remembered.

Fruit and vegetable talks and demonstrations became popular up and down the country with counties concentrating on what grew well in their soils. Shropshire focused on gardening and beekeeping while Staffordshire institutes began a drive to encourage poultry-keeping, whether in gardens, backyards or allotments. A produce guild member of Sevenhampton in Gloucestershire told her institute that she was keeping three old age pensioners, with a combined age of 244 years, supplied with fresh vegetables.

Mrs Milburn's garden in Leicestershire was a triumph that summer. On 8 July she wrote in her diary: 'Some thunder today and a sharp, three minute shower this morning. The garden is greatly freshened. The peas have filled out their pods, the leeks are upstanding and the cabbages are too marvellous for words – they have grown enormously in two days.' That day Lord Woolton announced, without prior warning, that tea was to be rationed to 2 ounces per head per week and margarine and cooking fats were also to be drawn into the rationing scheme.

It was not until Tuesday 16 July that she and her husband received a telegram from the War Office to say that Alan was a prisoner of war. 'There and then, saying "Thank God", we embraced each other for sheer joy at the good news. Oh how delighted we were to hear at last he is alive.'

Two months later, on 7 September, Hitler launched the Blitz. The war rained down on Britain's major cities for nine months. 'Germans bombing London every night', wrote Edith Jones in her little brown diary. Even for women living in villages well away from the bombing the sense of menace was ever-present. Patricia Kelly had been evacuated from Manchester to Cressbrook in Derbyshire. She said: 'My bedroom in the cottage in Cressbrook was high in the roof and I could see the red glow in the sky when Manchester and Sheffield were being bombed during the autumn of 1940. Sheffield to the right and Manchester to the left.' In October 1940 *Home & Country* came under attack. The editorial for the month began: 'this should perhaps more properly be headed, "From the Editor's Dug-Out", for it was drafted in the basement to which the staff of *Home & Country* retires when the air-raid siren goes off. The preparation and production of this number of the magazine has been carried on during a period of all-night and nightly Air Raids, and constant daytime alarms and raids.' She added that not only had the staff had to cope in these trying circumstances but so had the printers, who had battled on for months 'with air battles going on overhead more or less continually'.

As a result of the intensive air attacks on London during September the staff of headquarters moved to Puddephats Farm in Markyate, Hertfordshire. There were further apologies to readers of the magazine for the lack of the usual blue cover which had to be dropped since the heavy paper 'used up nearly one-third of the amount of paper allotted to us by the Paper Control'. Paper was controlled from the beginning of the war. Newspapers were limited to 60 per cent of their pre-war consumption of newsprint and magazines had to follow suit. Paper supply was officially limited and controlled by the Ministry of Production in 1942. Restrictions of all kinds followed in alarming succession as the bombing raids on London and other British cities intensified.

Sybil Norcott was responsible in large part for the kitchen garden at her parents' farm outside Dunham Massey near Manchester. Her mother was disabled with multiple sclerosis and her father was occupied by farm work. 'The farmhouse garden was no kaleidoscope or blaze of colour but a utility garden. During the war the name utility was apt. The garden was down to earth, a basic necessity but it provided luxuriant fruit and vegetables for family, friends and neighbours in a time of frugal living. We grew early peas and beans, strawberries with ruby-red jewel like fruits, Cox's orange pippin apples and any number of other wholesome produce. No fertilisers were used, just good sweaty, currant cake coloured, rotted donkey manure, either spread or well dug in,' she explained.

Sybil was born in Lancashire on Shakespeare's birthday in 1928. Her father was one of thirteen children from Liverpool and her mother, who had been orphaned as a child, was from Cheshire. Sybil's father had always wanted to farm and soon after her birth he was granted tenancy of Heath Farm in Dunham Massey. 'At last my father achieved his childhood dream. He had a farm of his own and it was there that I spent a wonderful childhood,' Sybil said. Although the farm was isolated she was very happy. She had a Manx cat, a dog called Peter Pup and a donkey called Tommy. She was an inquisitive little girl and very outgoing, so Peter, the farmhand, took her under his wing and taught her a great deal about nature. 'Peter could not agree with his extravagant daughter-in-law so he moved into an empty loose-box on the farm and converted it into a bedsit. He became the granddad I had never known.' Peter was a keen gardener and he created a kitchen garden for Sybil's mother, growing her soft fruit, herbs and all the vegetables she could ever want. When Sybil was old enough, Peter made her the child-sized spade which she still has, and he taught her to dig, sow and harvest. 'I even had a little plot of my own. I called it the secret garden for it was past the poultry houses and surrounded by a tall hawthorn hedge.' Peter retired when Sybil was still a little girl and her father took on another farmhand, an Irishman named Martin.

Like Peter, Martin was a great naturalist and he enjoyed nothing more than lying on his tummy observing the animals in the covert. He used to take Sybil with him and she watched with him as the fox cubs learned their skills while playing rough and tumble with one other. He showed her the barn owl which raised a brood in the loft over the stable and explained to her how the owl spread out the laying of her eggs so that they hatched at intervals. This meant the mother could feed the baby owlets at their individual stages of development and the oldest owlet would sit on the other eggs and keep them warm while the mother owl went out hunting.

Martin moved into Peter's loose-box and Sybil remembered him refilling the feather mattress on his bed whenever they plucked a duck. His ways with the natural world fascinated her. 'Martin carried a dried fox's tongue in his pocket. He would soak it, cover it in Vaseline and bandage it on wounds. It could draw out thorns, heal a cow's foot and even soothe a horse's hoof after shoeing. I always thought it had magic powers. And when he had done with it he would put it back in his waistcoat pocket.' He had a lovely gentle sense of humour, which always delighted her. On Saturday nights he would go to the pub 'to refresh himself well', riding on her father's bike. It didn't have a bell but the mudguards rattled so loudly that her father would hear him coming back late in the evening and know he was safe. One night he was later than expected: 'Dad asked him if he was drunk. "Nay Mester, I was just sober enough to know I was not quite drunk. Sure, it was the bike. It wouldn't stand still while I got on it."'

Sybil's father harvested potatoes in the traditional way, helped by Martin. 'Dad drove the horses, pulling the old-fashioned potato digger and Martin took charge of emptying the full hampers into the cart. The potatoes were stored at the edge of the field in hogs. Between cartloads Martin would dig a wide gully, leaving the soil in a heap on either side. The potatoes were tipped, then shaped into a triangle and covered with straw. The soil was replaced, leaving a gap at the top with the straw protruding to allow for the spuds to dry without sweating. Later the potato tops covered the whole hog to guard against the frost.'

Sybil learned so much about life and nature from the two farmhands and from her father but she also required formal education. This began at Partington Village School and then continued, from the age of eight, at Altrincham Girls Grammar School. When she was twelve her mother decided to join the WI. Sybil was too young to join the local institute, as the minimum age was fourteen, the statutory school-leaving age; however, Partington WI took girls from twelve so she and her mother joined that institute in 1940. She explained: 'My mother wanted very much to join but the track to the village was through the woods and my mother did not want to walk that route on her own. She was afraid. So she asked me to accompany her on my bike, which of course I did and that is how I came to join Partington WI.'

The war brought relatively little change for Sybil, though the proximity of the village to Manchester meant that she was only too aware of the so-called Christmas Blitz which reached its height on the two nights of 22 and 23 December, killing 684 and wounding four times as many civilians. When she left Altrincham Grammar in 1944 she worked on the farm full time as this was considered to be proper war work. She was already experienced at most aspects of farming and had learnt to drive a tractor at seven so she slipped easily into the role. Her mother, who had become thoroughly involved in Partington WI, was not able to work outdoors. 'My mother never complained about her condition, she was so brave, and she took on all manner of voluntary work during the war. The WI is not just an institution, it is a way of life and one that my mother embraced. So from an early age, when Mum was laid up, I did a lot in the house as well as working outside.' Sybil was perhaps unusual in that she had so much responsibility for home production at such a young age but she was certainly not alone. Peggy and Majorie Sumner down the road in Hale turned their back garden into a vegetable patch, though Peggy admitted she did not have green fingers and the only line of peas she ever grew to maturity provided but one serving. She was nevertheless a good knitter and she managed to combine that successfully with her civilian ambulance work.

One of the most useful propaganda tools the government had in encouraging people to grow their own food and to make their excess produce available was via the BBC Home Service. The weekly fifteen-minute gardening programme was fronted by Mr Middleton, who had been broadcasting to the nation's gardeners since 1931.

Cecil Henry Middleton was born in 1886 in Northamptonshire. His father, John Robert Middleton, was the head gardener to Sir George Sitwell, so that the young Mr Middleton grew up with the Sitwell children, Edith, Osbert and Sacheverell. At the age of fifteen he began to work on the Sitwell estate but by seventeen he had left Northamptonshire and moved to London, becoming a student gardener at Kew. During the First World War he worked in the horticultural division of the Board of Agriculture and Fisheries and was involved in food production, later going on to join Surrey County Council as a horticultural instructor. He had also had a spell working in the seed trade, so that by the time the war came he had experience of many aspects of food production as well as gardening. Although a modest man he was proud of the gardening tradition and resented the portrayal of gardeners as 'funny old men with battered hats and old moth-eaten trousers, and with whiskers and very little intelligence'. He was the complete opposite of the caricature, being neat and bespectacled but with a warm and engaging manner.

Just months after its inception in 1922, the BBC began broadcasting gardening talks which ranged from practical advice supplied by the Royal Horticultural Society to gardening traditions and history with luminaries such as Vita Sackville West speaking about their specialist areas. The advice given by the RHS, however, was described as 'entirely impersonal, read by an anonymous announcer, and peppered with Latin names'.[6] As the BBC developed, so it felt it had to offer listeners more appealing programmes and they asked the society to recommend speakers who could talk on gardening. Mr Middleton's name was put forward as one of a pool of gardening experts and he broadcast for the first time on 9 May 1931, with the opening words: 'Good afternoon. Well, it's not much of a day for gardening, is it?'[7] His easy manner and his conversational style of broadcasting made him one of the most popular speakers on the radio and by the outbreak of the Second World War he had been broadcasting his own programme *In the Garden* for five years.

Mr Middleton's programme reached 3.5 million listeners each week. It was a gift to the government, especially given his role in food production during the last war. When he was not working on his weekly broadcasts he was toiling in his own garden or travelling around the country giving lectures and offering advice to professional and amateur groups alike. His BBC talks were so popular that people who were unable to hear them broadcast would often ask for transcripts, so that in 1942 he published *Digging for Victory*, which included talks covering the autumn, winter and spring months from September 1941 to May 1942. In his preface he wrote:

> In happier days we talked of rock gardens, herbaceous borders, and verdant lawns; but with the advent of war and its grim demands, these pleasant features rapidly receded into the background to make way for the all-important food crops. But interest in the garden has never slackened; it has, if anything, been intensified by the urgent necessity of growing food, and presumably most of my old friends still listen when I hold forth on Leeks, Lettuces, and Leatherjackets, instead of Lilac, Lilies, and Lavender.[8]

The WI often quoted tips from his weekly broadcasts in their advice to institutes. He was particularly good on advising storage solutions for root vegetables, onions and fruit that could be kept through the autumn and winter, but he also had much to say on the subject of bugs and caterpillars, which brought out a playful side:

> I have noticed a good many white butterflies about and you know what that means – caterpillars on the Brussels and other greens if something isn't done about it. I find a tennis racket a

> very good thing for swatting white butterflies. I am getting quite expert at it and developing quite a good over-arm stroke, but even so, you can't swat them all and they still find their way to the cabbage leaves, so I usually have a look through the plants to find their eggs. These are laid in clusters and stuck to the underside of the leaves; they are bright yellow and easy to see, and if you squash them with your thumb and finger that means one colony of caterpillars less.[9]

One of the key messages he gave at the beginning of the war was that plants take time to grow. However much the government encouraged the nation's gardeners to plant, sow and reap, they could not speed up the growing cycle of, say, an apple tree. Patience was always required. A tree that was planted in one year and had its small crop of fruit picked in the following season would not do as well, longer term, as a tree that was allowed to become established and then crop better in the second or third season.

Apples vary enormously and some store better than others and people had to work out how the crops could be staggered so that not all the apples ripened at once and went to waste. The storage of apples is an art and the autumn pages of *Home & Country* were full of advice about how not to bruise them when they were picked, on the best form of wrapping, or indeed whether to wrap at all when paper was in short supply. With careful handling and cool, not too dry conditions, apples picked in September could be crisp and ready to eat the following spring. Mr Middleton told his listeners that he had once kept apples in perfect condition until the end of May by storing them outside, in old fruit boxes piled up against a wall and covered in old sacks, odds and ends and finally a few pieces of corrugated iron: 'We had some pretty sharp frosts while they were there and the whole pile was buried under snow for a time but the apples were well protected. We took out a box at a time as required, and there were very few bad ones among them.'[10] Mrs Van Praet, who was a land girl in the war but later a WI member, recalled storing apples and pears in a sturdy thatched building in their orchard at Broughton Hall on the Staffordshire–Shropshire border where she worked. 'The fruit had to be constantly monitored and with those going rotten being jettisoned for the compost heap.' Edith Jones stored her apples in a granary next to the wash house at the farm. Those that were not keepers she would bottle, along with her pears, plums and damsons.

Preserving food was a way of life that was still well understood in the countryside though electricity and fridges in towns and cities had brought more modern food-storage possibilities. Cold storage was already used by commercial growers and meant that by the 1930s people could buy fresh apples in towns more or less all the year round. The trouble came during the war and not just because there was a shortage of apples but owing to the government fixing the price of apples regardless of the time of year. The effect of this was that it did not pay the commercial growers to store apples during the winter and spring but to sell them as quickly as they could. 'This may lead to plentiful supplies between now and Christmas, but precious little after that,' Mr Middleton said in October. He recommended to his listeners they should put any good 'keepers' in store for as long as possible and buy from shops while supplies were still plentiful. He also encouraged those who had no apple trees to buy keepers and store them in cool conditions so that they too would have stocks of apples into the next spring. This is just another example of how the war changed attitudes towards food. Growing one's own food, even in small quantities, helped to protect families from the vagaries of the food supply chain.

The WI took this advice to heart and published a series of drawings and articles on how best to store apples. One showed a wooden box with troughs and furrows of newspaper separating the lines of apples. They explained how the fruit should be graded and each variety kept separate with plenty of ventilation so that the sweating of the crop in the first few weeks would not give rise to rotting. Once this process had been completed then the apples could be wrapped individually in newspaper or in the trough and furrow box system. The sweet smell of stored apples evokes childhood memories for many people and something that has all but disappeared today.

After the remarkable fruit harvest of 1940, when the WI alone reported 1,000 tons of jam, over one million kilograms, or 4 million half-pound jars, had been made, the ripening season of 1941 was disappointing and gardeners everywhere struggled to produce even a decent percentage of what they had enjoyed in the glut the year before. It was demoralising for those women who had taken on allotments and gardens in early 1940 and celebrated success over their excellent potatoes and carrots. But they soldiered on.

A vital prerequisite for a healthy vegetable crop is decent fertiliser. Edith Jones had excellent compost made from a mixture of straw with cow manure from the barns, hen droppings, which are rich in nitrogen, and garden waste. She was fortunate. Other women growing vegetables on allotments had to rely on artificial fertilisers to help their crops. Throughout the war, fertiliser was in limited supply so people had to resort to using kitchen waste and even night soil, the contents of their privies, to encourage their plants to grow. The government had control of all fertilisers but there was a serious shortage of potash until 1943 when Canada began to mine and export the precious mineral. Potash was hard to replace and it was much missed by industry as well as gardeners. Ashes from wood fires or bonfires contained potash and could be used on gardens but most households used coal and coal ash was no use, except for keeping back nettles.

But fertiliser itself was not enough to encourage the kitchen garden or allotment to flourish. 'If you take a cart-load of vegetables from the plot and put back a cart-load of farmyard muck, you will have made a fair exchange, the soil will be quite satisfied and produce another cart-load of vegetables.'[11] Farmyard manure mixed with straw was ideal as it is bulky and decayed slowly, releasing food into the soil gradually. It was difficult to get farmyard manure because the farmers were using it on their own fields in the absence of manufactured fertilisers and of course there was the question of transport. So the WI and other groups stepped up their campaign to use all forms of waste materials in various stages of decay to provide the bulk and slow-releasing nutrients that the straw otherwise provided.

Mrs Van Praet, the land girl, was taught how to mix potting soil from leaf mould, which she would collect in great sackloads from the nearby woods. She would add to this a bucketful of lime gravel taken from the derelict tennis court at the hall and stir them both together with garden soil and a little bit of sand. 'Thus we produced a wonderful, loamy mixture. It certainly worked well and our tomatoes were magnificent in both colour and flavour. This was an indoor job which I enjoyed as it kept us out of the wind and rain.'

Miss Hess, the agricultural adviser to the WI, was keen on compost heaps. She urged members to throw anything from the garden or kitchen onto the heaps, proposing two or three heaps about five feet square and four feet high for a modest-sized garden. There was even a lecturer doing the rounds in the early years of the war who spoke about composting. A member in Cirencester was so inspired by a description on the radio about how to construct a proper compost heap she was said to have constructed a 'lordly pile which is one of the sights of the village'.[12]

Vegetables and fruit were one aspect of country food production but the other was animals. WI members were encouraged to keep poultry, pigs, goats and rabbits for their meat and fur. Chickens, ducks and turkeys were relatively easy to manage, even in a small garden, and many people kept hens for eggs and later, for the pot, though a hen at the end of her laying days is fit only for a well-cooked stew. Ruth Toosey kept hens. Caroline remembered: 'We always had plenty of eggs though I do remember my mother making cakes with dried eggs, which were dry as a result. Meat was scarce during the war but the real horror was the soup that my mother made using a sheep's head. It had bits of meat and vegetables floating about it in and I remember it tasted disgusting. There used to be a race to see who could eat it up fastest and reveal the flower pattern on the bottom of the bowls.'

Nella Last, another prolific wartime diarist for Mass Observation, and member of her local WI in Barrow-in-Furness, kept chickens in her little back garden. She often referred to them in the diary, and sometimes had concerns. In September 1941 she wrote: 'I felt a bit worried over one of my chickens: it has "gone back" for some reason. I've got some chicken pills and gave it one today. Such a kind little hen, she took it quite well. I hope it does her good, for I'd hate to lose her now. The others all look well: they are thriving and eat a lot.'[13] Edith Jones wrote a great deal about her chickens in her diaries. Hatching chicks was always a delight for her and she would have at least three sittings a year. She also bought new pullets for laying and had a series of sheds around the garden and orchard which hens progressed to at various stages of their development. Some weeks she would take a gross of eggs to the market, which she would sell at 1s 6d a dozen, giving her 18s (£38.40 today).

Leigh WI in Lancashire encouraged their members to keep poultry and were pleased to report in 1940 that two members had started from scratch and others had increased their stock. 'The following increases were reported: 24 pullets, 11 cockerels, 12 day-old chicks, 12 ducks and 7 geese.' The total number of fowl in the village was not given but the minutes' secretary reported that 2,283 eggs had been preserved that season. Hookwood WI in East Sussex kept a meticulous log of all their members' produce and livestock activities. It was kept by Mrs Daisy Jackson and was subtitled 'Drive for more food production'. Mrs Jackson reported on one member's poultry: 'Mrs H Brown keeps chickens, ducks and bantams which have all done splendidly in egg laying. From January 1 to October 31 from 18 hens – 1429 eggs, from 5 ducks – 465 eggs and from 3 bantams – 91 eggs. The bantams didn't start till March and left off in September. The ducks left off at the end of September but the chickens are still going strong.'[14] Lady Denman had always been keen on poultry keeping, as was the Minister of Agriculture, Sir Reginald Dorman-Smith. He told his audience in a BBC broadcast:

> The hen is an excellent medium for the production of food, not only does she spend her life in providing us with excellent food – an egg is a meal in itself – but at the other end of her period of economic production she provides us with a well covered carcass of meat. When we realise that to maintain this production we can feed her on all sorts of household waste without much expenditure for other foods, the importance of the humble fowl in this war is clearly demonstrated.[15]

As the larger animals were a greater commitment the WI proposed setting up village pig clubs. These were started in 1940 and were initially not a success, with just eight established by the summer, but by the following July the WI was able to report that after just one year of campaigning over 1,000 pig clubs had been formed, and the 1,000th was for members of the royal household at Windsor Castle. The great appeal of the pig clubs was that members could cure bacon and hams from their own pigs in spite of rationing as well as selling them to the government for a profit.

A pig club was set up in the village of Barham in Kent in 1941 and celebrated success two years later with sales of twenty-seven pigs to the Ministry of Food and four killed for the village in December and a further two the following February. With the profits from the sale of those pigs the club purchased a further twenty-one piglets. The WI minute book records: '14 of those have been sold to the Ministry of Food bringing in £124 [£4,200]. There are now 7 pigs left. It is proposed to kill two of these for Christmas and send the others to market. Nearly all the pigs sold have reached top prices.'[16]

Classes were offered on pig-rearing and meat preparation in an article entitled 'Pig into Pork'. The advice ranged from curing a whole pig in a large wooden trough to making sausages and black pudding to preparing brawn from half a pig's head.

> Every bit of the pig should be made use of and here is an old country way of using up scraps and oddments that used to be counted a special dish. Wash and dry the pig's liver and sweetbread, and mince them together with some fat and lean bits of pork, beating the last named first of all with a rolling pin to make them tender. Season with pepper, salt, a little grated nutmeg and a very little finely shredded onion. Add a spoonful

> or two of stock, just enough to bind the ingredients. Make the mixture into a thick roll, cover it with the leaf – that is the inner fat of the pig – and bake it in the oven.

It is clear that the wartime country housewife was more than used to butchering and dealing with animals.

The WI pointed out that the pig club movement also brought benefits to agriculture. 'Since its 25,000 members do not breed pigs but only fatten them, their demands have had a steadying effect at a difficult time upon the market for weaners.'[17] They were also keen to point out that two pigs kept at the bottom of a 10-rod plot would produce 500 kilograms of manure a year, which would then go to dressing the plot at the rate of 80 tons per acre. That is a satisfactory covering sufficient to make Miss Hess and Mr Middleton smile. By 1943 there were some 4,000 pig clubs throughout the country with over 100,000 people involved. Many villages had large metal dustbins labelled 'Pig Food' where local people could contribute household waste and suitable vegetable peelings to the communal pig bin. Ronnie Spatch remembered being asked by his mother to help her fix the bin to the tree in the centre of the village: 'Mother was very institute minded and she liked to take on responsibility for things that would benefit everyone in the community, so we were involved in the Pig Club. We got an old dustbin, metal of course, with a lid and I pushed it round the village in a wheel barrow collecting swill and leftovers. It smelled pretty ripe by the end of a summer's day, I can tell you.'

Lord Woolton knew that one of the ways of keeping the WI on side was to make sure that from time to time their work was recognised officially. One of the most memorable visits was made by Mrs Roosevelt, accompanied by Mrs Churchill, to Barham WI. The build-up for the visit had started nearly a week earlier and although it was meant to be shrouded in the utmost secrecy with the identity of the celebrity visitor withheld, one member asked innocently: 'Oughtn't we to begin learning the Star Spangled Banner?'[18] Barham was chosen because it was close to the Canterbury–Dover Road and Mrs Roosevelt was on her way from Canterbury to Dover. She had told her hostess, Mrs Churchill, that she was keen to see a typical WI with its preservation centre, weekly market stall, communal allotment, rabbits, pig and poultry clubs. Barham also had a flourishing choir and drama club and had been knitting for the services and the prisoner-of-war fund as well as gathering herbs, hips and salvage material.

Mrs Roosevelt and Mrs Churchill and other dignitaries arrived on board a double-headed train of seven LMS coaches. Sixty members of the press from almost every national newspaper who were bussed in separately. Among the guests were Colonel Hobby of the WAAC, the Dowager Marchioness of Reading (WVS) and Mrs Lawton Matthews (WRNS). Lady Denman and Miss Erle Drax, the chairman of East Kent FWI, were on hand to welcome the visitors. Although the location of the village was meant to be kept secret one paper gave the name away and the following day, when Canterbury was blitzed, a train at Barham was strafed.

The minutes secretary, who was asked to record the visit, wrote: 'A film was made, flash light photographs taken, the garments for Merchant Seamen, the market stall, wool collected from the hedges and knitted, the toys and fur garments were admired. The preservation centre was inspected, a rabbit from the rabbit club, a pig from the pig club, two hens from the poultry club were commented on. Mrs Murphy, the WI president, took Mrs Roosevelt round the stalls and Barham WI showed America's First Lady what it did in wartime.'

She inspected the WI produce on show and was introduced to a pig called Franklin from the village pig club. The visit was reported on the news that evening, with film of Mrs Roosevelt joking with the member holding the pig. The clipped tones of the commentator announce proudly: 'Rural England shows America's First Lady how it is doing its bit. At the village hall the bazaar displays with evident pride the products of an industrious community. It meant a great deal to the residents of Barham and to the President's wife also. Nice people.' A week later Mrs Roosevelt sent Lady Denman a telegram to say: 'Before I return home may I again thank the NFWI for the extraordinarily interesting demonstration of their work arranged at Barham. I congratulate you on the fine contribution they are making to their country's war effort and wish them all possible success.' Mrs Roosevelt had endeared herself to everyone by announcing 'I felt very much at home at Barham.'

Such events were great morale boosters and Lord Woolton paid several visits to markets, canning centres and produce events and was always careful to write to thank the WI for their efforts in helping with the nation's larder, as he called it. Lady Denman was equally aware of the value of this form of acknowledgement of their work and she made sure that his letters were published in *Home & Country*.

One of the less-publicised contributions the WI made to production was in the collection and drying of fruit and leaves, both for food and for medicinal purposes. The foxglove, or *Digitalis purpurea*, had long been known to have useful medicinal properties. In 1775 Dr William Withering discovered that an effective medicine for treating heart conditions could be made from drying leaves picked just before the plant flowered and crushing them into a powder. He also discovered that if the patient was given too much it was poisonous. It was not until a hundred years later that the active properties of digitalis were discovered and the benefits, as well as the risks, of this medicinal plant could be fully exploited. During the Second World War there was a shortage of certain drugs which had formerly been imported into the UK and this shortfall had to be made up by collecting whatever medicinal herbs there were in the country. The British pharmaceutical industry processed huge amounts of foxglove leaves, many of them gathered in collection parties organised by the Women's Institutes.

One of the difficulties of exploiting the foxglove is the need to pick, carry and store the leaves without bruising or damaging them. The drying process is also not straightforward and required the advice of experts. In Oxfordshire the WI was fortunate in having Dr W. O. James from the Department of Botany at the university as their adviser.

Dr James was a plant physiologist who had a reputation for imaginatively prepared lectures that attracted many students. His wife, a fellow botanist, had written to the county secretary in early 1941 explaining how the previous summer her husband had made a survey of herbs needed for medicinal purposes, which were to be found in the Chilterns, particularly around Henley, Nettlebed and Peppard, and in large enough quantities to be worth collecting commercially. 'He had found the following: Belladonna, Digitalis, Datura and Hyoscyamus, and had had them collected and dried under his supervision. He was willing to extend the scheme this year in collaboration with the OFWI and suggest that members might collect herbs on specified dates and send them to depots from which he would collect them and superintend drying.'[19] Dr James was exploring the home cultivation of some of these medicinal plants and the success of his efforts led to national recognition of the Oxford Medicinal Plants Scheme.[20] When dried, the herbs could be sold, and after deducting costs of transport, drying etc. the profit would be available for the institute collecting, but 'Dr James asks us to emphasise that it will be very small. People must not expect to make any real money out of it, but to regard it as a piece of national service, by which they can help to supply life saving drugs which would not otherwise be available.'[21]

During the spring of 1941, members of Oxfordshire WIs and other willing volunteers collected foxgloves and belladonna which were dried at Islip by Dr and Mrs James at their home. This yielded 350,000 doses of digitalis. To put this into perspective I consulted Dr Nigel Stanley who explained that 'Digitalis was given as a single daily dose for long term treatment of heart failure and so 350,000 doses would have provided one year of continuing treatment for 1000 patients.' This was therefore not an inconsiderable contribution from just one county but more was needed. In April Mrs James wrote again to the county secretary, this time asking her to encourage members to grow foxgloves on any piece of spare land, so great was the demand for digitalis. The collection and drying of these medicinal herbs had proved so successful that they encouraged members to broaden their harvesting and bring in dandelion roots, nettles, chestnuts and rosehips. In 1942 the board of the Medicinal Plants Scheme wrote to thank the institutes for their work in collecting plants and in particular to those institutes who had taken no payment for the leaves they had collected. A film made about the medicinal use of foxgloves was sent around institutes so that they could see the value of the work they had undertaken.

Towards the end of the war the demand for rosehips grew. The WI and other voluntary organisations were asked to collect 500 tons. The reason they were so highly valued was that they contain a high concentration of vitamin C, something that was only established relatively late on in the war. While oranges and lemons were plentiful before the war there was no need to focus on other sources of vitamin C but once they became scarce another source was needed. They discovered that a pound of good-quality rosehips contained as much vitamin C as a dozen large oranges, as well as containing other valuable vitamins as well.

Rosehips could not be eaten in their raw state so they had to be collected and sent to manufacturers who could convert them into syrup, which was then sold through pharmacists for children and people in hospital. The advantage of rosehip syrup over orange syrup was that it was not so strongly acid, which made it an easier and more palatable drink for patients. In 1945 Miss Hess wrote that: 'During the past four years members of WIs all over the country have gathered hundreds of pounds of rosehips, so that it is natural that the Association should now appeal to them to assist in continuing production this summer at the rate of five hundred tons of hips a year. The demand is likely greatly to exceed the supply for children here and on the continent. Recently 1000 gallons of the syrup were flown to France for Polish children living in a war camp under appalling conditions, where they had been assembled by the Germans to harvest root crops.'[22]

Miss Hess suggested that pickers should take gloves, a large basket and a crook-handled stick, adding that if it were the blackberry season she would advise taking a second basket for picking those as well. Elsie Bainbridge used to collect rosehips in Cumbria after school. The price of rosehips was 3d a pound to the pickers, she remembered, but they did not use baskets.

> We put them in paper bags and then took them to the chemist in Penrith who would then send them on to the manufacturers.

> I also used to get a penny each for rat tails. Rats were a real nuisance around the village, on the farm of course when they nested in the hay and we were paid as children to trap as many as we could. You didn't need to take the whole rat in, just the tails. A councillor in the village would collect them and count out the cash. It was one of the many ways we got a little bit of pocket money in those days.

Elsie had to work on the farm too. She did not need gloves for picking rosehips but she certainly did for harvesting turnips. 'It was hard in the winter. We used to get chilblains picking them even though we had nice woollen gloves. The turnips were mainly for the sheep but we also grew potatoes, carrots and cabbages for ourselves.' Elsie's mother was in Morland and Newby WI in Cumbria during the war and she remembered her mother going to the meetings.

> A lot of people on farms were self-sufficient but it meant that women didn't have a lot of reason to get out. Going to the WI was an opportunity for farmer's wives to get out and be together. They were big on their weekly competitions and there were even county competitions which kept going during the war. My mother was very resourceful. When we didn't have sugar she would use Golden Syrup and I remember the biscuits she used to make with syrup in those days.

Mary Hodgson also came from Cumbria. Her parents had a farm in Howtown on the banks of Ullswater. 'My parents lived on a mixed farm and we had land girls. Women would take over men's jobs and keep things going. Everybody worked together, nobody was on their own. There were no selfish ways in those days. We grew carrots, turnips and potatoes for the servicemen who were

ıdy Denman, NFWI Chairman
)17–1946, was said to be worth
n men on a committee

Members of the NFWI Executive Committee 1937 with Lady Denman seated in the centre

·race Hadow was Lady Denman's Vice Chairman
·om 1918–1940. She was an academic from
)xford, an outstanding public speaker and a fearless
ıountaineer

Dame Frances Farrer, NFWI General Secretary 1929–1959, known for ringing ministers before breakfast

Edith Jones and her nephew Leonard, c. 1943

Edith Jones with her husband Jack ar
her great-niece, Chris Downes

Clara Milburn, prolific wartime diarist and member of Balsall Common WI

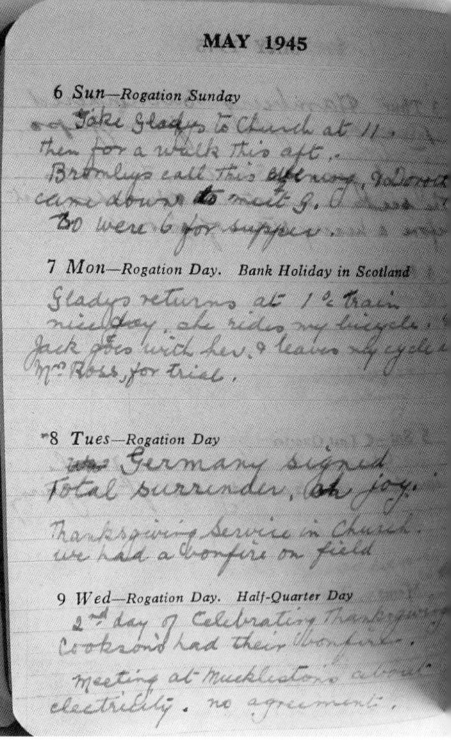

MAY 1945

6 *Sun*—*Rogation Sunday*

Take Gladys to Church at 11.
then for a walk this aft.
Bromleys call this afternoon, & Doro
came down to meet G.
So were 6 for supper.

7 *Mon*—*Rogation Day.* *Bank Holiday in Scotland*

Gladys returns at 1 o/c train
nice day, she rides my bicycle.
Jack goes with her. & leaves my cycle
Mrs Ross, for trial.

8 *Tues*—*Rogation Day*

Germany signed
total surrender, oh joy.
Thanksgiving Service in Church.
we had a bonfire on field

9 *Wed*—*Rogation Day.* *Half-Quarter Day*

2nd day of Celebrating Thanksgiving
Cooksons had their bonfire.
meeting at Muckleston's about
electricity. no agreement.

Edith Jones's diary entries for the last three day
of the Second World War

Thousands of tons of fruit were boiled in WI preservation centres

x canning vans were donated to the WI by the American Federation of Business and Professional Women

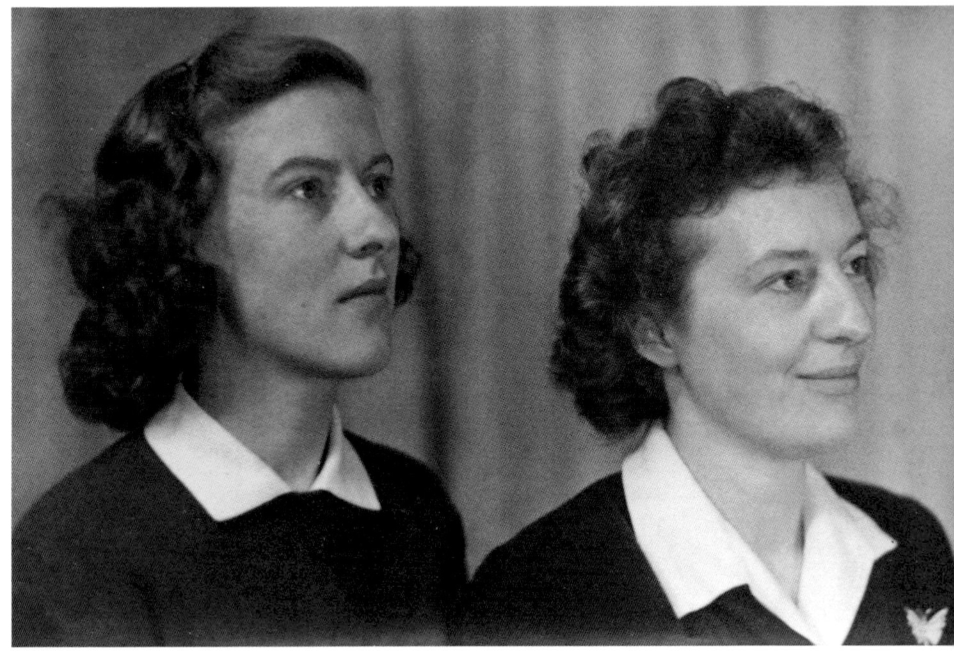

Peggy and Marjorie Sumner. Peggy (left) joined Dunham Massey WI in 1938 and was still a member in 2012

Ruth Toosey was the secretary of Barrow WI during the war

Sybil Norcott joined her local WI at the age of 12. She says 'the WI is a way of life'

r Gwen Bark was a GP and encouraged young
others to join their WIs to have a voice on
atters concerning their children

Betty Sims, mother of Ann Tetlow, was an active member of Bradfield WI for over 40 years

iriam Ward (right), with Aunt Phil, was a
under member of Bradfield WI and secretary
ring the war

Ann Tetlow (left) and Dorcas Ward's childhoods were shaped by the war and their mothers' involvement with the WI

Pies on sale at Toft in Cheshire as part of the meals in rural areas scheme

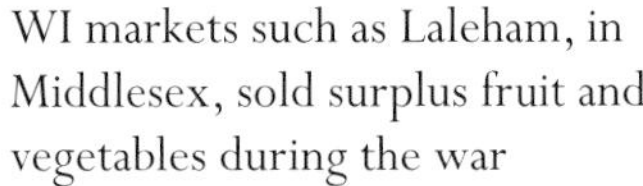

WI markets such as Laleham, in Middlesex, sold surplus fruit and vegetables during the war

Weighing vegetables at Muskham

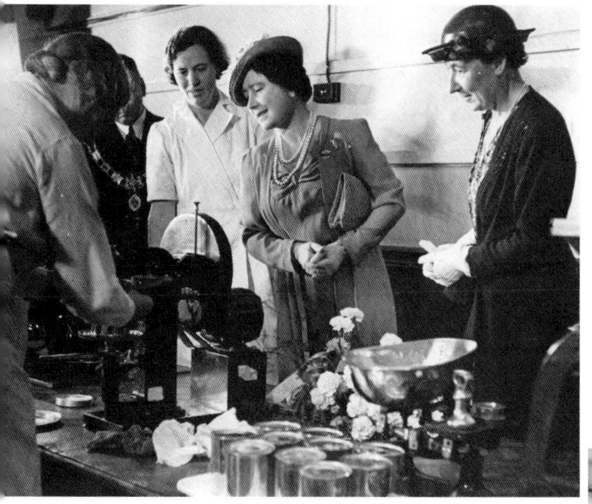

Queen Elizabeth at the WI canning centre at Reading in August 1941. She was a member of Sandringham WI with Queen Mary, who was president, and Princess Elizabeth, who joined in 1943

A WI ambulance being handed over by Lady Denman outside the London HQ of the NFWI

Mrs Roosevelt on her visit to Barham WI in Kent, October 1942

Lord Woolton, Minister of Food, visiting a WI, June 1941

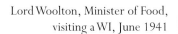

Mrs Milburn as Britannia in her WI pageant in 1941. That morning she had heard that her nephev
had been badly injured and his wife killed in the Blitz

Amongst many other activities the WI collected herbs for medicinal purposes

Community Singing at Flamstead WI in Hertfordshire during the war

The WI made potato baskets for th
Ministry of Agriculture

stationed locally. We didn't grow fruit but we used to get plenty in exchange for chickens and butter. And then I used to go to Penrith and sell chicken and butter at the market on Tuesdays.' Mary was still at school at the beginning of the war. She used to walk two and a half miles to Pooley Bridge. In the winter, when it snowed, she could not leave the farm so had to miss school.

Snow interrupted life regularly for farming communities and not just in Cumbria. The weather could be treacherous in the hills around Smethcote and in winter of 1941 there were six weeks of snow and blizzards. It began on New Year's Day and gradually got worse. On 5 February Edith Jones wrote in her diary: 'Gale, blizzard. Snow. What a day! Drifts everywhere, yards high.' The following day, 'Jack lent Jolly to Mr Silver to ride home. He himself rides the chestnut nag to bring Jolly back. Drifts over the horse's head in places.' At times like this it was impossible to hold WI meetings, so that year they only held nine meetings, for which they had to obtain special permission from county headquarters.

In addition to growing vegetables, collecting wild herbs and rosehips and keeping pigs, the WI encouraged women to breed rabbits. Rabbits had the advantage of being multi-purpose and were reared throughout the war for food and fur, latterly most especially so for Mrs Churchill's Fur for Russia Scheme which she ran in 1944. Edith's diary often refers to Leonard ferreting to catch wild rabbits with his friend Jim Middleton. They would regularly return with eight pairs. 'Monday, 10 Jan, Len and Jim Middleton go ferreting to catch 8½ pairs of rabbits. Len has unfortunately lost 2 of his ferrets through eating a bad rat. The best worker is left, one good thing.' Mrs Ward in Bradfield was also adept at catching rabbits, which she sold at the market for their meat. In 1941 an article from the ad hoc Subcommittee for Agriculture and Handicrafts outlined the advantages and somewhat surprising statistics about rabbits: 'The tame rabbit reproduces itself rapidly and can, in the course of a year, produce over half a hundredweight of meat, which is a little higher in proteins and minerals than most butcher's meat, but has a lower fat content. It can be made into a great variety of excellent dishes.' No mention of it tasting like chicken. Half a hundredweight is 25 kilograms, which is a very large accumulator on the average rabbit that weighs around 650 grams.

On the premise that nothing must be allowed to go to waste, the article explained how the skin, unless in very poor condition, should be removed with care and dried by nailing it onto a board and then sent to a reliable firm for dressing. Alternatively rabbits could be kept and killed for their fur. One advantage of rabbits was that they were more or less able to be fed on grass and vegetable scraps, with just the odd handful of hay, bran or corn. Does could be used to breed just two weeks after weaning their youngsters so that the cycle could be repeated every three months, since the gestation period for a rabbit is just thirty-one days. 'The weaned youngsters can be reared in groups if desired . . . in hutches with wire netted bottoms, so that they live mainly on grass. Under this system they can quite often obtain all the food they need, except a little hay, to raise them to killing age at three to four months old. Tame rabbits, like fowls or wild rabbits, are killed by dislocating their necks.'[23] The article continued, 'if more are produced than are needed for the family table, there is a very keen demand for tame rabbits in the principal markets, especially in London and other big towns, at 3s 4d to 5s each.'

Although skins were also much in demand there was a big variation in the price for them, depending on the grade of the rabbit fur and the age of the creature when it was dispatched. 'Those of common rabbits killed at early ages made 2d to 1s each according to grade, while the skins of the more valuable *fur* breeds, which are killed in winter after maturity, make from about 3s to 6s each, and very much higher prices for a few special skins in perfect coat.' However, Mr King Wilson warned that breeding for fur was a much more skilled job than breeding for the table. Mrs Heron Maxwell told the Consultative Council at their meeting in August 1941 that they should appeal to rabbit owners to keep Ermine Rex and to sell their white pelts for export to the United States. 'Unfortunately when the skin reaches its most desirable texture what lies beneath has long passed that stage and has qualified for stew pots only. A nice problem for rabbit fanciers. Which way lies patriotism?'[24]

Of all the schemes the government asked the WI to promote it was the bone salvage scheme that was the least savoury. There were severe restrictions on shipping and domestic livestock farming had been cut back, yet the country still needed to import 50 per cent of its meat. Argentina had been Britain's main pre-war trading partner and faced a significant cut-back to its exports. As a result a decision was taken to process the meat prior to shipping by means of de-boning, telescoping and canning it. This enabled Britain to maintain its meat imports at their pre-war level. However, importing meat off the bone meant that there was a lack of bones available for industrial use.

Mr Dawes, the Controller of Salvage at the Ministry of Supply in Tothill Street, a stone's throw from the Cabinet War Rooms, was in charge of addressing this issue in March 1942. He wrote to all town, borough and metropolitan councils, to urban and rural district councils and to the Special Scavenging Districts (Scotland) to ask them to organise an increase in the salvage of household bones. There had already been five circulars to that effect but the tonnage collected so far had been far below expectations and seriously short of requirements. 'Hitherto it has been possible to meet the deficiency largely (though not entirely) by reliance on imports. The present war situation with its repercussions on sea routes, especially from the Far East, has forced the position that the bone using industries must now rely continuously on home sources to provide the necessary supplies. Household bones must therefore assume equal importance with other forms of salvage such as waste paper, metal etc.'[25]

Every bit of bone, even rabbit and poultry bones were needed, though not fish bones. There was no substitute. Bones were routinely used in a variety of important war-related industries. Technical fats were extracted from bones and used for explosives, lubricating grease for guns and tanks, glycerine and medicinal products. Bones were also used for glue vital in the manufacture of aeroplanes, ships, shell carriers and other forms of equipment. Ground-up bone meal was used as fertiliser and processed bone meal needed for feedstuffs for the cattle, pig and poultry industries.

The average yield of household bones from the salvage schemes run in December 1941 was 45lb per thousand of population and that had dropped in the spring. 'The tonnage of bone issued for purchase at butchers' shops, either in the meat ration or separately, has been ascertained from statistics compiled by the Ministry of Food; carefully conducted tests reveal that less than one-fourth of this tonnage entering dwelling houses is at present recovered.'[26] This does rather beg the question as to how the calculations were made, not least as Mr Dawes revealed that the tonnage of bones returned to the trade by butchers had also been taken into account. He went on: 'There can be no doubt that this most serious loss arises because bones are put into dustbins with refuse, burnt or buried.'[27]

The solution was to organise a collection of bones, and this would have to be carried out frequently since, it was admitted, 'householders had shown a dislike of retaining bones for more than a day or so, especially in warm weather'. Experts had confirmed that bones could be dried, but not burnt, either in an oven or on a boiler so as to get rid of the smell but without damaging the industrial value. The suggestion was to set out bins for the bones but these had to be kept out of the reach of dogs, who had shown a keen interest in the bone salvage scheme and become a menace in some areas. Salvage stewards, who were appointed to encourage the collection of every piece of recyclable waste, were urged to emphasise to householders the necessity for saving every piece of bone. 'To prevent bins from being overturned by dogs, they should be fastened, where possible, to trees or standards. The bins must be clearly marked BONES so as to distinguish them from kitchen waste bins. Suitable posters are available from Salvage Department.'[28]

Inevitably the bone salvage scheme was incorporated into WI wartime duties and they were encouraged to run the scheme in their villages. And, more importantly, to explain to people why the collection of bones was so important and to get Boy Scouts and other enthusiastic collectors to help out with checking the bins, cleaning them, repairing them where necessary and making sure dogs could not get at the precious salvage material. Coningsby and Tattershall helped to collect 3 tons and 7 hundredweight of bones for the salvage scheme in 1942 along with 1 and a half tons of rags, 54 tons of paper and 3 tons of insulation material. At their January meeting they decided to buy a padlock for the yard as the material was potentially so valuable. The publicity for the bone salvage campaign was carried out by local authorities with advice, if required, from the Federation of Bone Users and Allied Trades, and run through towns and villages by means of posters, newspaper advertisements and loudspeakers. It is hard not to smile at the thought of some eager council worker bellowing through a megaphone: 'Bring out your bones.'

6

BOIL AND BUBBLE, TOIL AND TROUBLE

> 15 February 1941: This is another of Hitler's 'invasion' dates, but up till 9pm he has not arrived. Jack sprayed the fruit trees with a cleansing wash and I did another yard or two of pear tree border.
>
> *Mrs Milburn*

Jam. If you ask someone what they think the WI did in wartime they will probably answer 'They made jam.' It is true. They did and they made a lot of it. As we have seen, it is by no means the only contribution members made to the war effort but it is one of the two images that the general public has of the WI. The other being singing 'Jerusalem'. They have had to live with that cosy couplet 'Jam and Jerusalem' for over half a century and it risks ridiculing the enormous amount of valuable work done by the women of rural Britain.

The contribution the WI made to fruit preservation should not be underestimated. To be clear, the Women's Institute did not take over responsibility for the manufacture of all jam during the Second World War. Factories continued to buy farmed fruit and produce jam as they always had done. What the WI did was to make hundreds of extra tons of jam from surplus fruit. This was fruit that would otherwise have rotted on bush or bough, either growing wild, in village gardens or on allotments. In 1940 alone it was estimated that their efforts saved 1,170 tons of fruit and it was sold commercially as well as in villages and on WI market stalls. It was a wonderful example of how the WI network functioned to the benefit of the country as a whole.

Four years into the war and thousands of tons of jam later the NFWI's educational organiser, Cicely McCall, summed up the appeal of this work:

> Jam-making was constructive and non-militant, if you liked to look at it that way. It accorded with the best Quaker traditions of feeding blockaded nations. For those who were dietetically minded, jam contained all the most highly prized vitamins. For those who were agriculturally minded, the scheme saved a valuable crop from literally rotting on the ground, and it encouraged better fruit cultivation – though not, one can only pray, of plums only. And for the belligerent, what could be more satisfying than fiercely stirring cauldrons of boiling jam and feeling that every pound took us one step further towards defeating Hitler?[1]

Why was jam so important? There were two main reasons. First, making fruit into jam, canning it or bottling it, preserved it in a state that meant it could be used long after the fruit itself was out of season. Thus it saved a very large amount of seasonal fruit and vegetables from going to waste. Secondly, as jam contained sugar, it was a nutritious, easy-to-store foodstuff that added taste to restricted wartime menus and when made for the government, as the WI jam was, it used sugar that was in addition to that available on ration. They made a large amount of jam to make a significant contribution to the food supply. Rural housewives had a long tradition of fruit and vegetable preservation since, as we have already seen, there were very few houses with refrigerators and it was not until well after the war that freezers were introduced into the home and used as they are today. Thus every housewife had bottled, tinned, canned preserves and some dried peas or beans in her pantry, whether through her own industry or bought from shops and market stalls.

Edith Jones made preserves and jams as fruit came into season. She conserved pears, plums and damsons, dried beans and stored other fruit and meat. Her larder was full of bottles, cans and jam jars while her pantry, with its cool, north-facing aspect and a long slate shelf down one side, had a variety of dressed fowl, cured meat, pies, butter, eggs and cooked meats. The jars were earthenware and she used two sorts – one was a dumpy, cream-coloured cylindrical jar with a lipped rim, ideal for jams, marmalades and other forms of preserves; the other was a rounder two-tone glazed jar, with a body wider at the shoulders than the base, which she used to store her beans in. Both types of jar were sealed to keep out air and the contents would have lasted for more than a year in favourable conditions. Outside above one of the stables there was a first-floor granary, approached by a set of stone steps on the outside wall. Here she stored fruit and vegetables that needed dry conditions, such as winter apples, and broad bean and pea seeds for next season's planting. The granary shared an inside wall with the farmhouse's dining room so that the chimney from the fireplace ran up that wall and kept the store dry even in the winter. Only through such husbandry could she guarantee a food supply for her family throughout the year.

The war broke out just as the autumn crops were ripening. Word reached the National Federation's headquarters that fruit from all over the country was going to waste because the bumper harvest could not be gathered in owing to disruption caused by the outbreak of hostilities. Miss Farrer at national headquarters immediately contacted the Ministry of Food and secured 430 tons of sugar, worth £13,000 (£450,000 today). She then wrote to county chairmen telling them that a quantity of sugar had been secured from the government for the purpose of preserving as much surplus fruit as possible and this could be ordered by institutes direct from London. The minimum quantity supplied by headquarters was one hundredweight or 50 kilograms at a price of 27s 6d and at this stage there was no maximum quantity, though members had to undertake that the sugar was used for preservation purposes only. Within a fortnight the price of sugar had risen to 30 shillings per hundredweight and institutes were ordering by the ton. Edith's institute ordered two hundredweight.

The first wave of jam-making was done on an entirely ad hoc basis, village by village, organised either by institute members or other women in the village who had the space in their kitchens to offer jam-making facilities. Large pots and pans were borrowed and lent, jars and bottles collected from friends and relatives, ripe fruit was spotted and picked from gardens, orchards, trees and hedgerows. Estimates varied about how much jam was made in that first wave but the WI claimed that it had saved some 450 tons of fruit from rotting.

In November 1939 the editor of *Home & Country* was triumphant: 'After that, there could be no doubt that the institute movement is very much alive. One of its original purposes was to help in the production and preserving of food: the very first Institute effort of this new war carried on that purpose.'[2] Another correspondent agreed, writing proudly: 'It is not too much to say that the Headquarters sugar campaign won, for the WIs, the first round of the war. It came at what learned persons call the psychological moment, when many of us saw no future for the Women's Institutes but a prolonged work-party. What women faced with panic need most is an organized common effort and something friendly and sensible in their hands. The National Federation gave us both together.'[3]

Mrs Blagg, the president of Burton Joyce and Bulcote WI, in Nottinghamshire, spoke for many institutes when she wrote in October: 'Our 4 cwt has gone to about twenty homes. We had quite an enjoyable afternoon weighing it, and our members gladly paid more than they were asked – we got it before the Budget advanced the price and by this means we have obtained £2 to help with our sewing for evacuees and hospital supplies. The forethought of the NFWI seems to me to supply an excellent answer to the often repeated cry, "Why do we need national and county federations?"'

With a common aim and united strength, highlighted by Lady Denman as two of the WI's strongest points, the jam-making of autumn 1939 proved the extraordinary efficiency and speed with which the WI could galvanise its members and it undoubtedly helped the institutes to get over the feeling that they were fiddling while Rome burned. Perhaps the greatest success of the first jam campaign, however, was to convince the government and in particular Lord Woolton that the WI was going to prove useful in this war and that they were prepared to seize the initiative.

The press picked up on the story. The *Burton Chronicle* reported on 28 September 1939 that 'Although the separate institutes are vigorously individual bodies, the value of the centralised control exercised by the HQ of the Fed was evidenced last week when the local counties sent in a plea that preserving sugar was running short. Headquarters managed to secure 35 tons of sugar and despatched it forthwith to country branches, thus saving hundreds of pounds worth of fruit for jam making.'

Some counties let their institutes fend for themselves in the first wave of spontaneous jam-preserving whereas others, such as Warwickshire, sprang quickly into action and organised professional canning. One or two women would undertake to do the work for individuals. Canning was an art that many members learned over the next few years but initially it was a high-level skill shared only by a few who had learned it in the Produce Guild. One member described the method of operating the machine:

'You had to turn the handle and it had to be in neutral to start with and this is what caused so many problems. It had to be absolutely neutral to start with and it had to be turned exactly twenty times . . . I fell into it quite easily [but] the other four kept on having trouble with it.'[4]

The risk associated with canning was that if it were not done properly faulty cans could explode dramatically. Mrs Toosey borrowed the local canning machine as it went around the village but did not like it. Caroline recalled: 'My mother actually preferred bottling as she once had a can of tomatoes that was blown, which was dangerous. So she bottled fruit and vegetables and these were stored in the larder, along with some canned foods. Unfortunately the larder was very damp so that the labels fell off the cans. That made for interesting meals as on Sunday nights we would have eggs with tinned vegetables. Sometimes we got eggs with plums!'

After the success of the 1939 'boil up' and a result of rationing, the Ministry of Food asked the WI 'to extend its Co-operative Fruit Preservation Scheme organized under the auspices of the Ministry of Agriculture'. It allocated to the federation a further supply of sugar, which, members were told, 'can be used for co-operative preserving of all local grown garden, orchard and hedgerow fruit supplied by members and non-members alike. Institutes that have not already signed up to the scheme are encouraged to do so through their county office so that they can benefit not only their own members but people in the wider community in their neighbourhood or village.'[5] This was the call to arms. The editorial in *Home & Country* in July 1940 also dealt with the bureaucratic aspect of this work, which became for some institutes such a thorn in the flesh that they eventually backed out of the scheme: 'A strict account of all fruit preserved must be kept for the information of the Ministry of Food, and the preserved produce can be sold through WI market stalls, WI monthly meeting stalls, or to retailers for re-sale in the normal course of trade.'[6] This ruling was put in place prior to preserve rationing, which came into force the following spring and introduced greater restrictions on how jam could be sold. 'With the help of sugar and without it, our members are going to be instrumental in saving for future use hundreds of tons of the fruits of the earth from our home gardens and orchards.'[7]

Sugar rationing was foreseen by the WI and in the same edition there were recipes for sugarless jam. The editor wrote: 'Let no one think that fruit need be wasted if we are unable to get sufficient sugar to convert it into jam.' One method was described as 'the Old Method' or sulphur preserving. 'The fruit must be fully ripe and in good condition. Pick it over carefully and put it into the preserving pan. Let it cook gradually over a gentle heat until enough juice has been drawn from the fruit to prevent any danger of burning. Then boil for an hour. Never let it go off the boil, and let it boil well all over the entire surface.'

So far, so good. Now comes the rather more exciting chemistry experiment:

> The jars (any shape or size will do) should be scrupulously clean and well warmed. Turn them upside down on a table. Put some sulphur in an iron spoon and set fire to it. Slip the spoon containing the burning sulphur under the mouth of each jar in turn until the glass is evenly smoked with fumes. Put the jar down quickly, mouth downwards, on the table to keep the sulphur fumes in. Now turn up a jar and fill it with the boiling fruit pulp; wave the sulphur spoon over the top of it, cover quickly with softened bladder or parchment paper. Brush over the top and sides of this covering with thin glue or paste to make it airtight. Seal each jar as it is filled, before filling the next. The pulp must be kept boiling all the time.[8]

This recipe was not one for the faint-hearted or those of a nervous disposition.

Another sugarless jam recipe, which was recommended for gooseberries, plums and damsons, was called Cottage Bottling. This involved cooking the fruit in large jars in the oven and then, when the fruit had shrunk down a bit, filling the jar to the brim with boiling water and covering it.

And the third method was drying. Fruit could be dried whole or, if large, cut into halves or quarters. Dried fruit became a luxury during the later years of the war but in the autumn of 1939 it was still being prepared. The WI also provided advice on drying vegetables, which would need to be steamed first and then dried. There was a great depth of knowledge in the combined membership of the Women's Institute but no subject, except perhaps housing, elicited more comment than food preservation.

Elsie Bainbridge's mother was resourceful when it came to making best use of what she had to hand. When sugar was in short supply she used golden syrup to make her jam, as she had used it in biscuit baking. 'Mother's jam was lovely and sweet and using the syrup was a good way of making sure that she did not waste the fruit we picked in the garden and from the hedgerows.'

In addition to encouraging members to experiment with different kinds of fruit preserving, *Home & Country* also carried advertisements for preserving equipment which the NFWI had obtained at special prices for institutes. A small number of hand-sealing machines could be bought from the National Federation for £5 12s 6d (£195 today). The tins were also available for sale. Sybil Norcott's father bought her a canning machine that she soon learned to operate efficiently. She would offer her services to the WI but also to other groups locally and that way she earned a little extra money and helped many village women to preserve for the winter. Mrs Cowley of Botley in Oxford had a childhood memory of accompanying her mother to the WI hall where she opened up as caretaker. There, in the hall, she would see rows and stacks of shiny cans ready to be used by the WI workers who came in to undertake this work. She also recalled the noise of the canning machine. It was a proper cottage industry and was taken seriously by both the WI and the government, however not to the extent that the Ministry of Supply would grant them additional petrol rations for distributing the jam.

The WI has remarkable records and in no area are these fuller than in the records of the preserves made in the centres formed at the request of Lord Woolton. All over the country women had taken the minister's message to heart: 'This war may well be decided by the last week's supply of food. It is up to all of us now to see that our people have that last week's supply.'[9] By 13 July some 375 tons of sugar had been allocated to the preserving centres, and 'tons of fruit that would otherwise have gone to waste have been turned into health-giving food for the coming winter'.[10]

The Ministry of Agriculture could hardly have hoped for a better response from the Women's Institutes. Not only did they make jam from all surplus fruit but they also ordered thousands of extra fruit trees and bushes. Blackcurrant bushes were the favourite in many counties as they were easy to grow and produced good yields quite quickly. Apple and pear trees took longer to establish and the harvests would not be large for the first few years. As one member pointed out: 'The government is expecting us to stock the nation's larder but it takes time to get a decent orchard established.'[11] Mrs Milburn was impressed by the quantities available at her local farm stall after the bumper crop in 1940. In August she wrote: 'When supper was over I finished WI notices and took them out to the village, picking up six pounds of greengages at the amazing price of 2d per pound. Plums, damsons and greengages are all so very plentiful this year.' Edith Jones had equally high yields and a particularly good crop of apples she stored not only in the granary but also in the box room, which she had tidied during her spring cleaning.

At Copyhold Farm in Bradfield the Wards grew fruit, including apples, pears, plums, cobnuts and blackcurrants. They also had a small dairy herd and a few pigs. Their aim had always been to make themselves as self-reliant as possible, so that they grew their own barley and oats for the cattle. There were days during the war when Mr Ward would get up at 5.30 a.m. to milk the cows and do a full day's work, and then spend half the night on Home Guard duties. 'My memory of my father in wartime was that he was always exhausted,' said Dorcas Ward. Mrs Ward kept hens and sold the eggs; she trapped wild rabbits which she sold for their meat. The fruit was grown for commercial sale and was taken every week to Reid's in Newbury, where the key thing was to remember to get the wooden crates back from Mr Reid for the next week's delivery. Mrs Ward also grew fruit and vegetables for the family and took great pride in being self-sufficient. 'I remember the great calamity one Christmas when my mother had to buy Brussels sprouts because for some reason our own had not grown that year. It was the shame of her war.' Jam-making was part of Mrs Ward's annual work and she would record on the inside of the cupboard door how many pots she had made in a year. Dorcas recalled the climax being 119lbs. Her mother was always busy, and no more so than at harvest time when she would help with haymaking and organise the farmworkers' wives who volunteered to help her in harvesting the field of blackcurrants. There was about an acre of the bushes and in good years the bushes would be sagging with fruit. Picking the blackcurrants was back-aching work so the women sat on milking stools which they moved along as they picked. In the evenings her mother would sit mending clothes, while listening to the nine o'clock news.

Wartime jam-making was an additional burden for busy housewives. The preservation centres were set up in villages or close to where supplies of fruit were found and the conditions that the women worked in were seldom ideal. The list from 1940 included halls, domestic science kitchens, huts, WI markets, police stations, cafes, packing sheds, garages and private kitchens of all kinds. Mrs Denys Blewitt lived at Boxted Hall near Colchester in Essex. A wealthy lady and an active member of her WI as well as of the Women's National Citizen Association and the Conservative Party, she was very generous offering the hall when it was needed. From 1939 onwards for the rest of the war she made the kitchens in the servants' quarters at the hall available for jam-making. There WI members made more than four tons of jam on seven stoves. Boxted Hall's kitchens were well equipped and there was running water to hand, which was a boon. Where water was not laid on it was carried by relays of willing helpers to the 'kitchens' and the fruit very often had to be picked by the women doing the jam-making. 'At one centre half the members cycled five miles before breakfast to pick the fruit, other members prepared and served them breakfast and the rest preserved the fruit in the afternoon.'[12] Miss Cox, who checked all the forms that came in from the preserving centres, found one that had a note apologising for her form being late but 'my house was bombed and it was so difficult to find things afterwards'.

Lord Woolton visited preservation centres several times each season. His continued support and interest in their work was essential and the visits did much to sustain morale. In December 1940 he wrote to Lady Denman congratulating her on the success of the preservation scheme. 'This was work of national importance demanding administrative ability of a high order at the Headquarters of your organization and local initiative and cooperation which are a fine example of democratic action at its best.'[13]

But the National Federation also sounded a note of caution about the preservation scheme. They wanted to ensure fair shares for everyone and equality was never far from their minds: 'The Institutes have readily grasped both the importance of this piece of work, and the principle of share-and-share alike on which its products should be distributed. It is important that no one, member or non-member, should buy more than her fair share of these sugar-content foods simply because she is better off or has been able to supply more fruit than her neighbours.'[14] This concern fed down to the counties and several had a discussion about fairness at county level. In 1940 members were allowed to buy back their jam at wholesale prices and the executive committees were exercised by the question of how much jam it should allow its members to purchase. Was it fair, they asked, to permit people to buy back as much jam as they had supplied fruit for?

This would discriminate against those who had produced less fruit and also those who would not be able to afford to buy large quantities. They also asked the question: 'What safeguards are there that members getting jam cheap can't sell it expensively?' The National Federation recommended that everyone should be allowed the same quantity so that no one was treated unfairly. The following year rationing was introduced and there were no special privileges for anyone. That was easier for WI members but the public was unhappy. An article entitled 'Making Jam at Home' appeared in *The Times* in March 1941 explaining how the Minister had asked the WI to take on the task of preserving all surplus crops.

> Already there is some feeling against 'the plan for giving all available sugar for jam making to the Women's Institutes and allowing none for private persons.' Mrs Dulcibella Dalby of Castle Donington, Derby, writes that angry feeling will be aroused in people who are not members of the Women's Institutes and there will be a sense of injustice at a small body of the community having the handling and control of all sugar for jam and bottling.[15]

The criticism was understandable but the WI had to undertake to keep the strictest checks on the amounts of sugar used and if any were lost it caused a tremendous headache for the Jam Committee, as was the case when Boxted WI could not account for 80lb in 1942. Mrs Blewitt was in charge of trying to find out what had happened as the local police had been unable to trace the missing sugar. On 9 February 1943 she wrote to her daughter: 'I spent the afternoon with Nina yesterday. We were supposed to finish the Jam accounts, which should have been in by the New Year. I found a proper jam morasse, and as she had not got the Pass Book, or looked at it all the year, we did not get very far. If we have to do it again I shall have to take on the account keeping, it is not conceivable to be so stupid at them as Nina!'

Hyde Heath WI in Buckinghamshire had a welcome surprise on 2 August 1940 when the Queen, who had requested to see a canning centre in operation, arrived to inspect their preservation centre. The canning shed at The Wick was cramped and hot but, as one observer pointed out, the Queen kept her cool. She asked lots of questions of Mrs van Kerkhoven, who gave the demonstration, and was very interested in learning how the fruit was being gathered from local gardens and orchards. Her lady-in-waiting wrote to Lady Denman after the visit to say how much she had enjoyed herself and 'how greatly Her Majesty appreciated all the most valuable work they were doing'.[16] At the end of her visit the members presented the Queen with 'a gift of jellies, jams, bottled and canned fruit'.

Even where institutes had dwindling numbers of members, for example owing to compulsory evacuation from the coastal areas in 1940, women who remained tried to keep jam-making going. In Old Felixstowe there were only a handful of members remaining in the coastal town, yet a fruit-picking party visited the deserted gardens and sold the crops for their owners or for the WI. They said: 'It is hard to carry on but in our quietness and confidence will be our strength.'[17]

Above all, jam-making caught the WI's imagination. 'No common pen can do justice to it', one woman wrote of the great jam drive. 'In Northamptonshire, one canning day, a WI copper was worked so hard it set the chimney on fire.'[18] At another institute members complained of developing corns on their fingers through peeling pound after pound of pears and 'Earls Barton centre has nearly reached the 2000th jam pot . . . while Marbury in Cheshire made 1187 lbs of jam and filled 1132 cans of fruit.' The scale of the industry was quite breathtaking and so was the enthusiasm and appetite for news of their work: 'Wootton Bridge canning report shows 722 cans, 624 lbs jam and 228 bottles, plus a perfectly fresh jar of tomatoes bottled by a member 22 years ago. No wonder they sang the National Anthem!'

The year 1940 was a particularly good one for fruit, especially plums, and the quantities of jam and fruit pickled, canned and preserved were impressive. In perspective, that would have been sufficient to supply 2 million adults with a year's ration of jam based on 1/4lb of jam every two months. The National Federation felt proud that its members had responded so enthusiastically to the Ministry of Agriculture's call for increased production.

Germany launched its *Luftschlacht um Grossbritannien*, translated literally as 'Air battle for Great Britain', in July 1940, first targeting British shipping centres and coastal convoys. Winston Churchill announced to the House of Commons '. . . the Battle of France is over. I expect that the Battle of Britain is about to begin.' It was the first campaign to be fought entirely by air forces and it represented one of the most significant battles in the war. Germany failed in its objective of destroying Britain's air defences. There is no doubt that the success of the Royal Air Force in preventing the Luftwaffe from gaining air superiority ended the threat of an invasion.

In August Mrs Milburn wrote of the Battle of Britain in her diary: 'We hear on the news of airmen's experiences during these exciting flights, usually told very calmly, quickly and tersely. Tonight we hear that in fighting round our south-east and south coasts, as well as over Berkshire, Wiltshire and Hampshire, the Germans have lost 57 planes and our losses are 9 here and 14 on the continent.' The next day, 14 August, she wrote: 'Yesterday's "bag" of Nazi planes was 78 to 13 of ours. And everybody was tired today because we have all been up the best part of the night.' Dugouts, air-raid shelters, Morrison shelters all became an everyday, or rather every night, reality for millions of civilians up and down the country for the next few months as the Germans launched attacks on industrial targets and cities, with often devastating effect. There are thousands of accounts of people hunkering in shelters, some cold and damp, others like Mrs Milburn's bunk hole which was eventually rendered quite comfortable. In London thousands slept in the Underground stations; in Manchester Patricia Kelly hid in an underground canal while the world exploded around her. She had gone home from the safety of Cressbrook to spend Christmas with her parents.

In London during one raid alone on 19 December 1940 almost 3,000 civilians died. The cost of the Battle of Britain in civilian lives was high. Between July and December of that year over 23,000 people were killed and 32,000 wounded. Yet for some it was exciting. Schoolchildren would regularly flock to sites where enemy aircraft had crashed to pick up souvenirs. Elsie Bainbridge in Cumbria had a close encounter. In January 1940 an English plane crashed in a field next to her house in a severe snowstorm. Elsie was in bed with whooping cough and her mother in bed with flu.

> We heard this plane over the roof top. Next thing I heard my father shouting to my mother 'the plane has crashed'. It had hit a hedge and took the hedge half way across the field. When they went over to the plane they expected to see someone injured or worse but all they saw was a notice saying 'danger, bombs on board'. The next thing they saw were footsteps across the field and so they knew whoever it was had escaped. It was a New

> Zealand pilot who walked to the next door farm but there was no one in so he walked into the village. Very few houses had phones in those days but fortunately the first house he came to was the only one in the village with a telephone. So they reported it to the police who came and cordoned off the plane and guarded it day and night until the bombs were dismantled and then they took it away. The thing that made my brother and I feel awful was that we couldn't go to see it because we were ill. My father took us to see it when it had been dismantled but when we got back to school lots of the children told us how they had come to see the plane when it had crashed and how they had got bits of Perspex off it as souvenirs. We were very fortunate it didn't land on the house.

My own mother recalled seeing a plane coming down close to Ellesmere Port. She and her brother, Patrick, jumped for joy as they saw the swastika on the tail when it spiralled down in a plume of smoke. 'Now I think that is an awful thing to have done but at the time, we were just children, and this was an enemy plane and one of our "boys" had got it. I do not know what happened to the pilot.'

The Battle of Britain coincided with the fruit harvests and some WI members had become so engrossed in their work that they regarded the war as an interference rather than a threat. East Kent was in the danger zone during the autumn of 1940 as the Luftwaffe was locked in aerial battle with the RAF, often overhead, but it did not stop one WI member from expressing her frustration. Her husband was a surveyor of farms for the War Agriculture Committee and her job was to chauffeur him around the county. She also had responsibility for boys and Scouts billeted in various empty cottages in her village, and life on the farm and in the garden was busy as well. Yet, as she wrote, 'all these things have been interrupted day after day five or six times with incessant fighting. At first I was dreadfully afraid; it was horrid, my tummy kept shivering and after the fight was over my knees went weak and I had to sit down. But after the first day or two, that all wore off – and the only thing we all feel now is so *cross* at the waste of time. Just as you've got your ladders fixed in the plum trees, over they come. We stay put; but when they start with the machine guns low enough to see them, then the men make us come indoors until *that* scrap is over, and it just makes me mad.'[19] She said she would stay put in Kent, even though the danger from air raids was evident. 'The people of East Kent are grand,' she wrote, adding: 'not one in our village have I heard doubting that we can hold on longer than "That Man".'[20]

Nothing could embody this attitude of defiance more than the tale of Hawkinge WI in East Kent. Before the war it had been a large institute with over a hundred members but being just three miles from Folkestone it was in a vulnerable area. A large number of families evacuated further inland and thus numbers dwindled so that by the summer of 1940 the membership was just five. These five women had a canning machine, which the institute had acquired in anticipation of the fruit harvest. The county federation offered to buy back the machine but the women refused politely, saying that they intended to use it. Cicely McCall told their story:

> And use it they did. They picked their own fruit and the fruit from the gardens of their evacuated members. Their preservation centre was a farm kitchen, and they jammed and bottled and canned. The Battle of Britain raged overhead, so they took it in turns to go to the air raid shelter when the bombing was too intense. One day when the jam was on the boil, and a fresh lot of raiders roared overhead, the youngest member said to the others:

> 'You go this time. Go on. I'll stay and watch this boiling.'
>
> So she stayed and stirred and defied Nazidom.
>
> 'You see,' she said afterwards, 'they had children and I haven't.'
>
> But she didn't think she was doing anything spectacular. None of them did. 'We didn't think anything of it,' they said. 'We couldn't go away and do war work, and we thought, well, we could do *that*.'

This story must be one of the most famous in the history of WI jam-making and it was symbolic of the kind of defiance that Lady Denman told them would win the war. It was not simply the tough-mindedness of the childless member, but the sheer amount of work that it must have taken to produce the jam and canned fruit that they did. Not only did they have to pick the fruit and wash, boil, can, bottle and label it but they had to collect firewood, as they did not have sufficient funds for coal. When East Kent did their calculations for the quantities made by each of their ninety institutes Hawkinge appeared third on their list. The five members had made 350 kilograms of jam and filled 350 kilograms of cans and a hundred bottles. It was an astonishing achievement.

As a young member of her WI, Betty Houghton was given a variety of jobs to do when it came to fruit preservation. The jam-making took place in the garage of a house called Pilgrims in Chiddingly in Sussex. Mrs A. T. Baker and Betty's future mother-in-law, Mrs Houghton, were the cooks. There were many members of the Baker family in Chiddingly at the time, so that the ladies were known by their initials, Mrs A. T. and so on. Betty's job was to weigh the fruit brought in by members and others who wanted to turn it into jam. She gave them 3/4lb of sugar for every pound of their fruit. It then went into production and once the jars were cool she would stick on the labels and hand the finished jam back. This was in the early years before rationing meant that all jam had to be sent for commercial distribution. 'It was very important to make sure the labels were stuck on straight before the jars were put onto the shelves and stored. This was not amateur production. It was carried out to a high standard and had to be just so.' In 1943 Betty joined the Wrens and was sent to work at Bletchley Park. She lived in Woburn Abbey for the next two years and worked on the Colossus, the world's first programmable computer, which was used by the British code-breakers to read encrypted German messages.

In 1985 Mrs Muller Rowland from Surrey was asked to talk about her memories of wartime institutes at an evening called 'Forty Years On'. During the war she had worked as a canning machine operator. She recalled how some of the older members would be exhausted in the evening when they went home after a whole day working in a kitchen. Often they would have evacuee children to care for as well as their own households. It was a big extra responsibility for them, she said, 'but they always found time to do our jam when necessary. The members who worked in those centres never had one pound of jam or one tin of fruit. It all went to the shops and was sold on the ration.' She described the variety of facilities available to the institutes, some more satisfactory than others. 'At Peaslake [Surrey] we had a very nice village hall but the sink was very small and the cans had to be cooled down at once so we took them to the little brook at the bottom of the village and cooled them there. I can still see batches of jam, beautifully labelled, covered with parchment covers, named and dated, and a tiny jar at the front for the Inspector [to examine]. I remember being asked what happened to the little pot and replied "Oh! That goes into the next batch."'

Miss Tomkinson of the NFWI Agricultural Subcommittee wrote: 'We look back on our 1940 scheme with feelings rather like those of Alice in Wonderland when she was "opening out like the largest telescope that ever was".' They had made preparations for 200 preserving centres and at twenty-four hours' notice the Ministry of Food asked them to expand five-fold. By the end of the season they had 2,650 centres. 'Under our scheme, over one thousand tons of fruit has been preserved, most of which would otherwise have been wasted.'[21] Although the committee agreed that there was room for improvement in some centres, by and large the standard had been high. Teething problems for the centres had included cans turning up late, orders not arriving at all and bottles broken in transit. In Oxfordshire the lack of bottles was solved by a couple of members driving a car and trailer to London, escorted by the WVS, to raid a rubbish dump in the capital. They returned unscathed with plenty of suitable containers and the preserving work continued.

One other difficulty a number of institutes came across was estimating the quantity of fruit that would come into the centres for preservation. It had an impact on the amount of sugar they would need to order and there was some debate about whether those running centres should refuse surplus fruit delivered without notice as making jam without sugar required different types of preparation. Mrs Milburn illustrated the problem from the other perspective: 'A WI produce meeting took me to Mrs Ford's at 10:45 am to hear about sugar for jam and the arrangements to be made about getting it for WI members. We have to calculate the amount of fruit we are going to have in our gardens!'

Institutes all around the country debated whether it was fair to ask women to volunteer to undertake hot, sticky work for long hours for no pay and no gain. Was it enough to know that they were contributing to the nation's stockpiles of food? 'Would that be enough reward for the toil and sweat, the trouble of organisation, and the inevitable public criticism?'[22] They would have to accept that they would not even get their own fruit back in their ration unless they were fortunate that a local shop bought jam from their centre. The majority of institutes who had been involved in the jam scheme agreed to carry on.

The women's institutes received a huge boost when the United States donated six mobile canning vans to the jam effort in addition to the over 500 canning machines they and the Canadians also gave to the WI. The vans had been given, fully licensed, insured and equipped, by the American Federation of Business and Professional Women in acknowledgement of the role played by rural women. The great beauty of the mobile units was that they could be driven to orchards 'so that the fruit could go straight from bough to can'.[23] At first some members were suspicious of the canning vans, one claiming that she thought at first it was simply a very expensive toy. But she soon became an enthusiastic 'van fan' after seeing it in action. Miss McCall described a van:

> Painted grey, mounted on a Ford V8 chassis (and surely 'V' was never more applicable!) they looked workmanlike and they were. Inside they were equipped with well arranged cupboards and shelves, a copper heated with Calor gas, and a zinc-lined sink. A trestle table which folded neatly away when the van was in motion held the hand-sealing machine. On the roof of the van stood the water tank . . . Canning, at all times, even in a well ventilated kitchen, is an unsuitable occupation for those who like fresh air and a low, even temperature. But if you like dripping heat, cramped space and perspiring companions, then the inside of a canning van is just the place for you.[24]

Despite the heat and discomfort the canning vans were well liked, as they were efficient and helped greatly in villages with no canning centre. Using a van institute members could produce fifty cans an hour or about 100lb of preserves a day.

Up to the outbreak of war there was a strong sense that although vegetable production would improve (which it did) jam production would remain at the same standard – palatable, sometimes delicious but always looking home-made. It was a case of 'We've always done it like that'. When the preservation centres started the government appointed inspectors. There were loud outcries.

> It was bad enough to have to make jam according to Government recipes, but to be reproved for an unorthodox knot in the string seemed to many members the height of Government interference and absurdity. What did it matter if the cover was a little crooked? Yet at the end of the season when centre workers could gaze proudly at rows of shining jam pots with identical labels and neat string round closely cropped tops, they began to agree that there was something to be said for uniformity and method.[25]

Redlynch and District WI in Wiltshire was one of the institutes with the widest diversity of preserving undertaken. They made jams, jellies, fruit cheeses, fruit juices, chutneys and bottled fruits. Strict instructions were sent to remind them that the sugar obtained from the government could not be used to make home-made wines, cider or perry. All fruit had to be home-grown and not bought from shops or commercial growers. The range was impressive: 'Gooseberries, red, white and blackcurrants, rhubarb, loganberries, blackberries, apples, plums, damsons, crab apples and quinces were all used at some point, either singly or mixed, to make jams and chutneys.' Initially they used the Scout hut but that was taken over by the Home Guard in 1943 and so they rented a room in the Temperance Hall for a shilling a week. The government supervisor was impressed with the jam in 1943 and also complimented the women on the layout of the room in the Scout hut. The next year the report on their jam read: 'very good, beautifully covered and the pots very well filled'.[26]

Ministry inspectors travelled all over the country checking the preservation centres were working to the highest standards. Mrs Stevens was one inspector who worked in the Midlands. She reported on the good and the bad:

> Sub-standard jam was in nearly all cases made by Centres which had not attended the County Council classes at the beginning of the summer, and had not kept to the standard recipes. About 1000lbs of sub-standard jam has been made out of a total of nearly 12 tons of jam and jelly. This does not include a very large quantity of very bad jam made by Little Compton and Chasleton who made about 1700 lbs, much of which contained wasps, and a quantity of which had not set and was going mouldy. Mrs Stevens had seen the jam and Miss Munro had also been to advise on it. A good deal had now been boiled up again, after the wasps had been removed, and a further report is awaited from the Centre secretary to say how much is now fit for sale.[27]

Even after the war some villages still complained of 'centre jam' as something of unnecessarily high standard conforming to government red-tape regulations. 'One hopes that this is a dying resentment. For after the war amateur methods will not compete successfully with better finished and equally palatable commercial products. Fewer and fewer people think that everything which comes out of a cottage kitchen is necessarily delicious or even wholesome.'[28] How things have changed since the 1940s.

The German attacks on Britain and Northern Ireland continued relentlessly until May 1941. London was bombed on seventy-six consecutive nights during the Blitz and many other towns and cities were badly damaged. Plymouth was targeted on 18 March 1941 and the lives of its citizens shattered. The city's infrastructure was badly damaged and, as Gerald Wasley put it, Plymouthians became 'casualties of war without shedding a drop of blood. For them the consequence of the intensive aerial attack was that their set way of life was not merely inconvenienced, it was destroyed.' The authorities encouraged families to leave the city, issuing free train tickets, but it was not easy to know where they would be welcomed. Bickleigh lay just seven miles from Plymouth and was one of the many villages that hosted destitute families. The WI had a hut which had been built in about 1920, donated by Lord and Lady Roborough of Maristow Estate. About 300 people a night sheltered in the hut and in farm buildings during what was known as 'the evening trek out'. The WI organised a whist drive to raise money for the victims of the bombing and apparently managed to carry on with their regular meetings in the hut despite wartime dislocation. Bickleigh's women were as busy and resourceful as any other WI, and contributed to the preservation scheme, although a note in their minute book read: 'Decided not to use canning machine but to bottle fruit and make jam instead.'

As the 1941 season approached the jam and canning centres were well organised but restrictions from the Ministry of Food were greater. *Home & Country* reported that 'so far as the early fruits – strawberries, black currants, and raspberries are concerned, the Ministry of Food has issued an instruction that they may be used only for jam. Later crops will be made into jam, canned where facilities for canning exist, and in some centres bottled.'[29] Lord Woolton broadcast an appeal to countrywomen to help out in the great jam production in 1941. He knew that many people were disgruntled that he could not supply extra sugar for preserving that year but, as he explained, 'As Minister of Food I have to be careful and to save sugar in order to see that there will be enough to keep up our rations even though the Germans may sink more of our sugar ships.'[30]

He urged women not to let the fruit go to waste but to pick and sell it to jam centres, rather than letting it rot on the trees and in the bushes: 'Ladies, we are fighting for our existence: all of us are in this war and we must pull together, sharing our resources. Last year 2600 village centres worked under this scheme; already we have 4500 centres ready this year – ready with their workers, ready with their jam jars, and the covers for them; everything ready for your help in bringing in the fruit.'[31]

He told the women how he had visited a country village and admired the patriotic fervour of the womenfolk, eager to do their bit, and how the following day he had seen bombed-out families who had lost everything: 'They want more jam; you women of the country districts can give it them from the surplus fruits in your gardens. I appeal for your help and I applaud all those who are unselfishly giving their work to increase our food supplies. Good luck to all of you who are helping in a grand piece of work.'[32]

The harvest was disappointing that year and there was a lot of poor fruit, which had to be discarded. The price of fruit in the shops and on the market stalls was higher than the previous year and the quality questionable. Mrs Milburn wrote: 'Red currants are 2s 6d a lb, cherries 4s 6d, desert gooseberries 3s 6d (and Mr Malins said to a customer: "They're not worth it! Wouldn't pay it!").'[33] But the WI members were far from downhearted. They gathered quantities of wild fruit, such as blackberries, rosehips, elderberries and whortleberries. In 1941 2,250,000 lb of fruit was preserved and 1,764 and a half tons of other preserves and chutneys had been canned or bottled, which was 100 tons more than the previous year when the harvest had been outstanding. Oxfordshire's county minute book recorded: 'The fact that Institute members had not been able to buy the jam they made was noted and discussed but the general feeling of the meeting was summed up in one member's most passionately voiced remark: "We are *proud* that our members have not got anything for themselves out of this scheme."'[34]

Coleshill Fruit Preservation Centre in Berkshire was particularly inventive in the disappointing fruit season of 1941. They made apple jelly, flavoured with cloves and lemons using windfalls, even maggoty ones. They then learned about apple pulp which could be made without sugar and thus be sold without having to breach the rationing regulations. They soon got into the swing of alternative preserves: 'Mulberries came next and we made mulberry and apple jam – not much, because our retailer thought, rightly, that people would be scared of risking their small ration on an unfamiliar jam. Then the blackberries ripened, the apples continued, obligingly, to drop. When good windfalls became saleable we took the bruised and wasp eaten ones, with a little trouble we got plenty of sound fruit out of them, and we made pectin for blackberry jelly out of the peel and cores.'[35]

After their success with fruit they turned to vegetables, making green tomato chutney from green tomatoes touched with blight, so otherwise unusable. That went down so well that they then bought some enormous marrows to make marrow chutney for their local shop. 'Our totals were small, this being a very small village but the variety of things we made and the fact that we tried to run the centre as a public utility service, making what the village wanted as far as possible did mean that the Centre members enjoyed the job and that the community was quite enthusiastic by the end of the season.'[36] Almost everybody in Coleshill had been involved in the fruit and vegetable scheme. Schoolchildren and teachers picked blackberries and other fruit; the local shopkeeper agreed to take all the produce and even the local supervisor was impressed by the community spirit.

Over the course of the next few years the food situation in Britain deteriorated. There was little risk that the country would starve but the variety of food available outside the ration was limited and grew increasingly so. Mrs Milburn went shopping in Leamington Spa in June 1941 and remarked that so many of the shops had notices saying no oranges or onions, sweets or chocolates, saccharine or cakes 'but there is always bread and carrots'. Like many she stepped up her efforts in the kitchen garden, digging up more ground for planting and waging a constant war on the pests that plagued her vegetable beds. 'I kill all the wireworms, calling them first Hitler, then Goering, Goebbels, Ribbentrop and Himmler. One by one they are destroyed, having eaten the life out of some living thing, and so they pay the penalty.'[37]

By 1943 some 800 fewer jam centres registered with the National Federation but the Ministry of Food was anxious that the WI should continue to run the Fruit Preservation Scheme. The main problem was the lack of volunteers. At the end of 1941 unmarried women between the ages of twenty and thirty were conscripted. The following year saw further recruitment and in 1943, when mobilisation reached its peak, nearly half of all women of working age were either in the forces, working in Civil Defence or in some other capacity that was directly linked to war work. This meant that most younger women had left the villages and in some areas there was a marked shortage of workers. Nevertheless, an illustrated article on canning in *Home & Country* claimed that 'even four years of ever-increasing restrictions and Government statutory rules and orders has failed to quench the enthusiasm of the great number of members who work at the Fruit Preservation Centres.'[38] To their surprise and pleasure, the WI found that they received frequent high-profile visits. That year at least three centres hosted the Queen, who insisted on trying out the canning machine herself when she went to a centre near Reading. She stamped her initials on the lid of the can and it was handed back to her, with the label, and sent by her lady-in-waiting to Mrs Roosevelt, as a gift. Miss Craigen of the British War Relief Society visited Little Baddow in Essex and took a series of photographs which were then presented to the WI for their own use. *Home & Country* said: 'She was most impressed with the work being done and asked a lot of questions as she wanted to send a very full account to America.'[39]

The visit that received the most coverage was that of Mrs McLean, president of the American Women's Voluntary Service, who was in Britain 'studying the wartime work of British women. She went to see a Dixie Hand Sealer being used at River Centre, near Dover, where they apparently jam and can imperturbably through air raids and bombardments.'[40] The day before Mrs McLean's visit there had been a raid and several bombs had fallen close to the centre. 'Mrs McLean was so impressed with the day's entry in the Day Record Book that the page was torn out and given to her as a memento of her visit to take back to America. Some 160lbs of jam were made, but the item that impressed her most was the secretary's footnote: 'All done while shelling was in progress – Heil Hitler!'[41]

In 1945 an appreciation of East Kent's bravery in producing jam when under fire from the V-rockets was published in *Home*

& *Country*. It was written by a ministry inspector who was required to make regular visits to preservation centres to check the WI jam:

> I feel I must write and tell you about the Preservation Centres in South-East England, who carried on so magnificently all through last season, under the most difficult conditions. Some mornings, after a bad night in London, I wondered whether I could face the hazards of the country, and then the thought of those centre members carrying on under gunfire, shelling, and 'doodles', braced me to another daily tour of the centres. One lot of jam which was passed, was referred to as a 'doodle batch', because the members had to take cover three times during the final boiling. Another centre worked constantly under shell fire. Where villages had had these horrible visitors at very close quarters, the answer I always received to an anxious enquiry was 'We were glad that it was one less for London.'
>
> I cannot express fully my appreciation and admiration of the centre members in the South-East, but I should like the rest to know what wonderful work they have done with a courage and sense of humour unequalled, and I am very proud to have worked with them.[42]

7

KNIT ONE PURL ONE

Institutes still knit, no doubt as a rest from onion planting

Home & Country, May 1941

Along with jam-making, knitting is a strong image for the wartime Women's Institute. The number of garments knitted for troops abroad, sailors, ARP wardens at home, evacuee children, hospital patients and for home use was enormous. No exact figure of the overall number of garments has ever been calculated, though in September 1944 the WI ran a three-month campaign to knit for Europe and the figure published in March 1945 for this one initiative alone was 152,044 garments with not all returns submitted. It is the only published figure but individual institutes made note of annual tallies in their minute books which indicate that the numbers must have been in the millions by the end of the war. In the first year of the war alone, Audlem in Cheshire knitted 770 garments for the troops, Totteridge on the outskirts of London 400, Essendon in Hertfordshire 450 and Broadway in Worcestershire a staggering 1,300, which they divided between the Army and the WVS. Three years later in 1941 St Catherine's Institute near Guildford produced 5,077 garments for Poles, Finns and prisoners of war while Grayshott in Hampshire knitted over 11,000 articles for the forces during the six years of the war. There were 5,585 institutes with 288,000 members. Not every member knitted but a rough calculation would put the number of garments at over 20 million. Many sewed while others were busy with food production and preservation but every minute book refers to some members knitting during the war. It was a major industry and one the Army and Navy came to rely on.

There was a hiatus in September 1940 when a memo was sent out from a government department saying that no more string gloves were required for minesweepers. Mrs Hazelwood in the Scottish Women's Rural Institute wrote to Miss Farrer to say that she had spoken to a commander who said that was quite wrong and begged for 640 pairs by the end of the month. 'It seems clear from the enclosure I send you that there are two types of sweeping and that for one of them, in which the danger of jagged wires does not arise, the string gloves are urgently needed. It is of course essential that they should be correctly made & properly sewn but I do hope that something can be done to clear up this disastrous mistake which will disappoint countless men at sea.'[1]

There are innumerable references in minute books to emergency requests for a dozen pairs of socks here, eight helmets there, or gloves for a Civil Defence team who were posted on a chilly hillside in November. And the WIs responded, as they always did, enthusiastically. Miss Farrer had discouraged knitting and sewing activities at monthly meetings so separate knitting groups or knitting parties were set up, some in conjunction with other voluntary organisations. Edith Jones wrote that her institute had set up a working party with the WVS. They sewed, knitted and collected salvage for the troops and for their local hospital. Just one example of how quickly the WI could react was when the Council for Maternity and Child Welfare sent the national head office an SOS for fifty nightgowns for expectant mothers. It was received on a Monday evening in January 1940. The following morning Buckinghamshire County Federation received the request, since the hospital had been evacuated to their county. At lunchtime the county secretary had been able to confirm to the London office that six institutes had volunteered to make six nightgowns and two would make seven. The patterns were received on Wednesday lunchtime and the nightgowns were delivered by the end of the week. Sewing was almost as popular as knitting and one of the groups who really benefited from the WI sewing parties were the land girls who often came to institutes with hopelessly ill-fitting clothes which they had no idea how to alter. Sambrook WI near Telford in Shropshire decided to spice up their sewing party in February 1942 by making their members do it blindfold.

Audlem WI in Cheshire met for their first wartime meeting on 14 October 1939 at two o'clock. The September meeting had been cancelled owing to the outbreak of hostilities and lighting restrictions so the committee had decided to move their meetings from evenings on the first Thursday of the month to afternoons on the second Saturday. 'At the conclusion of business, scissors, needles and a sewing machine were busy and by 4pm 23 thrift garments were ready for distribution to children evacuated from the town to our village.' Twenty-three garments in two hours and while a meeting had been taking place. That is impressive. It is good to record that in their November meeting they heard from the mother of an evacuee child who wished to record her gratitude to Audlem institute's women for the 'kindness shown to the children by the sewing done on their behalf'. In the five and a half years between autumn 1939 and spring 1945 the institute secretaries filled four sets of minute books and only once did the three-letter word 'war' appear in any of those writings. They discussed how meetings would proceed in the future and the quantity of sugar they should order from the National Federation for their jam-making.

Materials for knitting and sewing parties could not be purchased from institute funds. Miss Farrer suggested that 'it is advisable that any money-raising effort for this purpose should be undertaken by the village as a whole, and not by the Women's Institute'. However, once money was raised then institutes could apply to purchase cheap materials and patterns from the Personal Service League, who had put out an urgent appeal for pyjamas, helpless-case jackets and shirts for Service and Civilian Hospitals, socks and pullovers (sleeveless or with sleeves) for the Services. 'The socks need not be of the regulation uniform colour, but the pullovers must be.'[2] This might seem cautious in the detail concerning fundraising but it was an important point for the Women's Institute, that they be seen to be neutral and not supporting the war effort with their funds, although their women-power was at the country's disposal. Some institutes ignored the directive from headquarters. Alphington WI in Devon reported in October 1941 that they had £200 6s 0d on war savings deposit. Members unanimously agreed to donate £100 towards a machine gun, £50 towards a Bren gun, £40 to parachutes, £6 17s for clothing for one soldier and £3 towards two stretchers. Ten months later they raised £500 in their 'tank drive'.

The Red Cross was a major beneficiary of WI efforts and fundraising. As early as November 1939 the Red Cross had been able to send supplies to hospitals and convalescent camps, thanks to the enthusiastic response to their first appeals. 'In that month, the base store at Dieppe was ready for the reception of goods, and a first consignment was dispatched by the Stores Department. It included over 30,000 hospital garments of all kinds, beds, bedding, ward accessories, surgical equipment, games and "comforts".'[3] However, it was to answer the need to put together prisoner-of-war packages in vast numbers after the fall of France and the evacuation from Dunkirk in 1940 that the greatest help was required. Although a trickle of men had been taken prisoner in 1939 and early 1940, it was following the Blitzkrieg of 10 May that the biggest single number of men was taken prisoner by the Germans: 50,000. The Red Cross had committed to sending each man a box of comforts once a week. It was a colossal undertaking and as the war progressed and more men were taken prisoner – some 200,000 in Europe alone – so the need for money, food and comforts for the Red Cross increased. According to historian Midge Gillies, 'During the six years of the war it sent over twenty million food parcels to POWs. In the peak year of 1942 five and a half million were delivered.'[4] Every penny for this vital work came from donations.

Mrs Milburn and several members of her institute used to go to a Red Cross workroom on a Tuesday to make whatever was most urgently needed at the time. In August 1941 she was asked to make lavender bags. 'The lavender bags are to be sold in America and someone suggested putting the Victory V on one corner.'

During the war years the Red Cross grew into a mighty machine. The WI was only one of the many voluntary organisations that answered the wartime appeals. In the official record of the Red Cross and St John published in 1949, authors P. G. Cambray and G. G. Briggs gave some idea of the way it worked:

> Functions of purchasing, reception, packing and distribution were carried out [by the British Red Cross's Stores Department] for voluntary organisations. Among them were the

> London Committee of Allied Red Cross Societies; regimental associations and next-of-kin parcel centres concerned with the contents of such parcels for prisoners of war; and many more. The Stores Department was, in fact, the clearing house for supplies for societies in London engaged upon voluntary relief services for war sufferers, for no other body had the organisation and facilities which it possessed.[5]

At first there was no rationing on wool and institutes could order as much as they could pay for, either on the open market for general use or from the Ministry of Supply for specific war-related items such as comforts for soldiers, sailors and airmen. The only restriction on acquiring wool in the early days of the war was the WI's own rule that wool intended to be used for knitting comforts could not be purchased using institute or county funds but had to be paid for by money raised from elsewhere. Over the next few years the WI became adept at raising money at whist drives and dances, as well as at other one-off events. There is no overall figure for money raised but individual institutes did keep records of money raised for wool and the amounts were considerable. Barham with Kingston WI in East Kent collected £238 13s 4d in 1942 and £259 3s 6d the following year, which they used to buy wool for the Merchant Fleet. That is the equivalent of nearly £20,000 in 2012.

It might be assumed that all women in the 1930s could knit and that therefore knitting was simply an extension of what happened in the home. This was not the case. By the middle of the nineteenth century knitting by hand had been superseded by industrial knitting machines and the production of cheap garments in factories meant that knitting individual items for wear or sale was far less prevalent than in the eighteenth century. When the Women's Institutes were founded during the First World War many handicrafts and skills had been lost or were limited to the smaller and most rural of communities. As Inez Jenkins pointed out in her 1953 history of the WI:

> the Industrial Revolution of the nineteenth century changed the British people in little more than twenty years from an agricultural to a manufacturing nation. It rang the knell of those crafts and skills of hand which, side by side with agriculture, had provided a livelihood for many and satisfied the personal and household needs of the community. It was quicker and cheaper to make by machine than by hand. So in most districts in England and Wales the old crafts disappeared and gradually were forgotten.[6]

One of the early aims of the Women's Institute was to revive those handicrafts and to encourage the practice of traditional skills. The National Executive was keen to promote cottage industries, for profit, with a view to giving girls a reason to stay in their villages rather than moving to towns and cities. This hope that institutes would provide a place where knowledge and interest might be passed on was well-founded but there turned out to be little stomach for turning it into a commercial venture. By early 1919 it was clear that a more profitable policy in terms of furthering the WI's own aims of educating women in the countryside was to encourage good craftsmanship and to meet home and local needs rather than aiming for industrial output that brought with it pressures and regulations that few felt eager to embrace. A loan from the Carnegie fund, who were supporters of the WI from the earliest days, was given to encourage the commercial exploitation of skilled crafts such as toy-, basket- and glove-making but by 1920 the grants were made solely for educational purposes. One great benefit of the

Carnegie grant was the provision for a collection of examples of fine craftwork.

The Craft Guild developed and during the twenties and thirties exhibitions of fine handicrafts were held at local, county and national levels. There was a focus on knitting, embroidery, sewing, basket-weaving, and slipper- and glove-making. It was popular and the standard of the work produced was very high. Edith Jones was a fine seamstress and entered competitions both locally and at county level with her sewing as well as her baking. On one occasion she was awarded third place for a calico patch she had made: 'My men folk were pleased when I told them. They would have been grateful too if they had seem some of the samples there showing very little sewing intelligence. A "dem" (demo) on plain sewing would evidently be useful.' However that night they had had a talk on poultry diseases, which was of equal interest to her.

Mrs Katharine Woods wrote a short history of Headington WI in 1974 to celebrate their 50th birthday and she was full of praise for the quality of their craftwork. She wrote: 'to have raised the status of home crafts to a useful and worth-while occupation to be enjoyed both in the doing and in the use, is no mean achievement when we remember the miserable conditions in which many "home industries" have been carried on in the past.' The main areas of expertise in Oxfordshire were glove-making and basket-making. Mrs Mannering from Evesham introduced WIs in the county to rush work, an ancient local craft that had all but died out. Rush work had been used predominantly to make horses' nosebags and she found a retired, highly skilled basket worker to share his lifetime's expertise with her WI. From this little beginning they began to develop the skill to make shopping bags and mats in the manner of osier basketry and floor mats in the East Anglian tradition using plaited rush sewn together with string. This industry continued during the war and proceeds from sales were used to bolster institute funds. Another WI member from the county, Barbara Cullum, had grown up in Wheatley and knew just when the rushes were in season and thus pliable enough for weaving. 'She is also an expert maker and a beautiful player on bamboo pipes – another ancient craft revived and developed and spread over many counties.'[7]

Glove-making was a highly skilled occupation. Leather from deer in Blenheim Palace park was made into gloves in the neighbouring little town of Woodstock. As late as the 1920s the leather dresser would cut out gloves and take them round to be sewn by hand in many local homes. The WI was keen on this fine work and continued to hand-stitch Woodstock gloves until the 1950s. 'The stitching demands much care and skill, and the WIs, with careful instruction through the guild of learners, have helped to raise the status of the craft to a fine art.'[8] A most exquisite pair of hand-made gloves was worn by the Duke of Wellington at the Queen's Coronation in 1953. The gloves were made by Mrs Andow of Netley Marsh WI in Hampshire and show the very highest quality of workmanship. Hampshire was just as proud of its handicraft skills as Oxfordshire and listed sixteen, including embroidery, smocking, tatting, spinning, upholstery and jewellery. At Burton and Puddington in Cheshire, a talk by Miss Clayton of Willaston on glove-making resulted in a series of classes for members. Willaston still possesses a lovely pair of leather gloves made by Miss Clayton in 1942. The minute book records that she donated her four guineas fee from teaching the classes to her own WI's handicraft section for the purchase of books.

It was not until 1941 that the government introduced rationing for clothes, dress material and shoes. Churchill had been against clothes rationing as he had been against food rationing. He told the President of the Board of Trade, Oliver Lyttelton, that he did not wish to see the public in rags and tatters. Lyttelton replied that he believed the man on the street wanted rationing, which produced an outburst of rage in the prime minister: 'Who are you to tell me what the public want? Why, I only picked you up out of some bucket shop in the City a few weeks ago!' Nevertheless it was obvious to the government that by introducing such a scheme they could save on 200,000 tons of cotton and wool per year and several hundred thousand workers who would have been required to provide civilian clothing could be released for other forms of war-related work. The argument was compelling and clothes rationing was introduced on Sunday, 1 June 1941. 'The great surprise of this Whit Sunday morning's news is that clothes are to be rationed. It has been a well-kept secret, and the rationing has begun!' wrote Mrs Milburn.[9] Churchill was later to apologise to Lyttelton and admitted that he had been right to insist on it.

Lyttelton made a radio broadcast in which he appealed to people in a new and unusual way. He wished them to consider it patriotic to be badly dressed. 'In war the term "battle stained" is an honourable one. We must learn as civilians to be seen in clothes that are not so smart . . . When you feel tired of your clothes remember that by making them do you are contributing some part of an aeroplane, a gun or a tank.'

Norman Longmate, in his book *How We Lived Then*, explained that clothes were put on coupons 'not because supplies were scarce but because they were too plentiful. The chief aim of rationing was to save factory space, and by closing down small firms to release 450,000 workers for the munitions industry'.[10]

Wealthier women with large wardrobes were affected far less by the clothes rationing scheme than less-well-off women who had fewer clothes and often of a poorer quality, so that it had an impact on them more quickly. There was more grumbling about clothes rationing than there had been about the food scheme and the government, aware that this would be the case, made a valiant attempt to mitigate the situation by commissioning top designers to design utility clothing. The Incorporated Society of London Fashion Designers, led by Norman Hartnell and Hardy Amies, created thirty-four smart Utility Clothing designs. The dresses were officially approved by the Board of Trade and a selection mass-produced to save labour; they were exempt from purchase tax. The designs followed the square-shouldered and short-skirted fashions of the war era whilst sticking to the regulations for minimal cloth usage. Buttons were limited to three and turn-back cuffs and trouser turn-ups were dispensed with. Skirts were still below the knee. In the event, utility clothing accounted for well over three quarters of all the clothes produced during the war, but not everyone liked it. Some people complained of poor quality and lack of durability, though others were still wearing dresses bought during the 1940s many years later.

Utility stockings came in for particular criticism. Silk stockings had ceased to be made, as the silk was needed for parachute production. *Home & Country* ran a series of advertisements and articles about how to mend stockings but they remained a sorely missed item until the end of the war, unless women were lucky enough to be made gifts of nylons by American GIs who apparently had limitless supplies of these glorious new stockings.

Clothing was rationed on a points system with coupons. The points could be used for buying wool, cotton and household textiles as well as individual items such as coats or dresses. No points were required for second-hand clothing or fur coats, but their prices were fixed and the supply of second-hand clothes was limited, though jumble sales run by WIs to raise money for wool and other purposes did yield odd articles of clothing that could be reused or reworked. In the first year of clothes rationing each adult was allotted sixty-six coupons. To give an indication of what this would buy, five coupons could be used toward a blouse, five for a pair of boots, seven for a dress, and fourteen for a coat. These four items alone represent half a year's clothing allowance for one person. Initially the allowance was designed to provide each adult with approximately one new outfit per year. However, this proved too extravagant and the number of coupons per person was reduced to forty-eight in 1942, to thirty-six in 1943 and finally, in 1945, to twenty-four, so that by the end of the war almost an entire year's clothing allowance would be used up buying just one coat. And of course coupons did not guarantee availability, nor could they be used as payment. In 1942 an even more unpopular ration, for bath towels, was introduced, described by many women as 'the last word'.

Children got ten extra coupons over the flat rate in acknowledgement that they were smaller and therefore their clothes needed less material but also that they were growing and therefore had a need for more changes of clothes during the year. A major problem for parents with young children was the shortage of shoes. Leather became scarce and it was more difficult to mend shoes, especially ones that had been worn out by energetic youngsters, than clothes. Collections of shoes and wellington boots for evacuee children were a recurring theme in minute books, as was making clothes for them.

Norman Longmate was critical of schools who, despite clothes rationing, insisted on school uniform. He wrote of the difficulties faced by parents who had to sacrifice a year's worth of clothing coupons just to equip their son or daughter to go to grammar school. However, it was his own school for which he reserved the sternest criticism:

> . . . which dressed its 800 boys in a ridiculous, uncomfortable and unhygienic Tudor ensemble of ankle-length gown, knee breeches, long, thick, yellow stockings and vast but shapeless shirts without collar or cuffs. A less practical and more wasteful outfit it would have been hard to devise, but though the school did allow new boys to dress normally for their first year or two, the rest of us continued to look as if we were expecting the Spanish Armada rather than the German Army and almost all our coupons were simply appropriated to maintain this fatuous tradition.[11]

Non-rationed items included boiler suits, workmen's overalls, hats and caps, sewing thread, boot- and shoelaces, ribbons and other fabrics less than three inches in width, elastic, lace, sanitary towels, braces, suspenders, garters, clogs and blackout dyed cloth. However these were never in plentiful supply and as the war progressed some things became impossible to find. Headgear, other than that made from scarves or 'incorporating handkerchiefs', was also exempt. Regulations governing the number of pleats in a skirt, the width of sleeves and collars, the number of buttons (3), the height of heels (2 inches), the size of pockets and the length of men's socks were introduced along with a raft of items that were either restricted or forbidden. Production of non-essential items such as jewellery was prohibited altogether. 'From 1941 onwards production of hollowware – pans, kettles, buckets etc – was permitted under licences which were only granted for essential items made to approved specifications. In 1942 this policy was extended to a wide range of consumer goods. Manufacture of pottery and pencils was controlled and many items such as floor coverings, domestic electric appliances, lighters and umbrellas could be produced under licence only, with output frequently being standardized.'[12]

Fripperies such as jewellery, metal toys, ornamental glassware and fancy goods were abolished. It is little wonder that people looked and felt drab, grey and tired by the end of the war.

The issue of men's socks became a hot topic and reached the highest levels. In April 1943 Mr Colman MP asked the President of the Board of Trade in a House of Commons debate whether he planned to relax the restrictions on the length of men's socks, as he feared traders would have difficulty in disposing of short socks and other 'style-controlled garments' after the war.

Mr Hugh Dalton replied: 'No, Sir. The reduction of the leg length of socks to nine inches saves a great deal of wool and the manufacture of longer socks for the civilian market cannot be permitted. I am glad to have this opportunity to give an assurance that effective steps will be taken at the right time to assist traders to overcome any such difficulty as my Hon. Friend has in mind.'[13] The reason that men's socks had been restricted to just nine inches was to provide more wool for infants' clothes and nightwear.

'Beating the Clothes Coupon' was a very popular talk that was given in various forms up and down the country. The land girls, who had less experience of mending clothes and less time to do so, were sometimes invited to this talk, which they found useful. Welford in Northamptonshire had regular visits from their young farm workers who liked to learn about how to use old clothes, or how to rope-sole slippers or make shirts from flower bags, while Welsh Frankton in Shropshire taught them how to make use of old mackintoshes. It was not just the land girls who wanted to know how to economise and save their clothing coupons: mothers were anxious to make as much clothing as they could for their growing children and evacuee visitors. Lamplugh held a competition for the best article of clothing for a child made from a flourbag. It was won by a woman who had made a boy's shirt which, the judge wrote, 'would have been no disgrace to the smartest tennis party'.[14]

The government's hope was that people would reuse and repair old garments rather than insisting on buying new outfits. The WI offered advice on how to give old clothes a new lease of life including rubbing hot bran into tweed skirts and jackets, cleaning white materials with ground rice and using powdered magnesia to clean delicate fabrics such as lace, embroideries, white kid and suede gloves. Oil of eucalyptus would revivify jaded silk and faded crêpe de chine while potato pulp could be employed to clean cloth gaiters and leggings. Grandmother's recipes for cleaning clothes were proposed but sounded very expensive: 'For cleaning silk . . . mix well together three ounces of strained honey, two ounces of castile soap and half a pint of gin.' As knitting patterns published by the WI were popular during the war, so were clothes patterns, though the problem was that it was difficult to get material. From 1941 onwards only 20 per cent of the amount of cotton and 40 per cent of the rayon that had been available prior to rationing was available. It was time for Make Do and Mend.

Make Do and Mend is one of the most famous catchphrases of the Second World War. The Board of Trade had consulted women's groups about introducing the campaign, designed to encourage people to save buying something new by reusing old clothes. The object of the campaign was to persuade householders that clothes-carelessness was effectively sabotage and should be discouraged as vigorously as food waste, since the same argument about merchant shipping applied to clothes as it did to food – every bit saved could spare the life of a sailor and help another ship to land with materials for the war. The government used all media at its disposal to get over its urgent message. There were advertisements in newspapers, women's magazines and on the radio. Exhibitions, leaflets, advice centres and 12,000 formal classes were held to bring the message home to Britain's housewives. There were even films screened in cinemas. The Board of Trade organised an exhibition with Harrods to show housewives how to turn something old into some useful and new. In a propaganda broadcast several garments were shown, made from old coats, patchwork material and even a dressing gown fashioned out of an old dust sheet. The pièce de résistance was a two-piece black costume made by a woman from her husband's old dress suit. The commentator on the film summed up Make Do and Mend assuring women that 'all garments made in Make Do and Mend are entirely exclusive' and warning the men to 'lock up your favourite old clothes before you leave home in the morning'. The film ended on the shot of a middle-aged businessman in bowler hat carrying an umbrella walking down the street in long-johns and a shirt.

Women in village institutes tackled making do and mending in most inventive ways and the minute books are of course full of competitions and demonstrations for garments, slippers, gloves and accessories made from salvaged material. Rural women had been used to reusing their clothes and mending things, so that the campaign simply endorsed their habits. The WI differentiated between Make Do and Mend and thrift. Thrift was prominent from the outbreak of the war and included different examples of how to make things, including meals and utensils, as cheaply as possible. When it came to thrift the WI was remarkably energetic and infinitely imaginative and were always keen to share their discoveries with other institutes. Holton-le-Moor WI in Lincolnshire had a roll call on soap saving and one member came up with a recipe for wartime soap. A member of Thornton Curtis WI, just down the road, made a pair of economy slippers from a home-cured lamb skin and brought them to a meeting to show other members. Burrough on the Hill's WI in Leicestershire had a competition to see who could make a child's dress for 1s 6d while at Harby WI in Nottinghamshire a thrift event produced examples of mittens made from stockings, coal gloves from old winter hats, a jumper made from scraps of wool, a sprinkler made from an old bottle with a carefully pierced lid. Members of Taplow WI in Buckinghamshire made babies' sleeping bags out of men's flannel trousers and bottle covers from boys' trousers.

A thrift exhibition in 1943 showed just how inventive some people could be when it came to reusing materials.

> The exhibition shows really handsome gloves made from chamois leathers, and the odd pieces left over from these wash-leather gloves have been joined together to make a leather for the shining of silver or the washing of windows. Women have made embroidered handkerchiefs from pieces of flour bags and one beautiful little garment with three rows of hem stitching has the blue lettering of the original left on the back to convince those who would not otherwise believe that the material really came from flour bags.[15]

Also on display were a shawl made from unpicked wool from a land girl's stockings, sandals made from odd strips of leather, a plaid frock made from thirty-two travellers' samples and handkerchiefs made from surplus linen.

Members of Preston Patrick and Preston Richard WI in Cumbria were evidently highly skilled at working with their hands, as demand for their knitted garments came in regularly from 1939 onwards, with letters of thanks flowing in equal measure. Betty Prickett, their honorary secretary, found references in their minute books to a great variety of different activities. In addition to knitting, sewing and making bandages they were also asked to supply walking sticks for wounded servicemen, though it is not clear from the minute books whether these were to be made from wood gathered locally or if these were unwanted or spare sticks. Sometimes only seven women were able to attend meetings, most likely because of haytime or harvesting, Betty suggested, but they still managed to produce large quantities of knitted goods and bandages, parcels for servicemen and raise money for the Red Cross, the local hospital and the WI ambulance appeal.

Glove- and slipper-making demonstrations had been popular before the war and became even more so once Make Do and Mend became more than just a byword. Demonstrators from local colleges and the handicraft guild were in high demand throughout the early years of the war and minute books were full of references to this or that demonstration of making felt slippers or leather gloves. One member of Rearsby WI in Leicestershire was heard to sigh with relief when told they would be offered three classes on glove-making: 'such a pleasant change from the knitting needles and leather gloves *are* wanted'.

Although the WI embraced Make Do and Mend wholeheartedly it did not mean that they were prepared to accept Mr Lyttelton's idea of being badly dressed. Demonstrations and lectures on topics such as make-up, hairdressing and dressmaking continued to be very popular. They learned about city fashions such as make-up made from boot polish, sugar and water mixture for hair-setting lotion or using a line of gravy browning or cocoa on their legs to simulate stockings. Advertisements for the Eugene permanent wave continued to appear in *Home & Country* throughout the war even though advertisements for clothes, stockings and underwear disappeared from the pages by 1942. Most women wore hats and competitions for best-dressed hats with fresh flowers were popular summer events. Edith Jones liked to dress up her hats and when she could she would buy another accoutrement. On 13 October 1943 she wrote in her diary: 'Italy declares war on Germany. I put new flower in my hat.'

By the time Edith wrote this entry the country had been at war for four years. In her annual report for her institute she said: 'The year 1943 has been one of quiet progress for our Institute which seems to have turned the corner after the difficult times experienced at the beginning of the war.' Listing the competitions, talks and demonstrations she concluded: 'The outstanding competition was for a shopping bag made from oddments. 20 members joined the course of Make and Mend classes which were very popular.' Hers is not the only annual report to mention a settling down after such turbulent times in the early years of the war. It had become a way of life and the extra duties taken on by WI members had gained a pattern within the strange structure of their weeks and months. Anxiety was never far from the surface, however. For the first two years of the war Edith's nephew, Leonard, who had lived with them since 1926, was on fire duty in Liverpool and was given farming leave at Red House Farm during haymaking, harvest or other busy times of the farming year, which were always recorded with great pleasure. She took him to whist drives, they went on long walks and he helped her in the garden and with the hens when he had more than a day at home. And his leaving always elicited a sigh of sadness in her diary: 'Len returns by train. How quickly the week has gone, he feels the benefit of the rest after so many disturbances,' she wrote after one visit. But in 1942 he went abroad and she did not see him again for three years. After this the war cropped up ever more frequently in her diaries.

Mrs Milburn was equally conscious of the war keeping her son from her. Alan had been taken prisoner at Dunkirk and the terror and uncertainty she felt until she heard he was alive are evident in her diaries. Then, in mid-July 1940, she learned where he was and that she would be able to write to him: 'How different was this morning's awakening! No dead weight of woe hanging over one, such as we have had the past six or eight weeks. The war? Yes, but not the war and the anxiety about Alan in the same way. Everyone overwhelms us with warm-heartedness.'[16] On 28 May 1943 she wrote: 'Three years today since Alan was made a prisoner of war – but it's no use moaning.' Alan was sent regular parcels both by his mother and by the Red Cross, so that he was well supplied with comforts and reading material from home.

It was not only prisoners of war who were fortunate enough to get Red Cross parcels. Troops and sailors all over the world were pleased to receive knitted woollen goods from, amongst others, the WI. In addition to making gloves, sweaters, balaclava helmets and socks for the forces the WI was also asked to mend for them. Initially they thought it would be more helpful to teach the men to darn their own socks and mend their own shirts but soon they were involved in mending for the Army on top of everything else that they were expected to do. Mrs Browne, who was a member of Albury WI in Hertfordshire from 1942, described a meeting:

> Volunteers were asked to go to the Newlands Corner Billet for Canadians on Mondays and Fridays from 3–5pm to mend for the troops stationed there. No one seemed too keen to go but offered to mend for them in their own homes. I had two young children and sometimes an evacuee so there was plenty to cope with. I was also on the roster of mothers who cooked and served soup to the children of Albury Village School, there being no school dinners then.

Buckinghamshire took the local anti-aircraft battery under its wing and announced that 'one institute mends and darns for them, one gives them craft lessons, one arranged hot baths, books, hot pies and general hospitality'. Gloucestershire reported that 150 soldiers arrived in a small village, each carrying a bundle of dirty laundry. The WI washed, mended and darned for the soldiers and told their country secretary that they would carry on doing so for as long as the soldiers remained in their area. A West Sussex institute had so many military shirts and socks to mend that they had to raise money themselves in order to get more material to carry out their task.

Some institutes were approached directly for help. A chaplain for the Seamen's Missions gave Greys WI in Berkshire a talk and they were 'so impressed by the tales of heroism and endurance of the merchant fleets of England that the whole Institute started knitting energetically through the black evenings.' Other institutes heard directly from members about men who were in need of their assistance. Mrs Close of Westbourne WI in Dorset wrote to the editor of *Home & Country* with her appeal:

> Among all the war efforts there is one part of our Army which is likely to be forgotten. I mean the Home Battalions. Many of these men are on Out-Post duty and need socks, pullovers, mitts and scarves, just as much as the men overseas. They are stationed on hill tops, bridges and tunnels, often only quartered in tents. There are camps now all over the country and I appeal to my fellow members who have working parties to spare some things for the men quartered in their district.[17]

In 1944, Albury was asked by Ewhurst WI in Surrey for 'Housewives' to be made and sent to women in France who would need them after the liberation. Mrs Browne was once again involved:

'Several were made. They consisted of a long piece of material, with cottons, needles, tapes, pins, buttons, etc fastened inside, rolled up and tied with tape. Peg Parfree and I cycled to a WI meeting at Ewhurst to deliver them, pursued by doodlebugs, one of which rumbled over during the meeting and crashed a couple of miles away.'

Barham with Kingston in East Kent knitted for the British Sailors' Society which supplied the Merchant Navy, the fishing fleet, and shipping not under the Royal Navy. 'No one needs telling what *they* mean to the food supply of Great Britain,' said their president. As far as they had been able to gather there was no fund for supplying free materials so they had to raise every penny they spent. By raising money from entertainments, small donations and raffles they succeeded by January 1940 in sending 146 garments, including shirts, pyjamas, helmets, pullovers and socks. They also sent a parcel to the Dover Patrol.[18] It was this institute that raised nearly £500 in two years for wool for garments for the merchant seamen and which also received a visit from Mrs Roosevelt and Mrs Churchill in 1942.

Getting wool was not always easy. Later on in the war there was the problem of supply but in the early months it was as much a question of how WIs could raise the money to buy it. One resourceful member made use of the car and trailer her husband had left her when he joined up. She gathered a couple of willing helpers and drove round the village hoping to collect waste paper. But the villagers, she explained in her report to the county, had more ambitious ideas. They offered any amount of salvage, from bedsteads to bicycles, fire irons to broken gates, as well as books, magazines, cardboard wrappers and even three rabbit skins. They loaded up the trailer and drove it down to the nearest dealer three miles outside the village. At one point there was a resounding crash as a bath fell off the trailer. People rushed out of their houses to laugh and help them get the bath back on the trailer. When they weighed all the goods at the dealer's they were thrilled to receive 32s 5d for their load. 'Now we can get on with the socks.'

The WI were warmly thanked for their efforts by everyone who benefited. A letter, published in January 1940, is from E. Hastings-Ord, the Honorary Secretary of the British and Allied Comforts and Victims of War Fund. Under the title 'Comforts for Friendless Serving Men' *Home & Country* published the letter from Mr Hastings-Ord who had been sending parcels of comforts to sailors, soldiers and airmen who had no relations or whose relations were too poor to be able to send them anything. 'The thanks we get are quite pathetic in their gratitude and we should like to let all those institute members who have enabled us to give these friendless men the pleasure of opening a parcel of their own to show how much their generosity is appreciated.'[19] Some institutes received so many letters of thanks during the early years of the war that they set aside a short slot before the end of the meeting so that the president could read them out.

In March 1941 the Secretary of the Comforts Committee of the Red Cross wrote to Miss Farrer asking for her help:

> In the last war the Women's Institutes were pioneers in the starting of toy making in this country, an industry which has now firmly established itself. This present war has brought to light another almost exclusively foreign industry, which I feel could be started with advantage in this country, that is the making of Chess sets. There is a tremendous demand for them among active forces, particularly Airmen, and we also receive many requests from Hospitals and Convalescent Homes.
>
> One of our workers has recently made a set out of broom

> handles with a sharp penknife and polished with sandpaper. The cost is negligible and it is a very fascinating and pleasant work.[20]

This was a popular request as making toys provided a break from endless knitting, though as one member pointed out ruefully, knitted dolls and soldiers were popular as well as wooden toys. A year later the Ministry of Health appealed to the WI for toys for the nursery schools being set up for refugees coming from Malta and Gibraltar to London. The WI were asked to supply home-made toys – knitted dolls, felt animals and second-hand toys in good condition to keep the children entertained in their new environment. The Ministry even offered to pay for the materials for the toys.[21] Edith Jones was delighted when she won first prize for her home-made doll in 1942.

In 1942 Miss Farrer passed on a request from the Society of Occupational Therapists for 'some form of occupation which will help to pass the time more happily for the prisoners [of war] and, if possible, give warmth, comfort and a creative outlet'.[22] County federations were encouraged to set up groups to put together suitable crafts, material and games that would entertain the prisoners. They were told that although they were not permitted to send sharp or dangerous tools, short-blade scissors and safety razor blades in holders could be included in the packages and that 'special concessions have been made for the inclusion of printed or typewritten instructions'.[23] Everything could be collected up and used, they were told: 'unwanted and disused apparatus, odd pieces of material, cardboard from books, pencils, paints, craft books, all types of material for slippers, coat hangers, small pieces of good wood for models, mesh shuttles and sticks.'[24] In short, anything that would entertain the POWs.

In June 1941 Hitler launched Operation Barbarossa and began

the largest invasion in the history of warfare when 4.5 million troops invaded along an 1,800-mile front in Russia. In Britain people could only imagine the horror of women's and children's suffering to come in the Russian winter. In November of that year Mrs Milburn wrote: 'Russia's winter has begun and the Germans are having a hard time. Some have been found frozen to death and some are clad in women's fur coats.'[25] Later in the year the Joint War Organisation began an Aid to Russia fund with Mrs Churchill as the chairman. Around £8 million was raised for the fund to pay for warm clothing and medical supplies as well as portable X-ray units, ambulances and other medical equipment. What they also wanted to do was send something specifically for the women: fur-lined garments. Mrs Churchill turned to the WI for support. She appealed to them to line garments with home-grown rabbit skins and allocated a sum of money for curing the skins as well as providing coats for lining. 'The keen desire of our members to help Russia has been amply proved, not only by the number of rabbit skins already received, but also by the almost embarrassing quantity and variety of fur coats, muffs, capes, stoles, sheepskin rugs, fox skins and even dog skins that have been received. Even a cat skin was attempted but proved incurable.'[26]

The National Federation advised counties who could not supply their own rabbit skins to offer to help in making up garments, and expert advice about patterns and handling was available from head office, who even offered to send an expert to work with a group of WIs if necessary. Once again the emphasis was on care: 'It is essential that we should be economic in the use of the skins – nothing must be wasted. Each skin costs about 1s 6d to cure.'[27] The Red Cross had supplied the coats for lining but smaller garments such as gloves and hats were made from scratch by members. 'WI members made coats, waistcoats, hoods and caps lined with rabbit fur for Russian women, members not only made the clothes but also reared the rabbits and cured the pelts. Sympathy for the women of Russia was strong. Warm clothing would be needed for the winter of 1942, they were told, so they stepped up their efforts. During two and half years of work 2,071 fur-lined garments were sent to Russia via the Red Cross. Mrs Churchill came to the WIs Consultative Council in 1943 and admired examples of the work and some garments were also on display at an exhibition organised by the Society for Cultural Relations with the USSR.'[28]

Mrs Roberts of Trefnant WI in Denbighshire received a warm hand-written letter from Mrs Churchill in February 1942 thanking them 'with all my heart' for the gifts sent by the institute for her Fur for Russia fund. She said donations were flowing in from all over the country: 'I feel they are particularly significant because they show the vivid and intense concern of the citizens of Great Britain for the glorious struggle for freedom of the Russian people and for the sufferings so silently and unflinchingly borne by them for their national life and ideals.'[29]

The Isle of Ely reported on the great success of its appeal for rabbit skins, the total of which had reached fifty-four 'and many parcels of lovely fur' for Mrs Churchill but sent an urgent word about skins to its members: '*Do please dry them before sending them through the post*. I am so pleased to receive them but prefer them dry.'[30] The editor of *Home & Country* wrote: 'The arrival of a moist and unpleasant parcel of rabbits' skins had a most unpleasant effect upon the County Secretary of Derby.'[31]

Another job required of the WI was camouflage net garnishing. This was a vital job where little bits of green, black and brown material were sewn onto nets. Some of the nets were made by WI members in Cornwall, where the headquarters of camouflage net production was based at St Ives. The Ministry of

Supply put out a call for fishermen, whose livelihood had been severely curtailed by the war:

> Hundreds of thousands of camouflage nets are wanted by the Min of Supply and thousands of fishermen and their wives are wanted to make them. Double hemp twine nets varying in size from 14 feet square to 35 feet square of 2 inch or 3 inch mesh are required. They are needed for work in obscuring guns, ammunition, wagons, tanks, buildings, stores and many other things which it is desirable to conceal from enemy aircraft.[32]

Britain had the largest net-making industry in the world and factories and looms, which formerly supplied fishing fleets around the world, were busy round the clock making nets for camouflage purposes. In addition large numbers of women and girls were employed in the cottages of the fishing villages braiding nets by hand to supplement the output of the machines. 'Here, it is suggested, is an opportunity for work – much of which could be done at home in the fishing villages – of real national importance. Camouflage nets save lives!'[33]

For those women who agreed to make the camouflage nets by hand the WI was able to obtain the twine and patterns. This was paid work whereas the garnishing, which went on in WIs around the country, was not. Arnside WI in Cumbria were busy garnishing camouflage nets for several months. They had hooks screwed into the beams of their meeting hut and the nets had the added benefit of dividing the space in two so they could proceed with their work or hold their meetings while the other side of the hut was used for ARP and other purposes, including weighing babies. Members of Bickleigh WI near Plymouth offered to make small nets for camouflage which used string rather than the twine employed for the larger nets. Dealing with the twine was hard on the hands so the Ministry of Supply sent pots of hand cream to the WI and WVS volunteers. Miss Walker, who was responsible for overseeing volunteers making potato baskets for farmers, wrote to Miss Farrer complaining that her women's hands were just as raw as those of the garnishers and netters and she hoped they would be able to get some extra cream. Unfortunately the baskets were made for a different ministry, one that did not consider the skin on volunteers' hands of sufficient importance to supply hand cream.

As the war progressed so the pressure increased to save and salvage whatever could be reused. Some items were collected in vast quantities. Stamps were a favourite and Blackwell WI collected 300,000 stamps in 1943. Empty cotton reels were also in demand, though no one was ever told why they were needed. Janie Hampton described their use in her book *How the Girl Guides Won the War*: 'Declassified files show that they were used by MI9, the secret War Office department set up to help prisoners of war escape. Tightly rolled silk maps of Europe, microfilm of contacts and German paper money were carefully inserted inside them, after which MI9 arranged for firms in the cotton industry to refill the reels with thread and to attach fresh paper labels to them.'[34]

Salvage became a byword for helping with the war effort and minute books are full of quantities of paper, metal, milk-bottle tops and wool that were found, collected, scavenged, saved and put to good use, either by being reused by WI members or being sent to scrap and salvage schemes organised by the government. The WI was keen to make use of everything they could, so parties of women would collect wool from the hedgerows and tufts left on wire to spin into precious fibre for knitting. Some women experimented with other types of fur. An article on knitting with dog fur explained that as dog 'wool' had been spun in the last war there was good reason to believe it would work well once again.

They recommend collecting the fur from dogs using wire brushes and spinning it in the usual way. The best dogs' coats they had found were collies, sheepdogs, chows, keeshonds and Pekinese but the group had also experimented with golden retriever, spaniel and poodle, though these had been less easy to spin and thus they had had to mix the different kinds of hair. Raw sheep's wool had become so scarce that towards the end of the war it was only possible to collect it from the wild. In the end the knitters concluded that articles knitted with dog wool did not turn out satisfactorily as the wool has little natural loft, unlike sheep's wool. However, some women wanted to persevere, as articles knitted with dogs' wool could be sold without coupons whereas anything made with sheep's wool, even if gathered from the hedgerows, required coupons. The bureaucracy of the rationing and coupon system had extraordinary reach.

Joan Simpkins of Whitstable in Kent recounted a story told by her late mother-in-law, who belonged to Aldington WI in East Kent and whose neighbour was Mrs Elsie Hueffer, widow of the author Ford Madox Ford. 'She was a somewhat eccentric lady, spun and wore her own garments, and was of course connected with the Pre-Raphaelites.' Mrs Hueffer taught Mrs Simpkins senior to spin and after the outbreak of the war, once clothing became scarce, Mrs Simpkins saw an opportunity to pass on the skill and so allow other women to have wool. Her husband was a keen woodworker, so he set about making spindles and soon she was visiting institutes all over Kent and elsewhere. Mrs Simpkins junior wrote to me: 'My husband and his brother were set to gather stray bits of wool left by sheep on hedges and fences. By the time I met the family it was all systems go and I was roped in to help make spindles.'

The lovely twist in this story came in the final paragraph of Joan Simpkins's letter: 'On one memorable occasion the WI held an exhibition at Barham (E. Kent) during the war which was visited by Mrs Eleanor Roosevelt, and I have photographs of Mother speaking to them.' This is of course the famous visit organised by Lord Woolton and Mrs Churchill in 1942 described in chapter 5. This letter brought that historical account to life.

The war in the Far East had had a dramatic effect on supplies and thus further rationing and salvage campaigns. On 7 December 1941 the Japanese attacked Pearl Harbor and brought the Americans into the war. Three days later the British suffered a terrible loss when the *Prince of Wales* and the *Repulse* were sunk off the coast of Malaya. Two months later, on 15 February 1942, Singapore fell to the Japanese in the biggest defeat in British military history. Within weeks the Japanese had taken over almost the entire Far East, creating a new empire which they called the Great East Asia Co-prosperity Sphere. With one blow they cut off all supplies from that area, including rubber, which now became scarce and had to be saved and salvaged. The WI was told to collect everything from car tyres to tap washers, every bit of rubber except proofed material such as rain coats. For the town-women this meant the banning of crêpe rubber soles for shoes and for the country wives a shortage of wellington boots. Elsie Bainbridge and her brother had special dispensation for wellingtons as they lived two miles from their school and had to walk down a cart track for half the distance. The track was often wet or frozen in the winter so that the boots for them were a vital necessity. 'My mother used to knit lovely, thick socks for our wellingtons and that kept our feet dry in winter. In the summer we would wear clogs with wooden soles and leather uppers. These were much better than shoes and were waterproof against wet grass and shallow puddles and were very warm, provided you didn't step into a deep puddle.'

By the middle of the war many things were restricted, unavailable or severely rationed. After the success of the clothing coupon scheme (from the government's point of view) the Ministry of Supply put out a fierce directive about what could or could not be done with paper. No paper should be destroyed unless it was to prevent spreading infectious diseases. All waste paper had to be disposed of to a collector or buyer.

Norton and Lenchwick WI in Worcestershire held a competition for waste paper and took delivery of 800lb of paper and cardboard while Little Aston in Staffordshire collected 2 tons in the same month. All these collections brought the institutes small amounts of money. Some was ploughed back into coffers to buy wool for knitting but much of the profits made from collections and sales were given away to hospitals, canteens, the Red Cross and other local good causes.

It is hard to imagine that some members did not feel a little downhearted when they received yet another request for voluntary assistance during the long years of the war. There is seldom a complaint recorded in the minute books and there is perhaps even a sense that grumbling would somehow undermine all their patriotic good work. The range as well as the quantity of hand-made articles that they made and distributed is simply astonishing and it is hard to imagine that they had time to squeeze all the activities into daylight hours. Yet they did. And they even found time to entertain one another. And the troops.

8

GAIETY, SONG AND DANCE

> Mrs Brown agreed to enquire into the possibilities of getting a band and also an extension of leave to carry on after 10pm for a dance to be held some moon-light night in November.
>
> *Bradfield WI minutes, 1939*

Mrs Blewitt of Boxted Hall in Essex wrote 195 letters and telegrams to her daughter, Maria, who was a Section Officer with the WAAF in England, Scotland and the Middle East and Italy during the war. She wrote 490 letters, telegrams and cards to her son, Major James Blewitt, during his war service in North Africa, the Middle East and the Mediterranean. Maria bundled up all her mother's letters and returned them to Boxted for safekeeping. Mrs Blewitt commented that, being filled with 'such very parochial matters', the correspondence would probably 'share the fate of most old letters of going into the paper-basket, considerably dusty and yellowed some years hence without further reading'. Fortunately this immensely rich treasure trove was deposited with the Department of Documents at the Imperial

War Museum in London and has been preserved for posterity. Far from being filled with parochial matters, it offers a wide-ranging and fascinating view of life in the 1940s from one woman's perspective. Much of the correspondence deals with family matters but Mrs Blewitt, like Mrs Milburn, was a brilliant observer of everyday life and as Cicely McCall wrote in 1943, 'The real stuff of a nation's history is just ordinary life.' Mrs Blewitt had an eye for the quirky or amusing angle on any story or snippet. As a prominent and wealthy member of her village she was involved in her WI, often hosting the annual garden party at the hall. In June 1941 she wrote to Maria telling her about the plans: 'It is the summer's meeting where I have to provide games etc. We are being very topical and having a gas mask race – a stirrup pump competition, dropping bombs on Berchtesgarten – and as a variant to placing the donkey's tail or the pig's eye we are having putting Hitler's moustache on his face blindfolded.'[1] Garden parties, winter dances, whist drives and games offered the WI some relaxation and laughter after all the hard work. That had been the intention from the outset.

A WI meeting consists of three distinct parts. First there is the formal business, which is led by the president and recorded by the institute secretary in the minute book. Then there is a talk or demonstration, most often given by an outside speaker. It can be educational or entertaining and is sometimes both. The talk is followed, after a short refreshment break, by the social half-hour. Almost the first instruction given by Lady Denman at the outbreak of the war was 'to keep the social side of the WI alive however hard this may be and even if our usual generous tea has become only a cup of tea and a biscuit! To laugh together will send us home heartened and cheered for our daily work.'[2] The WI is serious about its educational work and is equally serious about entertainment. WI choirs and drama productions often reach a very high level and during the war, as we shall see, some important musicians were involved in rehearsing and conducting choirs. The social half-hour was designed to allow people the freedom to let their hair down a little. At no time was this more important than through the war when demand on their time, expertise and goodwill was so enormous. As we have seen, the government expected women who were not directly employed in war work to give up an extraordinary amount of time to 'do their bit' and to do it for free, with no personal gain other than the satisfaction that they were contributing to this or that campaign.

At first some institutes faltered, overwhelmed by all the other work that had been heaped onto their plates by billeting officers, WVS duties, food production committees and extended family responsibilities. A sympathetic editorial in *Home & Country* acknowledged these extra commitments and tried to make light of them:

> Of course, we know the difficulties are enormous. Life in reception areas is not all blackberrying, nor even wholly knitted squares. One government department tells us to double our activities for the doubled rural population, another seizes our halls. County Federations beg us to meet before dark: school shifts fill up the rooms till 5:30pm. Above all, there is the black-out, the universal pall that falls on England's gaiety and activity every night at sunset. Ah, what a peace party the National Federation will hold some day, with one gigantic jumble sale of a hundred miles of black, ill-dyed and malodorous sheeting.[3]

Membership of the WI dropped from a pre-war high of 331,600 in 1939 to a low of 288,000 in 1943, the year that mobilisation peaked. The majority of women who departed were under thirty, unmarried, and could join the forces or do war work. It marked a big shift in the demographics in the countryside. As the Queen acknowledged in her speech to the Annual General Meeting that year: 'Today our villages are sadly empty. The young men are away fighting for the land they love so well. The girls too are away at their war work, and the great responsibility of carrying on rests with the older women. How gallantly they are doing this, shouldering every sort of job with such a grand and cheerful spirit and planning and praying for the day when their dear ones come home again.'[4] She was right. The average age of a Women's Institute had gone up after the beginning of the war and the women left behind were usually older members who had been with their institutes from the beginning and valued the social half-hour. It had always been part of the WI meetings and it was popular. Sometimes it comprised a dramatic production, at other times a beetle or whist drive, often a sing-song and sometimes a more rumbustious game of musical chairs. As the war dragged on so the desire to keep cheerful grew, and far from becoming demoralised it seems that women became more resilient.

The third edition of *Games for Playing at Women's Institute Meetings*, printed at the University Press in Oxford in 1941, ran to thirty-two pages and included eight sections covering acting, miming and speaking; guessing; moving about games; musical games; outdoor games and sports; sitting games; team games and writing games. The games had been gathered from a variety of books written for the Girl Guides Association and the Central Council for Recreative Physical Training. Miss Mary Hirst Simpson, who wrote the introduction to the booklet, emphasised that playing games in the right spirit 'can be a true piece of communal work, one which is not only worthwhile, but which may even be a duty of the Institute member'. She was a champion of the social half-hour and took it seriously, berating institutes that neglected what she saw as the all-important part of the meeting that allowed women to relax in each other's company.

Miss Hirst Simpson was almost a WI institution in her own right. Born to a wealthy family in Northamptonshire in 1871, she never attended school but was educated at home by a governess and later, as she had trouble with her eyes, by her mother, who read to her in a darkened room. When she recovered she was allowed to explore the lovely landscape around her home. Her real gift was her intimate knowledge of the countryside. She understood rat-catchers and hedgers and ditchers, farmers and farmhands just as much as she did the local doctor, the parson and the lawyer. She always felt that there were gaps in her knowledge so she continued to do correspondence courses throughout her life to catch up. She was exactly the kind of woman for whom the WI offered so much.

She joined the NFWI in 1919 and worked as the agricultural adviser from 1925, having been an organiser in the Women's Land Army during the First World War, for which she was awarded an MBE in 1919. She was described in the short biography compiled by the WI after her death as 'a personality, a great countrywoman, with the heart of a child'. Like Lady Denman, she was a notable sportswoman and had captained the hockey team for the county. She rode to hounds, was a good judge of a horse and always had a dog at her heels. Throughout her life she claimed she had one straightforward aim, which was to work 'for God, King and Country', and was proud to belong to the County of Spires, Spinsters and Springs – Northamptonshire.'[5] An obituary in the personnel files of the WI listed her interests and abilities:

> She showed sweet peas and bred dachshunds, sang in church and taught at Sunday School. Loved and respected by her colleagues at the national federation as someone who rejoiced in the little things in life, Miss Hirst Simpson brought common sense and clear thinking to her WI work. She understood what it felt like to be an outsider, given her lack of formal education, and was very kind to shy women and tried to help them to develop their talents, though she was tough on women who grumbled. She was particularly well known for her passion for the social half hour and she often left her own WI out of breath after an energetic spate of games.

When on one occasion women at a council meeting complained how inconvenient it was for them to attend meetings as one lived a mile from the bus, another three quarters of a mile, Miss Hirst Simpson jumped to her feet and demanded of the delegates: 'Have the countrywomen of Oxfordshire lost the use of their legs?'

At early WI meetings in newly formed WIs the social half-hour helped to break down the class barriers and create a bond between the women, which in other circumstances would have been hard to establish. Quick reactions, decisive moves and powers of deduction are not limited to background or education, Miss Hirst Simpson would point out: 'We find unexpected qualities of character among our fellow-players. Shyness and reserve break down during a game, ingenuity and initiative emerge, and all round us is friendliness and goodwill.'[6]

However, the games were mainly intended to offer a little light relief in the lives of women who may have viewed the monthly meeting as their one opportunity in four weeks to let their hair down and behave in a way that they could never have done in mixed company or in front of their children. Miss Hirst Simpson hoped that 'hearty cooperation in games would help to bring a measure of cheerfulness and laughter into many lonely and weary lives, and surely to help to combat weariness and anxiety in others is worthwhile.'[7] Miss McCall, in her brief illustrated history of the WI, celebrated the pleasure of the fun side of the Women's Institutes. About the social half-hour she wrote:

> In practice it may be a childish game played rowdily for ten minutes before going home, or it may be community singing for forty minutes. It may be entertainment by the drama enthusiasts of the institute or it may be dancing. Games are nearly always popular with the middle aged. In fact the older the members the more hysterical they become over musical bumps or passing the halfpenny. Younger and more sophisticated people may smile. But if you have been up at six, cooked two or more sets of breakfast for the variously employed grown-up members of the family, sent the children off to school and packed their dinner for them, cooked dinner for the others and washed up afterwards, looked after the fowls, swept the house, fetched the water from the pump; if you have done this every day for twenty years with no holiday and no difference except that sometimes you're bearing a child, then you deserve a laugh once a month. And if musical bumps is going to give you one, let's have more musical bumps.[8]

Musical bumps, sing-songs, parties even, all continued during the war years. Institute members soon realised that entertainments were one of the best ways to include newcomers into the villages or communities. By the middle of the war these had increased beyond offering parties and games to evacuees and visitors to well-organised entertainment for British, Canadian and American soldiers, dances and even drama productions with other local groups. But the social half-hour itself was to be kept for the end of their WI meetings.

As the WI was very often the largest organisation in their village and also the most structured, it fell to them to put on village-wide events. Particularly at the beginning of the war when so many extra, new people had arrived in the villages and needed some sort of diversion. In Ringmer in Sussex Mrs James and Mrs Hills ran a canteen in the Parish Rooms every Sunday so that parents could meet their children in the hall and buy a cup of tea and, as this was before rationing, a piece of cake. That stopped within six months but it had been a useful safety valve for the parents of the evacuees and also the foster parents. The war had disrupted village life but Christmas was such a significant festival in the annual calendar of the country that it had to be celebrated, war or no war. Christmas 1939 had been labelled the 'Economy Christmas' although much worse was to come in future years. Even the turkeys were leaner, the WI members were told, 'because nothing can stop our young London visitors from chasing them. Probably they have never seen a turkey on its legs before, only in skinny and anaemic rows in a poulterer's shop.'[9] Suggestions for Christmas arose such as having a communal tree in the village, as was the tradition in Scandinavia, or giving away family heirlooms such as silver spoons and old snuffboxes rather than purchasing expensive new items and, finally, not having icing on the Christmas cake. But the National Executive did not want the WIs to forgo their traditional Christmas party. They urged institutes to get around the difficulties by being inventive and getting everyone in the village to help.

> That's the spirit for Christmas 1939. We might be expected to black out our windows and doors but not our heart, intelligence or hospitality. The season of plenty must, like a well run

> WI, make a little go a long way. The festival, in fact, must tie its Christmas sash a little tighter. And be thankful that *our* Government doesn't tell us to wear imitation wool and make our tea of blackberries, as Dr Goebbels was recommending the Germans to do the other day. Poor old Germans! Once the best Christmas keepers of all.[10]

The British government had indeed spoken about Christmas, suggesting that 'reasonable expenditure on Christmas festivities will help trade and lessen unemployment'. There were still plenty of toys in the shops that year. Toy soldiers and models of the Maginot Line were hot favourites among the little boys. Parents and children were all keen to keep the spirit of Christmas going and when the calculations were made the economic figures showed that spending was up on the previous Christmas by 10 per cent.

Goostrey in Cheshire had initially planned to have their party from 6 to 10 p.m. but at their November meeting they decided to run with their usual format after all and to start at 7.30 p.m. and go on until midnight. And there would be dancing. The Christmas party was a great success, allowing the secretary to note in the end-of-year minutes: 'all felt that the WI was carrying on in a splendid way in spite of the difficult times'. Barthomley, just down the road, decided not to hold their Christmas party and 'Members resolved instead to give a party to the children, both Barthomley children and the evacuees in the village'. Lindsey WI in Suffolk was one of hundreds of WIs who decided to have a village-wide Christmas celebration. It started at noon at the institute hall with a meal for a hundred children. After lunch there was a grand procession to the school led by Father Christmas and followed by a jazz band of small village boys. The under-fives rode in decorated handcarts or pranced behind the procession on hobbyhorses, the whole scene was made yet more magical by the light snow that fell during the walk to the school. After games, carols and the lighting of the Christmas tree the party went home to tea, each with a little bag of goodies. Ashover in Derbyshire had so many children to entertain that they had to hold a series of parties in order to be able to accommodate them all.

The following year things were completely different for large swathes of the country and most especially in the cities. The Blitz was at its height and some 40 per cent of the population spent the majority of their nights in shelters. Christmas 1940 was 'under fire'. Parties, though still held, were often disrupted. Radley WI decided in December 1940 that it was not possible to put on a Nativity Play since 'it had been considered inadvisable to undertake anything that would bring children out at night or assemble them in one place in considerable numbers'. A New Year's Party held in January 1941 in Audlem was not unusual: 'The Party had just got livened up when our unwelcome visitors were heard overhead after which the lights went out and we were left high and dry. Anyway we managed to have something to eat and drink in candle light and then all had to leave to report on various ARP duties.'[11] Barrow WI had a Christmas meeting when they invited guests, including children, to join them. Caroline Dickinson said:

> I remember those Christmas meetings. The women were all dressed in slightly tight dresses and the hall was decorated. There were dances held to raise money as well as monthly whist drives. The war years were not unhappy times for us children but I think they must have been very difficult for women like my mother. So much was expected of them and many of them had husbands away from home so that in addition to all the extra work they also had to look after all aspects of the household, even things that previously would have been done by men.

The fact that so many women had been members since the First World War meant that they had a great understanding of the suffering of those who were being damaged by this current conflict, whether at home or abroad. 'Women who were grown up in the last war remember, as hardest to bear, the thought that young lives were being paid for their safety. Young men are defending us now, in a manner beyond praise. But this time we have the honour of sharing a little of the danger.'[12] The Second World War had a much bigger direct impact on the civilian population than the Great War. Out of the 752,091 British deaths attributed to the 1914–18 war only about 1 per cent were civilian – some 8,000 casualties. The number of civilian casualties in the Second World War was far higher – about 20 per cent of all deaths, or 63,655 out of a total of 334,342. Like Mrs Milburn and Edith Jones, many of the women living in the rural communities had sons or husbands in the forces. Some were prisoners of war, others were missing and more still fighting in far-off countries. The constant stream of letters to and from family members provided a welcome link but also a constant reminder of the pain of separation. The King broadcast a message on Christmas Day 1944 in which he acknowledged this, saying that the separation of families was one of the great trials of the current war. 'Indeed it is. No one can imagine what it means until they have experienced it,' wrote Mrs Milburn that night.

The war was never far from people's minds and despite it usually being referred to as 'this difficult time' it does occasionally find a way into minute books. On 15 July 1941, Mrs Dainty in Oxfordshire was warmly congratulated on her son being awarded the Military Medal. At that meeting the WI had enjoyed 'a delicious repast of fruit shortcake & coffee with real sugar'. At other times the news received was of tragedy, husbands, brothers, sons of members. And then there was the general loss in the Blitz and other aerial attacks that killed, wounded and rendered people homeless. In almost every edition of *Home & Country* from late 1940 there were tales of bombed-out families being rehoused in villages, of collections for specific areas of London, Coventry, Bristol to give people the most basic of materials. Warwickshire 'rolled up its sleeves in earnest this morning after the bombing of Coventry', wrote the county secretary to Miss Farrer. 'Thousands of refugees slept at the WVS Rest Centre, and WI members who have been on duty all night served early breakfasts to men going to work, and women returning to ruined houses in the hope of salvaging their belongings.' Mrs Milburn lived just a few miles from Coventry and her diary is full of stories from the air raids on the city and the terrible destruction and loss of life. 'Poor, poor Coventry! The attack is described on the wireless as "a vicious attack against an open town comparable to one of the worst raids on London, and the damage is very considerable". The casualties are in the neighbourhood of a thousand, and the beautiful fourteenth-century cathedral is destroyed. I feel numb with the pain of it all . . . the loss of life and the injuries make one's heart ache.' Her institute catered for refugees from the city and she had people staying at Burleigh. 'They just want bed,' she wrote after she had shown a couple up to Alan's bedroom.[13]

The city came under attack again, the following spring. On 28 May she wrote:

> The morning sped swiftly away and at the WI this afternoon we were glad to welcome evacuees, three of whom had been injured in air raids. One young woman, a native of Coventry, rode here on a bicycle with plaster cases on her legs! Her husband was killed in the raid on Coventry. He was on duty that night but looked in for a moment to see how his wife was

> getting on in their shelter. When a direct hit was made there, he threw himself upon his wife and saved her life, but lost his own. Poor girl, she does not want to go back to the house again. It is too full of memories.[14]

A personal tragedy struck her family when she heard that her nephew, Colin, had been badly injured in an air raid on London and had to have his foot amputated. His wife Peggy had been killed. That evening Mrs Milburn was meant to be playing the lead part in her WI's sketch, which she and others had written and rehearsed over the last four months. During the afternoon she worked in the garden, sowing seeds and digging: 'one just had to be *doing*,' she wrote in her diary that night.

> Then the evening came and I went across and did my part with the 'properties' for the entertainment and stood at the end as 'Britannia' with a very sad heart. But it is best to go on, with whatever is one's job at the moment . . . The young go and we old ones are left. They seem the ones so fitted to build a better world after this madness is over. Peggy, so capable and so sane, killed by this ruthless enemy. And what of Colin? If only we could hear more.[15]

Mrs Blewitt's family suffered several bitter tragedies. Her nephew, Bill Blewitt, was killed over Tunisia in January 1943. He was in the Parachute Regiment. Fourteen months earlier another Blewitt nephew had been killed: Richard Budworth died in North Africa and was commemorated on the Alamein memorial. His remains were never found and his mother, Helen, was completely broken by his death. She had lost her husband, Major General Budworth, in 1921 in the First World War and his body too had not been found. Mrs Blewitt was deeply touched by both the deaths. And then, in 1944, came the closest tragedy. Her sister Kitty's only child was killed in Burma. The war took its final toll on the Blewitt family when Johnnie Fenwick, another cousin, was killed in France. Every time a death was announced her concern for her own son, James, grew stronger, but he was fortunate to survive the war and she was spared the horror of losing her only son.

These were personal tragedies and individual families bore the pain. One event over all others united the Women's Institute in collective grief in January 1940 and that was the announcement of the death of their vice-chairman, Miss Hadow, after a brief attack of pneumonia. She was only sixty-five and the news came as a terrible blow to everyone. Lady Denman wrote: 'How ever shall we do without her? – not only her great ability, but her absolute unselfishness, her cool judgement, her cheerful confidence, her complete integrity, her warm understanding of and sympathy with the weakness of others, her oratory and her wit: qualities which made a combination we cannot hope to find again. The loss to the Institute movement is irreparable, as is the personal one to her friends and colleagues.'[16] A member of her own institute of Quarry in Oxford, which met the night she died, said simply: 'worse than the war'. One of many stories that abounded about her after her death was that of a day in Oxford when she, as the newly appointed Principal of the Society of Oxford Home Students, was invited to take part in commemoration events. She was seen dressed up in her smart grey dress and shoes 'with her academic hood, the trickiest part of her costume, already pinned on, gardening zealously to the last'.[17] She felt it summed up Miss Hadow perfectly: the academic with the countrywoman's touch. The WI set up a holiday fund in her memory and asked institutes to contribute to it. Several sent in the profits from their jam-making work while others made special collections and the amount of money raised reflected the very great affection members felt for this remarkable woman.

One effect of the war was the strong sense of camaraderie that it created. A WI member wrote that the local ARP had celebrated its 100th air-raid warning. 'Later, after the "all clear", in the strange stillness that follows the noise of battle, we agreed that there are things about the war that we shall miss in the peace. Beautiful things – searchlights, weaving those flat, milky patterns across the sky; balloons, like bubbles rising out of our seething cauldron; the amazing loveliness of stars and dawn, that for years we have slept too soundly to think about at all.'[18] She went on: 'We should miss, indeed, if we lost them now, the general friendliness, the humour and courage, common sense and imagination, that break out in such unexpected places. Most of all we should miss what the Prime Minister calls the feeling that "we all stand in together".'[19]

That sense of standing together was celebrated at every meeting when the women stood to sing 'Jerusalem' and closed with the National Anthem. This routine seldom changed, except for special occasions or events. In November 1942 the Audlem minutes' secretary recorded: 'As this week the news had been broadcast that the Eighth Army in Egypt had won a great victory against the German and Italian forces, Mrs Williams suggested we opened the meeting with the National Anthem.'

Mobberley WI in Cheshire, founded in 1928, prided itself on working hard to ensure the highest quality in everything they did. During the 1930s they engaged a conductor to help them sing 'Jerusalem', as members had decided it was badly sung. 'This must have done the trick for in 1937 the visiting VCO, Miss Forbes, in her Organisers Report writes: "I have never heard 'Jerusalem' sung with better rhythm and spirit; it gave the keynote for the whole meeting which was excellent in every way."'[20]

Music has always played a major role in WI life, from community singing at social half-hours to performances at national events by WI choirs. In 1940 six musicians were appointed by Sir Walford Davies 'to inspire and organise musical activities among civilians in rural areas'. The scheme was originally funded by the Pilgrim Trust. It was later taken over by the newly formed Council for the Encouragement of Music and the Arts, which was the forerunner of the Arts Council of Great Britain. One of the six musicians was the composer Imogen Holst, who had returned from Switzerland at the outbreak of war. In February 1942 she attended Oxfordshire's annual general meeting in Oxford and the minutes read: 'Miss Imogen Holst conducted community singing and practised members in singing "Jerusalem". This was her farewell visit, a spray of Christmas roses and other winter flowers was given to her as a token of affectionate appreciation and gratitude for her music and her help given in the County.'[21]

Oxfordshire also supported a school for conductors, specially designed to encourage village choirs. The school was taught by Sir Adrian Boult, and Mrs Woods, a Headington WI member, recalled her own experience of it:

> His demonstrations in handling the baton to give clear and well-timed directions are unforgettable. Sir Adrian Boult has recently written of the Deneke Sisters, both of whom were members of our Headington WI that they were 'a great beacon in Oxford Music'. The beacon spread its light far into Oxfordshire villages through Helena Deneke's devoted and untiring work during the long years of her secretaryship of the OFWI. Of Margaret Deneke Sir Adrian writes: 'that one could not meet her without sensing the great power of character and musicianship which was poured out for others, and for so many others'.[22]

Her most poignant memory, however, was of the WI choir of Charlton on Otmoor singing 'Jerusalem' unaccompanied. 'The singing was delicate but assured – it stays in the mind like the fragrance of wild flowers. Too often we have heard Parry's beautiful but difficult piano part played on a bad piano – why do we not more often sing unaccompanied?'

Surrey County Federation had an exceptionally successful music festival in 1943 when 200 members met at Guildford Technical College to sing under the direction of Ralph Vaughan Williams. They rehearsed for two and a half hours before giving their performance. One member wrote about how much she had enjoyed singing under his guidance and that she lost herself in the beauty of the music and being part of something that was bigger than herself. 'We learn from this to find our true selves in others – and here music can help.'[23]

Bradfield WI had elected to hold its meetings in the afternoons rather than the evenings during the war. They lost their meeting place, the Connop Room, in early 1941 so met in the president's house, Horseleas. As Mrs Sims was keen to attend the WI meetings she had no option but to allow her two children, Ann and John, to come to the house after school to meet her. Ann said: 'I remember cycling down to WI meetings. I must have been about six or seven. We used to be allowed to sit in the back of the room as long as we were mousey quiet. I suppose we used to arrive in time for the social half-hour because my main memory is of music and the drama. Some of what they put on was excellent and of a high standard.'

A particular success that Ann remembered, and that the minute books recorded 'how greatly did we enjoy it', was the dress rehearsal for two scenes from *Pride and Prejudice* which were to be performed at the county drama competition in 1943. 'Mrs Bennett was played by Mrs Bird and Elizabeth by Mrs Clarke. She was an evacuee from London, young and very pretty. She brought a great deal to Bradfield WI including her talent for acting. We missed her sorely when she went back home.' Mrs Clarke rented a house in Bradfield for the whole of the war and became a liked and respected member of the community. 'Mr Collins was played by Mrs Reeves. She always got the man's role because she had an Eton crop and could carry it off with great success. She was a real stalwart of our WI. She was keen on bell ringing and she rode around the village on a bicycle. She was one of many great characters in the institute. When the younger postmen were conscripted she took over as postwoman.'

Music was as popular in Bradfield as amateur dramatics. Ann recalled an entertaining performance of 'Riding Down from Bangor', an American student's song in which a bewhiskered student takes advantage in a long train tunnel of a pretty young girl in his carriage. As the train comes out of the tunnel evidence of his amorous advances can be seen: 'Maiden seen all blushes when then and there appeared/ a tiny little earring, in that horrid student's beard.' Mrs Bird with a false beard took the part of the horrid student.

Mrs Sims had to play the piano at WI meetings but she struggled with 'Jerusalem', as clearly other pianists did too, so on one occasion she brought a gramophone to the meeting. Unfortunately she had put the record on the wrong side and instead of hearing 'Jerusalem' the ladies got the B side, which was 'Rule Britannia'. Fortunately everyone saw the funny side of it. Music was an important part of their WI and Ann remembered Mrs Howlett's lovely contralto voice. She would sing songs from the current favourites but also older melodies. Mrs McCaskie, Mrs Howlett's daughter, was good at whistling, which Ann thought was wonderful. She told her mother she wanted to learn to whistle like Mrs McCaskie and her mother replied that she would be able to once her permanent front teeth had come through. She never did learn but she remembered Mrs McCaskie entertaining the WI with popular tunes. Ann found her rather exotic, with long red-painted fingernails and long dark hair. As most women wore muted colours during the war, those who wore bright colours stood out and made an impression on the children. Ann said:

> most women, as far as I can recall, wore hats and gabardine macs. Mrs Adams, who helped my mother with National Savings and village gossip, always wore the same outfit in drab colours but a few wore what we called 'frumpo-artistic clothes' – hand woven skirts and the like. Miss Brooks, the dancing teacher, wore a red and white jazzy dress and Mrs Leyton, who was evacuated to live with us, had blond shoulder-length hair and wore make-up, which was considered a bit fast by people like our parents.

One of the land girls was even more fascinating for Ann. She had dyed her hair with henna and wore mascara as well as make-up. 'I'd never seen anything like it,' she admitted with a twinkle.

As for millions of other children, the Second World War dominated Ann's childhood. Everything about village life was affected by the war. The predominant change was of course the number of men who left the village to fight. However, the incoming evacuee families also made their mark on Bradfield and, prior to the construction of an American camp at the end of the village towards the latter part of the war, the most significant development was the new school in Bucklebury, the next-door village. A Mr Stapleforth from Purley, south of Croydon, evacuated himself and his family to Bucklebury in 1940. He took a house in Paradise Lane, where he lived with his two daughters and two grandsons. One of the daughters, Eileen, was unmarried. She was a violin teacher and, determined to do her bit for the war effort, she offered her services to Mr and Mrs Ward as a land girl. The Wards did not require her help on the farm but Mrs Ward told Miss Stapleforth that she was in need of a school for her two young daughters, Dorcas and Marion, and of course other children in Bradfield and the surrounding area whose numbers had been swelled by evacuation.

Ann explained: 'The upshot was that Miss Stapleforth took over the Orchard Tea Room in Bucklebury, which had closed for the duration, and opened the Orchard Kindergarten there in September 1940. At first she was the only teacher, but as the school flourished she took on more staff and opened a second classroom in a summerhouse in the garden of Mr and Mrs Castello at Green Meadows.' Even that was not sufficient and Miss Stapleforth purchased a prefabricated building which provided two further classrooms. Bucklebury was just over a mile from the Southend area of Bradfield and the children either walked, took the number 11 bus or cycled to school, in the later war years through the American army camp. 'Miss Stapleforth was an inspired teacher – she took us for English and needlework as well as singing. Her sister, Mrs Pritchard (whose two young sons were in the school), was an elocution mistress and under her tutelage we produced either a concert or a play at the end of each term. Our theatre was the kitchen of the Old Manor. I well remember walking in crocodile down the hill to Bucklebury village for rehearsals.'

The third of the three Rs was catered for by a trained teacher, Miss Wilson, who taught the children arithmetic. They remembered her as being very strict and had been told that she had been governess to an Indian prince or maharajah. The Vicar of Bucklebury taught scripture and Mademoiselle Bouvier came from Reading on a bus to teach French. They even had a German teacher in Fräulein Oberländer, who had escaped from the Nazis by fleeing from Austria. 'She was an excellent teacher, and, with the consent of our parents, taught us German counting rhymes and singing games which we still remember over 60 years on. I remember "Eins, zwei Polizei, drei, vier Offizier!" and so on.'

Ann kept her exercise books from school and her English book gives a flavour of the times. 'Mrs Brown has been fined for buying some bananas at the Black Market.' 'Mr Jones is a bankrupt' and 'Mr Williams got a posthumous VC'. Slightly less easy to fathom is 'Charles Dikons is a notorious highwayman'.

The WI featured as part of that wartime backdrop to Ann and Dorcas's lives. They greatly enjoyed the children's parties organised by the institute for the village children each summer at Horseleas. In June 1940 the WI was not sure the village party could take place. The war had taken a dangerous turn and the threat of invasion was real, so that the announcement of the date for 11 July suddenly seemed optimistic.

Bradfield was not a target for bombs but suffered, as many villages did, from planes opening their bomb bays over the countryside on the return flight. Ann recalled sitting under the stairs with John and her mother, who told them stories, while her father was out in his tin hat on air-raid duty. 'Not once did she infect us with the fear that she must have felt at the thought of my father out there, unprotected, looking for bombs. His tin hat would not have offered him much protection if he had ever been close to an explosion, but thankfully he was not.'

In 1944 there was the children's party, which was recorded by Mrs Ward in the minute book: 'After tea they enjoyed competitions and races in the garden organised by Mrs Sims and Mrs McCaskie. Mrs Dartford judged the competition for pencil sketches and awarded 1st prize for the over 10s to Mary Bird, 1st for the under 10s to Dorcas and Marion Ward jointly. At six o'clock the children gave a hearty clap first to Mrs Sims for organising the games and then to Mrs Howlett for once again welcoming us all to Horseleas.' In return the children would entertain the WI at their Christmas parties with singing and carols. Ann remembered: 'Mrs Howlett was the tenant at the house so she made the garden available to us for those summer parties. They were wonderful, I remember, we had swing boats and roundabouts and ice cream – an unheard of treat.' Dorcas said: 'It was a wonderful time to be growing up.'

Children accepted the war as part of their lives, and not always a bad part of it. Caroline Dickinson was equally positive about her childhood in Cheshire. There was a great deal of freedom in Barrow and the addition of her two cousins to the family during the war years meant there was plenty going on and always someone to play with. Sadly the final legacy of the war for her was that she was left without her father. He died in Normandy on 15 July 1944.

For some the war was even exciting. An article that produced a critical response in ensuing issues of *Home & Country* described the thrill for one young woman:

> We country and little-town people are getting the best of the fun in this war! A big town is rigid and impersonal. Air Raid Wardens and Local Authorities are 'them' in a town. In the country they are 'us'. We seem sometimes to be living in a John Buchan story, set on an enormous stage, and each one of us with an acting part. It is a story of passwords and signals, emergency rations and prohibited areas – all the best thrills of romance! – and with our own men going out to guard us from dusk to dawn. Who would have believed that an official paper

> would have told you and me to 'keep watch for anything suspicious', what to do if an armed German invader were to drop from the sky?[24]

On her way to an institute meeting, the writer and a friend stopped to watch a dogfight in the sky above. They were enthralled by the acrobatics of the British fighters 'like terriers' on the tail of the German pilot. 'When the wireless told the world of enemy aircraft shot down off the coast we felt we had done it ourselves!'[25] She had stopped being afraid when the air-raid siren sounded and pointed out that even in the shelters they were able to carry on with their war effort since 'we get through a lot of knitting underground'.

Amongst all the other requests received by institutes there was one from their own National Executive. The WI ran a fundraising drive for ambulances during 1940 and raised sufficient funds to buy five: one for the War Office, one for the Royal Navy and three for the Royal Air Force. The fund also raised sufficient money to buy a mobile X-ray unit for the treatment of civilian casualties and three smaller, portable X-ray units, which would be most welcome, Dr Ulysses Williams assured the WI in his thank-you letter: 'a most useful piece of apparatus that will solve many of our difficulties. In the case of air raids, when the lifts at the Royal Free are possibly not working, we shall find it very useful indeed.'[26] It was one of the few national campaigns by the WI; most others were instigated by bodies such as the Red Cross, or the government itself, or begun locally by the village institutes.

A list of the activities undertaken by individual institutes gives some idea of the enormous breadth of support that one village could provide, from knitting string gloves for sailors or parcelling up toys for prisoners of war, to providing vegetables for the local elderly or volunteering to cook school meals. Every year members of Mobberley WI made a donation towards a good cause in addition to all their other work on behalf of others. Over a five-year period from 1939 they gave £221 (£7,500 today) to charities. In 1942 they offered to raise money for the Christie Hospital in Manchester. When they told the hospital that they had raised £70 they received a request from the surgeons to allow them to use the money to purchase surgical instruments rather than putting the money into the general fund. 'Later we were invited to the hospital and there saw these expensive things displayed with a large card on which was printed, "Presented by the members of Mobberley Women's Institute." The surgeons told us they had wanted these instruments for a long while but could not afford them.'[27]

Most counties had military bases or camps billeted in their area and these were not just British units. From 1940 there was a contingent of Canadian troops and two years later the first of the American soldiers arrived, reaching a total of 770,000 by 1943. At the beginning, when the camps were predominantly occupied by British forces, the institutes became involved in washing and mending clothes, organising parties and dances as entertainment. These were encouraged and were popular with both the men stationed in far-flung corners of the country and the women who were able to put on the events. These might range from a supper and dance for a few dozen men to a fully fledged party for 200. The WI was also involved with running military canteens, sometimes in cooperation with the WVS but often on their own initiative.

Thornton Hough WI on the Wirral had their own hall which had opened in 1931. It was used for catering for local troops and hospitals. They were only a small institute but were open on Sunday afternoons for soldiers based at Levers School and Raby camps. 'Members took it in turns to serve egg and chips or poached egg on toast to provide comfort for the troops.'[28] The WI also catered for the summer fete at Thornton Manor and members helped with catering when a convalescence hospital for the forces opened there later in the war. They also had a canteen for troops housed in huts at Clatterbridge Hospital. Grayshott WI opened a canteen in the Scout Hut in the village and served 670 meals a day. The canteens were a great boon for the soldiers but it was a lot of work for the women. Nella Last did a regular slot at her local canteen in Barrow-in-Furness, which she enjoyed, though not when the soldiers got too rowdy. As well as working in the canteen she served in a charity shop and also did a stint at the Red Cross Centre. It was exhausting work but when she wondered to herself why she did it she came to the conclusion that it was because she hoped someone, somewhere, would be serving her son, Cliff: 'Every soldier I serve has my Cliff's face – every merchant seaman has Frank Larkin's,' she told a woman who asked her why she was so determined to carry on. Coningsby and Tattershall WI in Lincolnshire ran a canteen for soldiers in the local Temperance Hall. Mrs McFeeters, who was the local doctor's wife and president of the WI, helped to staff the canteen. She was asked to go in front of the hall committee one day as it had been reported that the soldiers had been heard to sing 'Roll out the Barrel'. The canteen closed in May 1941, not because of the singing but because it was no longer possible to get supplies.

The appreciation felt by soldiers for the efforts made by the WIs is evident from the many references to letters of warm thanks for entertainment, refreshments, hot baths, clothes repairs and sock-darning. It was not a given that all WIs would be prepared to undertake mending work. Mrs McFeeters asked her membership to vote on the issue of whether they should undertake darning for the RAF. The result was 10:1 in favour but by 1942 they had to give up their knitting party as there was no coupon-free wool available. Some WIs, such as Warton in Lancashire, received so many such letters that reading them became a permanent feature of their meetings. Private Fred Evans wrote to Mrs Walker: 'Thank you so much for mending my shirt. I couldn't see the tear anymore and it was comfortable again. You did a grand job. Give my love to Missy and say I'll see her again soon.' Gloucestershire institutes made such an impact on a regiment stationed temporarily in the county that the week after the soldiers left a cheque for £5 was received by the county 'for WI funds'. At another party an aircraft engineer won a teapot full of chocolates as a prize. 'He returned it to be sold and a colleague won it, kept the teapot for a lady friend and returned the chocolates.'[29]

It was not just men that the WIs entertained. There were women's units stationed around the country too. Radley decided to invite girls from the WAAF to a party in August 1942: 'It was decided to entertain the guests from 7.30–10.0 with progressive games followed by dancing and community singing. It was agreed to buy bread and cakes from WI funds, the members to provide tea, milk, jam, butter, margarine and tomatoes. Prizes were promised by Mrs. Wrinch (jam), Mrs. Talboys (toilet soap), Mrs. Paton (toilet soap), Mrs. Hellard (cake), Miss Greening (book) and Mrs. Drysdale (fruit). Cigarettes (to be handed round) to be provided by members not giving prizes.'

Lady Denman had particularly mentioned her Women's Land Army girls when she asked her institutes for help at the beginning of the war. Many of these young women, she told them, would come from the cities and have no experience of the countryside. In 1940 she published an appeal to farmers' wives to help her out by considering how best to approach the thorny issue of persuading farmers and gardeners of the potential value of employing members of the Women's Land Army, for which she was responsible. 'The Women's Institutes and the Women's Land Army are each helping in the campaign for more food production. Women's Institute members can do much by their influence and encouragement to enable the Land Army to take its full share in this task. The prejudice against a woman attempting to do a man's work dies hard.'[30] The main problem was that most girls who joined the Land Army had never worked in the countryside. Many had been barmaids, waitresses, hairdressers or millworkers before joining up. They came in great numbers from London and the industrial cities in the north and found the outdoor life in the isolated countryside a big change. Initially almost all the girls lived in lodgings or billets close to or on the farms where they worked. These could be cottages with the families of other workers, or in the farmhouse with the farmer's family. Farmers and their wives often looked down on them if they came from the poorer areas of cities. Many WI minute books record kindnesses extended to the Women's Land Army, from offers of hot baths when none were available in their billets, to invitations to WI meetings and events, high tea or lunch on Sundays with individual members and invitations to dances if troops were stationed close by.

Ruth Toosey had responsibility for the welfare of the land girls in her village, of which there were about fifteen. They used to come to the White House where the Tooseys lived for a weekly get-together after tea and Mrs Toosey would listen to their stories and hear their complaints or worries. One unfortunate land girl got pregnant during the war, so her advice was clearly needed, if not always listened to. Mrs Milburn referred to the nine land girls who regularly visited Burleigh for baths and tea as 'my' girls. She wrote to them regularly after they were moved on to another farm as they were part of a mobile unit that went where work was required. The WLA reached its maximum strength in July 1943 with 87,000 workers. As the food shortages increased and the amount of available male labour for farmers decreased so they began to see the value of the land girls. One wrote:

> They drove a tractor, harrowed up twitch, which they carted and burned, had a whole week's threshing, one on the corn stacks and the other on the straw stacks, taking a man's place in each case, and keeping pace with the men. They fed and cleaned out pigs and learnt to milk daily, they picked potatoes and took on four acres of beet, of which they made an excellent job . . . I found them cheerful and willing, with never a grumble in rain or storm, always sensibly clad and happy. Girls like this cannot but help to win the war.[31]

British troops, Women's Land Army, Civil Defence units, RAF and the WAAF were familiar territory and easy to deal with. The influx of hundreds of thousands of Americans leading up to D-Day was a slightly different issue for the WI and those counties that had US military camps were encouraged to make friends with their guests. The majority of the 426,000 US airmen in Britain in 1944 were stationed in Norfolk and Suffolk and their camps and airfields swallowed up over 100,000 acres of the countryside in those two counties alone. Suffolk also had 71,000 GIs, which had a profound impact on the population of the county which, in 1943, stood at 400,000. In Wiltshire there were so many Americans that, according to historian Juliet Gardiner, the English only just outnumbered the GIs by two to one. The WI were encouraged set up welcome clubs: 'The aim of these clubs is to give American troops the chance of meeting English people socially and to introduce some of them to English family life . . . it may be an opportunity of giving Americans who are missing home life the chance of being welcomed by Institute members.'[32] The letter went on to describe how members should familiarise themselves with the geography of the USA and find out the difference in character between the eastern states, those in the Midwest and those on the Pacific coast. They might find their customs and speech easier to understand if they took the trouble to do the research before the visitors arrived. In fact there was relatively little opportunity for any organised mixing since the Americans were to some extent cocooned in their camps and entertained with American food, movies and even their own daily newspaper. There were of course encounters between Americans and the British and many, famously, led to relationships, but in terms of what the WI could do to entertain them, that was limited.

By 1945 there were over 155,000 Italian and 400,000 German POWs in hundreds of camps around the country. These men frequently worked on farms and local families often had contact with the camps. The prisoners, missing their own families, particularly liked to see the children and many school-aged boys and girls were given hand-made toys by POWs. A few WIs adopted local prisoners of war and offered to help out with mending and sewing for them, though not with cooking. The Italians were particularly inventive with cooking even with the most basic rations and the smells coming from their camps were delicious. 'They seemed to have knowledge of wild herbs and used them in their cooking pots to make their rations tasty,' said Sara Downey.

Most WIs were more concerned with the 300,000 British POWs in Europe and the Far East and contributed to the weekly Red Cross parcels that were prepared by the thousand after Dunkirk. Nella Last and a group of women in Barrow managed to negotiate the loan of a small shop from which they could sell merchandise, all donated, to raise money for POW parcels.

While busy entertaining others at parties and dances, the institutes also kept up their own talks and demonstrations as well as their social half-hour. Some talks were topical, others were deliberately light-hearted debates and still more helped them to understand the plight of individuals in the war. In 1942 members of Bickleigh WI had a 'nice talk on Chemical Warfare which everyone thoroughly enjoyed'. Mrs Ward recorded more detail than most minutes secretaries about the content of talks given to her institute. In 1943 they had a visit from a refugee and noted in the minute book: 'Mrs Eiffler gave us a most interesting talk on her native land, Poland. Her description of the picturesque customs and ways of peace-time Poland made the present condition of that unhappy country seem all the more ghastly. The speaker herself had escaped shortly before the German attack but her brothers are now in concentration camps and her mother and sister deported by the Russians to Siberia.' A few meetings later they had a talk from Mrs Hall, 'a refugee from Nazi oppression who spoke of life in Nazi Germany as she had known it. Though she spoke with a studied restraint she brought home to her audience the sufferings endured in Germany by those who are not of the favoured race. Members found the talk absorbingly interesting and realized more than ever that it is indeed Evil things which we are fighting.'

Sometimes the lecturers and demonstrators failed to arrive at meetings, often due to transport problems, so it fell to members to entertain one another. Mrs Ward recorded one such event in Bradfield when Mrs Wilson 'stepped valiantly into the breach' and said that she would demonstrate trussing if a chicken could be produced. 'By good chance a fowl was forthcoming and members watched fascinated as her expert fingers performed the job over which our own had often fumbled.' How did that chicken materialise? Unfortunately Mrs Ward did not reveal that secret.

The editor of *Home & Country* enjoyed collecting stories and would publish brief anecdotes that caught her fancy. In November 1943 she entertained the readership with stories from all over the country: Reculver in East Kent put on a show written by a member called *Women Who Wait*, which looked at what happened when the men were away fighting. It was extremely popular in the village and there was so much pressure for tickets from WI and non-WI alike that the president had to ask for 'four thinnish people' to take tea round after the performance. At Alphington WI in Devon there was a competition for the perfect husband. The answer had to be no more than ten words and the winning answer was: 'Makes plenty *dough*, never *crusty*, calls me his little *flour*.' A debate held in several institutes was 'Should husbands help with the housework?' One WI concluded that there was no point in taking a vote since 'useful or not, we shouldn't like to be without them'. Another debate on a similar subject held in Kirkham, Lancashire, 'that it is advisable for menfolk to help in the kitchen', was won, after a brief discussion. These and other debates such as 'Should husband or wife get up first in the morning?' or 'Should women wear trousers?' are a reminder of how very different life was for women seventy years ago.

Competitions remained a feature of WI monthly meetings. Some institutes were more inventive than others in their ideas for what could be fairly set as a competition and judged. The funniest potato, the longest carrot or the most peculiar-shaped vegetable were all staple competitions. Some were serious and highly competitive, with certain members being serial winners. Edith Jones often won at Smethcote: 'Our WI meeting at Leebotwood. I win 1st prize with Victoria Sponge sandwich (Green's competition). There were 27 entries. Olive Gretton 2nd and Phyllis Munslow 3rd. I must be a fair cook as this is the 3rd time I have won prizes for cakes in big competitions.' And then there were more creative competitions that delighted the membership and drew comment: the most inventive buttonhole, the best decorated hat, the best thrift shirt and the best hand-made toy. Thrift competitions were great favourites, with Findon in West Sussex inviting members to come along wearing or carrying something they had made which, the minutes secretary wrote, 'turned into a whole exhibition'. Almost as important as the competitions were the prizes. One prize that absolutely stunned members at Goffs Oak in Hertfordshire in 1942 was *a lemon* brought from South America by a member's seaman son. Such was the reverence in which this precious delicacy was held that no one remembered what the competition was, merely the prize, and it was recorded in the minute book in capital letters and underlined several times. Crowthorne in Berkshire held a whistling competition which silenced the birds outside their hall.

Members always tried to find a light side to work that was mundane. Salvage collection might not seem to be particularly amusing but Mrs Thompson, the president of Wigtoft WI in Lincolnshire, wrote: 'Our institute has derived a lot of fun from our salvage efforts. At the time of writing our depot (a disused cottage) is stocked with empty tins so we have appealed to the County Surveyor for his help and he has promised to send a steam-roller to our aid for flattening operations. I hope that before this letter is in print our tins will be well on their way to help meet the great demand.'[33]

Sharing stories was an important part of keeping up morale. One of the most extraordinary was that of two women who belonged to Ningwood and Shalfleet WI on the Isle of Wight. They met regularly at meetings, Mrs B, the elder, having returned to the island from living abroad for many years. Mrs T, the younger, came from Sussex to live at Ningwood during the war. One day they were chatting over a cup of tea and discovered that they were sisters, who had been separated for thirty years. Mrs T suddenly discovered to her surprise and delight that she had eight nephews and great nephews, all in the forces.

Communication was important during the war, and in addition to writing letters to friends and family, the WI communicated with institutes abroad. In February 1940 the NFWI announced a push to establish letter friendships between villages in this country and villages in neutral European countries, in America and in the Empire. Hundreds of institutes were involved in the scheme and people delighted in tales from all over the world. They were particularly grateful for supportive letters during the Blitz but what really interested them were stories of what was happening in countries where the war was further away. A letter from New Zealand made Mrs Denny from Billericay smile: 'You will be pleased to know, well rather, I am to tell you that "New Zealand *Home & Country*" is adopting the same cover as your *Home & Country*: that is, the map of NZ, and it was through you it has come about . . . Up to now we have had photographs of towns, and this has caused controversy one way and another because the North Island have never had a picture in. The map will stop all that.'[34]

At the end of June 1944 Miss Mary Leslie looked back on the women who had welcomed her into their institute in a little south-east coast village when she was evacuated from her home in London in September 1939. She wrote: 'Each year, when June approaches, when the chestnut trees lift their splendour to the skies and buttercups carpet the green fields, my thoughts return to a small village near the South-East Coast which was my home at the time of Dunkirk. Those were days of anguish when all day the guns thundered across the Channel and we saw the little ships return from hell with their human cargo.'[35] She remembered the last meeting she attended when the strain of the past weeks showed on the faces of all the members present but how with great determination they conducted the business in the usual fashion, followed by a demonstration and then a sing-song to lift their spirits before they each went their separate ways.

> I looked around at that little group of women in their sombre blacks and browns, their shabby housekeeping purses clasped in work-worn hands, at their patient kindly faces, now infinitely sad in the golden evening sun. The thought came to my mind '. . . we are all members one of another' and I felt strangely comforted. The next week I left my village, but they stayed on, working, knitting, preserving and keeping the wheels of life turning in that perilous corner of our small island home. Their names may not be written in the annals of history, but to me they are heroines – these, my fellow members.[36]

9

BUILDING FOR THE FUTURE

While our country is at war our duty is generally obvious, but when peace comes it will need much thought to make certain that we strive for those reforms which are essential for the well being of country people and especially country children.

Lady Denman, AGM 1943

On 20 July 1944, Edith Jones noted in her little brown diary: 'Hitler's life threatened by bomb. Puppy is very lousy, so Margaret is sorry for him & gives him a sound bathing and dressing.' Two weeks before the attempt on Hitler's life, the D-Day landings had taken place and the long, drawn-out end-phase of the war in Europe had begun. Around 24,500 British, American, Canadian and Free-French airborne troops landed in occupied France shortly after midnight on 6 June, and six hours later 160,000 troops made amphibious landings on the beaches of Normandy. By the end of the month the Allies had established a firm foothold in Normandy and by mid-August they had crossed the River Seine. The cost was high with over 12,000 casualties but there was a great feeling of excitement in the country that there was serious movement against the Germans. 'Announcers of the BBC cannot conceal their delight at being able to give such good news, and the war correspondents nearly tumble over themselves with the thrill of telling the story of this most spectacular advance. As Robin Duff told his story we could hear the victory bells ringing from the French church nearby,'[1] wrote Mrs Milburn on 18 August.

People sensed that the war would soon be over and for the WI this was the time to redouble their efforts and focus on rebuilding after the war. Mrs Ward, in her perceptive way, contemplated the role the WI would have. She wrote in her 1944 end-of-year report for Bradfield:

> Membership and attendance has fallen off considerably of late. It is difficult to say how much this is due to everyone being harder worked and more tired as this war goes on and how much that we are not providing the type of programme to attract attendance. I think a great drive for increased membership is called for . . . When the war ends there should be great scope for organizations such as this if those who return from the services and other war activities are not to feel village life [is] empty. Meanwhile in a world largely reverted to barbarism and destruction it is up to us to keep the light of civilization and kindliness burning as brightly as is in our small power to do.

From the outbreak of the war Lady Denman and the National Executive had tried to reinforce the message that the war should not stop the WI from its campaigns for improving life in the countryside. Although the war interrupted normal proceedings of the administration in many ways, the WI tried as hard as it could to keep going with national committees and urged their county colleagues to try to keep to their regular schedule of meetings as well. The annual general meeting was traditionally held in London but for the first four years of the war this was not possible. Restrictions on travel prevented many women from attending and the bombing meant that all but essential visits to the capital were to be avoided. Other national meetings could take place in cities outside London. In March 1941 Lady Denman announced at a Consultative Council meeting that the WI should begin preparing for a post-war world. Planning for reconstruction was not easy, she conceded, since so many WI officers at national and county level were committed to other jobs and the work had to get done with fewer meetings. But it was vital work and the meetings had to go on so that they could get stimulus and guidance from one another.

> A great opportunity has been given us through the food production and preservation work. We should not forget the permanent results: (a) sounder diet, (b) the opportunity to get more County Council teachers. To carry out this work, the best possible machinery – WI and Council Meetings, Produce Guild rallies – are all as necessary as in peacetime; so is the election of good committees. Only through WI meetings can members realize the importance of their contribution to the national effort.[2]

This last point underlines once again the extraordinary reach of the WI, from the grass roots in rural villages to the National Executive Committees who had the ear of government. Now, in the middle of the war, Lady Denman urged institute presidents not to overlook their WI work while helping with other war work such as the Red Cross or WVS. 'We are a permanent body and reforms such as an increase in the number of women police, the provision of milk for necessitous town evacuees and of school meals for children are very much our concern, more so than that of the wartime organizations.'[3]

It was the permanence of the WI over the other organisations and the many bodies concerned with wartime food and rationing that gave planning for the future relevance. Issues that had been of concern to the movement in the lead-up to the war – rural housing, sewage and electricity provision, more women police, equal pay, school meals, analgesics for women giving birth at home – continued to occupy the WI throughout the 1940s. They lobbied ministries and badgered MPs as much as they had ever done.

In June 1942 Lady Denman broadcast a fifteen-minute speech on the BBC to her membership. It was a propaganda coup since many more listened in to the broadcast, including non-WI members, than could possibly have heard her speak at an AGM. She talked about how hard it was to run the WI in wartime when meetings were so difficult to organise, particularly national ones, and she likened herself to a captain of a ship unable to get messages to her crew about their destination:

> The crew carries on, but it must do its best to guess what course to take. If I am considered as captain of the ship I must say that all the other members of the crew have done their utmost to find out the wishes of Institutes who should be directing our course; and we look forward to the day when you can again take charge. I do not want to press this simile too far but you Institute members not only direct the course of the ship of the National Federation, you also provide its motive power, its engines. Engines of about 300,000 woman-power sound pretty powerful to me.[4]

Never one to miss the opportunity to point out the value of the WI, she went on to say: 'I hope that this figure will also impress those who are planning for the future and that they will remember that our powerful woman-power machine should be used to the full for the improvement of country life . . .'

One issue that had been bothering the WI since the 1930s was the question of water and sewerage in villages. A questionnaire had been sent to institutes in 1942 and the response had been overwhelming. In 1939 some 30 per cent of villages had no running water and over half were not on main drains. Pumping and carrying water was a daily chore for thousands of households and made the task of washing and cleaning that much more difficult, especially in frosty or especially dry conditions. In 1944 the National Federation circulated the results of the questionnaire, which showed that in some villages 75 per cent of inhabitants had no piped water in their homes and nearly 100 per cent had no main drains. Herefordshire, which had a particularly bad water supply, commented: 'No village in time of drought or frost has an adequate supply and quite 50 per cent have an inadequate supply at all times.'[5]

Bradfield took part in the survey and Mrs Ward made notes about who surveyed which parts of the village. The request had come from the county and she wrote: 'The question of water and sanitation in rural areas was considered so urgent that it was decided to undertake the detailed survey asked for in the letter.' Nine members volunteered to conduct the house-to-house survey with Mrs Ward taking responsibility for Mariner's Road. Their survey revealed that most houses managed with 'earth closets or primitive water closets that drained into malodorous cess pits or more scientific septic tanks'. It was not until the mid-1950s that the village would get main drains. Ann Tetlow remembered perennial problems with the septic tank at their house which constantly overflowed, leaving the garden and the farmer's field beyond in a smelly, soggy condition. 'The trouble was that my father had a cold bath every morning, my mother bathed us every evening and she herself would have a bath before she went to bed so that the septic tank was overwhelmed and the garden was often a bit rank.' When Ann moved into her own cottage in 1966 just down the road from her family home it had no mains water, no drains and a bucket loo. Electricity was also missing. All these were speedily rectified but it illustrates just how much work had to be done even in villages that were not so far from towns with good amenities.

Mrs Walshe from Danbury WI in Essex had written to complain that

> in many little houses all over the country there is no sanitary appliance except a pail. The gardens of these houses, many of them very small, cannot grow food because the soil is polluted. There is also the question of the many rural schools which still have no sanitary appliances except pails. The Ministry of Health is very busy organising inoculation against diphtheria, but surely one essential method of fighting this and other dangerous diseases, such as scarlet fever, is to raise the standard of sanitation for all the people.[6]

As late as 1944, *Home & Country* published an article on how to manage an earth closet. It started with a cheerful assertion that if you have no drains in the house then there are no drains to go wrong. 'But, and there is a very big but, an earth closet can be the most unpleasant thing in the world if it is not managed correctly.'[7] Sybil Norcott's family home outside Dunham Massey had an outside privy and she remembered a funny story when one of her mother's friends, Aunt Rose, who had married a shipping director and lived in a smart house with modern sanitation, came to stay on the farm for a holiday.

> Aunt Rose was used to a flush lavatory at home whereas here the lavatory was outside – a scrubbed wooden seat over a bucket in an outhouse not far from the kitchen. Martin, our Irish farmhand, was bringing the morning milk into the house to be sieved when Aunt Rose came in from the loo and said: 'Hannah, you have no lock on the toilet door.' Martin remarked: 'Eh, missus, we've never had anyone pinch a bucket 'a shit yet.' Poor Mum!

Earlier that year the government had published a White Paper suggesting what might be done to bring water to nearly every house and farm 'where practicable'. One of the problems was that there were over 1,000 water companies in Britain at the time and the government had to decide how to amalgamate the companies in order to provide water to remote households.

> Sceptics too will find themselves wondering over those words 'a piped water supply where practicable'. Practicable according to whom? There are WIs who before the war appealed in vain to the rural district councils for a piped water supply. They were told it was impracticable. Yet with the building of an aerodrome or an American camp a piped water supply was provided without difficulty. In Switzerland and in Sweden it is found practicable to supply even remote villages with water, electricity and telephones.[8]

This rankled many village householders and in their report the NFWI asked the question: 'There appear to be ample supplies for Military camps. Water is practicable and reasonable for soldiers in wartime. Are we ratepayers and housewives going to insist that it is practicable and reasonable for civilian family life in time of peace?'[9]

The government had spent money on providing water supplies to rural villages during the 1930s and had succeeded in bringing water to 70 per cent of these areas. As the WI pointed out, however, these were the easiest 70 per cent to reach, the remaining 30 per cent being more inaccessible. In 1944 the government agreed to allocate grants for water and drainage. How far would the money stretch? the WI asked. 'Many of the houses already served with water have no drainage. Even some of the agricultural cottages built this year have no water laid on, in some cases in spite of ample water being available.'[10]

Bedfordshire was one of the counties that had a good piped water supply with only one or two villages relying on a private scheme. Nearly all the houses had taps or standpipes, with the majority being served by the latter. Nevertheless five villages had to rely on wells and in three, Dean, Turvey and Milton Ernest, several villagers had to go more than 200 yards for a piped water supply. Counties further north, like Lancashire, were worse off. In Hoghton thirty-six households shared five wells, Great Dalby in Leicestershire was a village where eighty houses had to share three pumps, and Farley Hill in Berkshire had to pay water rates, yet 80 per cent of their householders had to carry water half a mile.

Answers to the sewerage question were even more shocking. In twenty-six English and Welsh counties half the houses surveyed had only earth, bucket or chemical closet and in Hampshire the figure rose to 77 per cent. In the worst case they could quote Bidford-on-Avon in Warwickshire, where twenty-one people living in three houses shared one bucket lavatory. The summary ended: 'In Cerne Abbas (Dorset) sanitation is described as deplorable and not much improved since Tudor days.'[11] What irritated the women carrying out the survey more almost than the insanitary conditions for the householders were those in the country schools where in twenty-one counties half of all schools had only earth or bucket lavatories. In Shropshire five schools were entirely without any form of water supply and 'earth closets in village schools of all counties are quite usual and with the wartime difficulty of finding adequate school cleaners, school hygiene – if one can use that word in connection with earth closets – becomes a nauseous mockery.'[12] At a school in Gloucestershire the pails were emptied into a drain which had not itself been emptied for forty years. Eighty yards below the drain was a pump supplying fourteen houses with water in times of drought. There was much to be done and the WI promised to lobby the government and follow closely the official survey into water supplies to ensure that the maximum pressure was put on local councils not to shirk responsibility for what they regarded as a scandalous situation. The battle over piped water and drains continued for another decade and it was only in the latter half of the 1950s that the majority of village homes had their own water supply. As the WI had pointed out in 1942, it did not seem very much to ask to be able to turn on a tap in the home and have running water.

In 1943 the WI decided to hold its AGM in London. As usual it was organised over a period of two days in June and despite 'stygian travel', as Lady Denman put it, almost everyone managed to arrive at the Royal Albert Hall on time, though the guest of honour was gracious enough to delay the start of her speech by a minute in order for delegates who had been held up on trains and buses to get to their seats. The National Executive had tried to keep the identity of their special guest a secret and there was tremendous excitement and anticipation as the Queen stood up and addressed the 8,000 women in the hall:

> Through the institutes the energies of thousands of countrywomen have been organised in directions essential to victory. The care of evacuated children, the preservation of thousands

> of tons of fruit, the collection of salvage – these are only some of the jobs tackled by village women through their respective institutes. As Joint President with Queen Mary of our own Institute at Sandringham – where I am glad to think that we have three generations of our family as members – I know how deeply concerned our members are in these problems.[13]

The next speaker was the Minister of Agriculture, Mr Robert Hudson MP, who elicited a huge roar of approval when he began:

> I could not help wondering, when I came into this great hall this morning, what the Nazis would think of a gathering like this. That is, if you can imagine them allowing women to have the audacity to organise and run a national movement of this sort. Your gathering is a tribute to the living force of democracy. In the fourth year of a world struggle, it is a very great achievement to have gathered together so representative an audience from all corners of England. I should like to congratulate you, Lady Denman, and your Federation on its wisdom and initiative in reviving the full democratic working of its machinery.[14]

Lady Denman used her speech at this AGM to encourage the members to start planning for the peace to come. She told them how proud she was that their water and sewerage survey had met with almost universal praise and she reminded her audience 'that there had hardly been a government department which had not asked, through this organisation, for the help and cooperation of country women. Both have been given freely by the Institutes all over the country.'

Another topic that concerned the WI from the mid-1940s was the *Report of the Inter-Departmental Committee on Social Insurance and Allied Services.* Presented to Parliament in November 1942 by its author, Sir William Beveridge, it recommended principles that he believed necessary to abolish poverty from Britain. The Beveridge Report, as it soon became known, was radical, suggesting as it did that the war provided the opportunity for a fundamental change. He said: 'Now, when the war is abolishing landmarks of every kind, is the opportunity for using experience in a clear field. A revolutionary moment in the world's history is a time for revolutions, not for patching.' The report was well received by the public, and the WIs were as vocal in their praise as other groups. They particularly liked the emphasis on 'social expenditure to the care of childhood and to the safeguarding of maternity'. They had long been arguing the case for an allowance for families with children under fifteen, claiming that it would help towards 'preventing widespread malnutrition, encourage the birth rate, and remove children from the consequences of those modern world diseases – slumps, industrial disputes and so on – which they should not have to bear'.[15]

The WI welcomed the Beveridge Report as a real advance on current thinking: 'Evolutionary not revolutionary. The logical outcome of the national insurance we already know. Everyone is talking about it and yet there is hardly anyone who disagrees with its general principles.'[16] Lectures, discussions and debates on the report were held in institutes throughout the country from the time of its publication in December 1942.

An article in *Home & Country* in January 1943 addressed specific issues relating to family life in the report: 'In order to understand some of the recommendations of the Report, we have to consider a very important fact which underlies them. This is the fact that in England today we have a great many old people and *far too few children*. It is a matter of common sense that many hands make light work, that if there is no one to speed the plough there can be no harvest.'[17]

The birth rate in Britain had been on a downwards curve since the 1920s and by 1942, when the statistics for the previous year were made public, it was a gloomy picture. The rate had declined by some 40,000 live births per year since 1938 and the 1941 figure of 579,091 was an all-time low. In fact the turning point had been reached and the birth rate began to rise from 1942 onwards, so that in 1944 nearly 200,000 more babies were born than in 1941. It marked the beginning of the so-called 'baby boom' that would last for the best part of fifteen years. But this was all in the future and the WI was concerned about how the country would function with an ageing population and no new blood to boost the working population in the future.

In 1943 an article appeared in *International Women's News* entitled 'Mothers and Homes: Need for Outside Interests'. The author, Gwen M. Bark, argued that it was wrong to expect women to be forced to spend their entire lives in their homes and to devote themselves solely to the running of the house and the care of husband and children. She herself worked as a volunteer with the cadet corps of her local Girl Guides and she asked herself why so many of the young girls in her group showed evident interest in and fondness for babies yet Britain was suffering from a decline in the birth rate. The conclusion she came to was that motherhood was not particularly appealing, especially in the countryside, where it could appear to be one long lifetime of drudgery. She argued in the article for women not only to develop outside interests but to become involved in local affairs so that they could have a say on water, electricity, sewerage, education and so on. And, of course, being a member of her local WI, she recommended joining at as early an age as possible so as to have some say in things that would affect not only the women but their children in the future.

Gwen Bark had trained as a doctor in Liverpool before marrying in 1938. Her husband had been called up but was invalided out of the Army in 1940 during the evacuation from Dunkirk. Their house in Wallasey had been destroyed by a bomb so they moved to Tarporley, in the middle of the Cheshire farming community. Her husband joined a spinster, Dr Clifton, in practice and during the war Dr Gwen, as she was always known, ran baby clinics. She also lectured on child welfare and contributed to the WI's war effort by knitting, sewing, growing vegetables and keeping goats, pigs and geese. She played the piano and loved music as well as walking, all of which passions she passed on to her children. At the time she wrote the article, she had two young children and went on to have two more. She was very keen on encouraging better conditions for children and working mothers. In 1944 she proposed 'that this institute should notify their MP of their opinion that the proposed allowances for children, under the Beveridge Report Scheme should not be paid to the father as suggested, but to the mother', giving the reason that the father was more likely to spend it on other things.

Another report from 1942 that pleased the WI was the Scott Report on *Land Utilisation in Rural Areas*. The NFWI had been represented by Lady Denman, who was appointed to the committee in October 1941, and evidence had been given by Mrs Vernon and Mrs Neville-Smith of the Executive Committee, Miss Farrer in her capacity of General Secretary and Miss Walker, the NFWI Agricultural Secretary at the time. The committee had as its brief the question of post-war planning, housing, water supply, electricity, rural industries and seasonal employment for women. They were so pleased with the report that they felt the Scott Committee deserved a vote of thanks from WIs 'for keeping so steadily in mind the vision of *Jerusalem*'.[18] The National Executive urged local institutes to take a lively interest in the Scott Report and to attend or even organise meetings and discussions about it in their village. Norfolk led the way in this by combining forces with the Parish Councils Advisory Committee, inviting speakers to come and explain points in the report so that they could make recommendations to their local MPs prior to the report being discussed in the House of Commons. It told women that they had a once in a lifetime opportunity to preserve true local government in England and although this would be a weighty responsibility it was one that they should welcome for the post-war era.

In June 1942, following a national House and Planning Conference on 28 May, the WI sent a housing questionnaire to county federations for distribution. They also announced a county competition, observing that 'Institutes seem to be taking to house planning like ducks to water,' adding that 'since the majority of members are housewives that is only to be expected'. The Ministry of Health had set up a Design of Dwellings Subcommittee to which the WI was asked to submit evidence. Houses mattered far more to rural working women than to their menfolk, since the home was run by the housewife for her husband and her children. This was the point emphasised in the opening paragraph summing up why the National Executive felt the response to the survey had been so positive. The editor of the questionnaire challenged the membership: 'In order to get really reliable ideas as to what most people want there must be as many answers sent in as possible. So cast your net wide, Counties, and see that the Committee has a huge catch to deal with.'[19]

Some WI surveys were accompanied by lectures or leaflets from experts giving advice to institutes on the topic in hand but on this occasion the National Federation was anxious to find out members' views on what kind of house they would like to live in. They asked for plans for a house, including fitments, its sanitary arrangements, outhouses and garden, and finally any other points of special importance. The subcommittee responsible at national level was particularly taken with the replies to the last point in the questionnaire, which had clearly captured the interest of members who were given the chance to vent long-pent-up feelings. The authors concluded that the combination of evacuation and films had meant that the country housewife 'had developed a healthy desire for an improved standard of housing'. Many said they had never enjoyed anything so much as answering the questionnaire and 'it showed the sound common sense of the average cottage housewife. It showed, too, how much she has suffered from the daily irritation of badly designed interior fittings . . . Nearly every member wants electric light and there is hardly one paper out of the hundreds returned that does not plead for built-in cupboards in every room, upstairs and down.'[20]

What makes both fascinating and sobering reading seventy years on is the fact that so much of what today is taken for granted, even in remote rural homes, was considered something to be desired but not expected: Aga stoves (or their equivalent) and fridges for example. 'A small number asked for some form of central heating and an Ideal boiler to burn rubbish.'[21] It is worth remembering that few rural villages had rubbish collection more than once a month at the time.

A picture of a typical rural cottage was painted by Kitty Blanche, whose aunt, Delyth Jones, lived near the Welsh village of Corwen in a farm cottage. It stood at the bottom of a lane, about half a mile from the main farmhouse up on the hill. At one stage the cottage had been tied to the farm but now her aunt rented it from the farmer.

> The cottage itself faced west and stood back from the lane. In the front garden my aunt used to grow lovely cut flowers but as soon as the war came she dug them up and planted potatoes. They grew quite well, except for those against the wall, which never got quite enough light. The back garden could be approached

through the cottage or through a gate on the left beside a shed that kept all our garden equipment, auntie's bicycle, an old pram and two wooden frames, one for coal and one for wood.

Kitty spent all her summer holidays at the cottage and remembered the basic amenities:

I had come from a nice house in Nottingham with electricity and running water and of course a flush loo. My mother cooked on a gas stove and we had central heating. Staying with my aunt was like going back half a century. Inside the cottage was low and dark. Facing east/west you might have expected it to be light but it had tiny windows and thick walls so that the sunlight seldom penetrated far into the rooms, except in winter when the sun was low in the sky. Downstairs there was a parlour to the left of the front door, stairs straight ahead and a tiny front room on the right which my aunt used as her sewing room. Along the back of the house was the kitchen. It was a long, thin room with three little windows overlooking the garden. On the left hand inside wall was a big fireplace which shared a chimney with the parlour and on the right was the dining area with a table and two dressers with crockery and cutlery. There was no sink in the kitchen but my aunt had a long work surface opposite the fireplace which was half wood, half slate and there she did all her cooking and baking. The sink was in the scullery which was two steps down from the kitchen between the house and the shed. Not long before the war they had had a pump installed in the scullery so that my aunt no longer had to heave water from the well up by the farm. The scullery also had a long, slate surface where she stored her cooked and uncooked foods. Jars of jam, vegetables and fruit were stored on shelves above and the washing copper lived in a corner of the scullery but was trundled outside under the awning outside the scullery on wash days. There was a mangle too, of course.

Upstairs the cottage had two bedrooms, one at the front for my aunt and one at the back for me. In addition there was a tiny box room which she used to store clothes before the war but during the war she converted it to an apple store so that for all the world when I close my eyes and think of my bedroom in the cottage I can smell nothing but apples.

The privy was outside, beyond the hen house in the back garden. Kitty described it as a superior brick building with a green wooden door. Her aunt had asked the local builder to put in a concrete floor to make it easier to clean than the old slabs that had been there before. 'Unfortunately the levels were not right and rainwater tended to run in rather than out of the privy, so we then got our friendly carpenter to make us some slatted boards which meant we could use the loo in shoes and not wellington boots. During the war my aunt cut up newspaper as loo rolls were scarce. Funnily enough, I have no recollection of that privy smelling bad. She must have managed it very well.'

The housing questionnaire was completed by women who lived in properties like Mrs Jones's and the authors of the report were struck by the two basic needs emphasised in every reply – the need for an adequate water supply and the need for female architects and for working-class women on housing committees. 'A woman would avoid the only too usual mistake of building sinks at a back-breaking level, or fixing cupboard doors so as to prevent the light from reaching inside. As for the need for an adequate water supply, it is so vital that some Institutes could think no further than this. It would be time to discuss bathrooms and lavatories, they said, when the village was supplied with water.'[22]

Betty Houghton's family lived in a bungalow in the Gun Hill end of Chiddingly village, which had its own well and tank, so with the use of a petrol-driven pump they were able to have water in the house. The heating was paraffin stoves and a coke boiler but they also had open fires that burned logs and coal. They had an Aga range from 1935 and two flush loos, so that their house was well equipped. At first, lighting was by paraffin lamps but by about 1935 they ran another Petter engine to charge up the accumulators. These methods of water production, heating and lighting were still in use in 1955 when Betty's parents left Chiddingly. Although they had no electricity they had a telephone. Their number was 14, so they too were early adopters.

Ruth Toosey also had a telephone. Her number was Tarvin 23. The woman who ran the telephone exchange made a point of knowing a lot about what was going on in her area and on one occasion someone rang the exchange and asked to be put through to Tarvin 23 but was told: 'You won't get Mrs Toosey. She's just gone into Chester on the bus, wearing a new hat.'

The demands of the institute members were not extravagant. Most women wanted three rooms downstairs with a separate hall or scullery for storing muddy boots, a perennial problem of the country housewife the report notes, but women in Durham and Gloucestershire said they would prefer just two rooms. A sign that so few women had fridges or expected to have one in the near future, since a large number of villages still had no electricity, was the insistence on a north-facing larder fitted with a cold slab.

'There was no unanimous opinion about the aspect of kitchen or living room except a general demand that both should be light. It seems clear that new housing estates should be planned with a choice of aspects except for the back door. Everyone agrees that there is only one possible aspect for that – *away* –

from one's neighbour. Side-by-side or face-to-face back doors have no supporters.'[23]

The interesting point about the report is the intimate detail it provides of the inside of a country cottage in the 1940s and, judging by the relatively modest demands of the members who contributed to the survey, the quite primitive conditions which must have prevailed in many homes. It is striking, for example, that a majority of women wanted electric lighting but some expressly preferred gas. Coal was preferred for heating, while gas and electricity were equally popular for cooking. In Wales many households still cooked on open fires and a few women were sceptical about cookers, though these were in the minority. Ranges were popular as they served the purpose of providing hot water and a place to dry clothes in an emergency as well as giving off heat for the kitchen. Some women who focused on the minutiae even suggested that a small drying room could be built off the back of the kitchen with a gap in the wall to take advantage of the heat from the cooking range. What surprised the authors of the report was the fact that no one opted for oil as their first choice of solid fuel, either for heating or cooking. What surprised this current author is the revelation that members thought there should be heating provided in at least one of the bedrooms. Just one?

Edith Jones considered submitting a design for a house. Although only ten miles from Shrewsbury and just two miles off the A49, Smethcote was and remains today very quiet. The village had no electricity or piped water, nor was it on main drains. In fact houses still use septic tanks, though water and electricity did eventually come to Smethcote well after the war. Red House Farm was similar to other houses in the area, with an outside privy, oil lamps and a pump in the kitchen. Chris explained what the house had been like when her parents moved to the farm in 1947 after Edith and Jack retired:

> The house had a phone – Leebotwood 69 – long before it had electricity. The only tap in the house was the pump in the brown sink in the kitchen and the loo was a good twenty yards from the house. You went out of the back door, up three steps and along a path, passed an old brick building which had hens in it and to the loo beyond the yew tree. Not a nice experience in the cold, wet or dark. And it was a two seater. One of the neighbours had a three seater as I recall. I was lucky not to have used it!

In the back of her 1944 diary she sketched out the floor plan of an ideal farmhouse with a list of notes that included central heating to one room downstairs, a water supply and a veranda under which she could hang her washing even on wet days. It is striking, looking at the sketch, how very similar the layout is to Red House Farm, where she had lived since 1914. The main difference was her requirement for a few more mod cons such as electricity and mains water. Though she had a pump in the kitchen that brought water from a well close to the back of the house, it was hard water and not ideal for her uses. On wash days she would heat water drawn from a wooden rainwater butt that she also used to water the garden. When there was a shortage of this soft water, she was obliged to use pumped water from the well. 'I added Carbosil which answers very well,' she wrote after one dry spell. 'Because of the drying wind, the clothes were dry at midday. Washed Len's smock not before it needed it!' When she could not get the clothes dry outside she would hang them in the Dutch barn at the other end of the farmyard.

Most of Edith's cooking was done on a black range, though she did have a brick oven in the wash-house, but she also liked to experiment with other methods. On one occasion she wrote: 'I have some spare time so make a hay box for cookery. I have often thought of doing this but it never materialised till now. I wonder if it will be a success.' It was. The following day she was able to report: 'I tried the hay box. It cooked the carrots nicely after 5 or 10 minutes on the fire, so it does act.' The trick when using a hay box was to make sure that the pan was well heated on the fire prior to being put into the hay box so that the food inside would continue cooking, well insulated by the hay. It was the predecessor to the slow cooker and Edith gradually gained confidence using it, succeeding in cooking hams as well as vegetables.

What occupied the minds of the contributors to the questionnaire more than cooking, heating or aspect was the question of storage and the need for more cupboards. 'Storage space is a special need of country families and too often it has been forgotten by the urban-minded architect. Some members ask for a perambulator porch, and many ask for a covered way to the coal-shed. Some ask for a chute from coal-shed to kitchen. A few would like cellars and many would like a loft for storage.'[24]

Another reminder of the lack of modern conveniences is the request for an 'outside copper for washing'. Mrs Watt's dream in 1935 that with unlimited money she would give every rural housewife a washing machine was well ahead of its time. A few institutes came down in favour of having communal wash houses in their villages, but that was the exception, most women wanted to have such amenities privately available and to have some form of facility, as well as an airing cupboard, for drying clothes indoors on wet days. Pulleys hanging from the ceiling in the kitchen that could be lowered on a rope were common in many village houses and people alive today still remember the overwhelming smell of damp washing hanging around the house after wash day, traditionally a Monday.

There was no assumption, either, that public transport would be laid on for the village, in fact one WI suggested that having a communal bicycle might be desirable as a way of getting around.

Welsh members felt it was reasonable to be expected to walk or ride three to four miles to get to local schools, shops, chapel or church and the WI hall, whereas English members, both north and south, preferred a shorter distance of just half a mile, although most were prepared to walk up to twenty minutes to get to a bus stop to take them into town on market days.

The questionnaire asked for very specific details about the hard furnishings such as doorknobs, windowsills and stairs, all of which were answered by the women in the same way. They had to be easy to reach, clean and maintain. It is a reminder of just how much of a woman's time in the 1940s was spent dusting and cleaning, mainly on account of the dirt and dust produced by open fires. The annual spring clean was a feature of life which has now all but disappeared. Most women requested washable wallpaper, picture rails, a bell and letter box on the front door. They wanted large windows that could be reached and cleaned from the inside and varnished paint on woodwork that could be wiped down with a damp cloth.

What is clear from the report produced by the WI is that women felt very strongly about how the home could and should be improved and there was no sense in their conclusions that what had been good enough for their mothers was good enough for them. They saw this as a real opportunity to make their voices heard and to push for significant improvements that would make their day-to-day lives easier and more efficient. An upshot of the housing survey was the determination felt by many institutes that no significant changes could be made without a strong representation of women's views.

In 1943 two WI members were appointed to two government housing committees. The first was Mrs Methuen to the Rural Housing (Hobhouse) Committee and the second was Miss Haworth to the Design of Dwellings (Dudley) Committee. Their greatest success, however, came just after the end of the war when Mrs Jew of Wilnecote WI in Warwickshire received a letter from Aneurin Bevan asking her to join the Central Housing Advisory Committee in 1946. Mrs Jew was just thirty-two years old and had a young family. After her appointment she gave an interview to her local newspaper spelling out her ideas for the perfect home, which was not the one she was currently living in. She wanted a kitchen with utility room for drying washing on wet days. She also wanted a kitchen diner – too much running about for housewives with food. But she realised that most of all the country needed houses and the key was to build them with space to accommodate fitments if possible. She pointed out anomalies, like building prefab houses without fireplaces in mining communities where miners got a coal allowance. Mrs Jew brought an intensely practical approach to considering housing questions.

An article that appeared in the *Daily Mirror* reminds us of the attitude towards women in 1946:

> **Busy Wife Will Be Advisor On Labour Saving.**
>
> When the Ministry of Health asked Mrs Verena Jew to serve on a committee advising on domestic equipment they chose a woman with ideas. Plump Verena knows from experience all the snags of the average house. In the Warwickshire village of Wilnecote, Tamworth, she runs a 7 roomed rambling house single handed, copes with a four year old daughter and an eighteen month old son, rears pigs, poultry and runs a garden as well.

Just to put the record straight on 'plump Verena', she was far from the homely housewife implied in this particularly patronising piece.

The seventh of eleven children, she had come from a poor home. As a child she had lived in a house with paraffin lamps where all cooking was done over an open fire. Her family had not been able to afford to let her study at college so she had worked as a nanny but she was determined to continue with her education. She studied at evening school and by correspondence course to become a writer. She wrote children's books before the war that were published by Pitman and used as school readers in the 1940s. During the war she trained as a nurse and was a busy member of her WI. She was invited to London in 1943 to speak at a London Housing Brains trust representing Warwickshire, which she did and loved. Being chosen by the WI for the Housing Committee came out of the blue but was a very welcome challenge. She said: 'Country life can be made just as easy as town life. Electricity, power plugs and running water are essential in every house. Why should some of us go on living like our grandmothers?'

In 1943 the National Executive once again canvassed its membership for views. This time it dealt with education and once again there was an enormous response. Out of the total of 5,800 WIs 4,000 sent back answers to questions such as what the advantages might be of raising the school leaving age from fifteen to sixteen; if state boarding schools were available would you send your children to one for all or part of their school career? Should part-time education for children up to the age of eighteen be compulsory and which subjects should be offered? Should country teachers be paid the same as their town counterparts? Finally there was an open question about what other points women felt were important. Interestingly a majority of women favoured sending their children to boarding school for a part of their education in order to broaden their horizons and give them the opportunity to develop independence and learn to mix with other children from different walks of life. They also all favoured raising the school leaving age to sixteen as they thought the extra year would offer the children more time to consider what they might do in the future and how vocational training could help them in their desire to continue to live in the countryside. The biggest concern they expressed was for the state of rural schools and time and again the answers to the question about raising the school leaving age was prefaced with the proviso that only on condition that the state of the schools was radically improved. In answer to the open question the majority of women argued for broader subject teaching so that children from an early age learned about the wider world. One institute summed it up: 'The child should be taught to be a unit of the home, the home a unit of the neighbourhood, the neighbourhood a unit of the country and the country a unit of the world.'[25]

In March 1943 the WI held a conference in London at which the post-war relief of Europe was discussed. The overall message that came out of the conference was that the WI would be involved in doing more of the same for several years to come: that is to say there would be a continued need for food production and surpluses would be made available to the European countries that most needed them. This would lend new impetus and purpose to the Produce Guild. Members of the Guild of Learners would be asked to make increased use of their skills in teaching thrift crafts – knitting, sewing and making garments, toys and household furnishings for people abroad. There was also an emphasis on learning more about the international situation that would be so very different after the war, and a renewed challenge to the WI membership to make a contribution to the new world that would emerge from the dust and rubble of war-torn Europe. Miss Tennant, who was chairman of the International Subcommittee, summarised what the WI's role would be: 'It would have been easier and more exciting if we had been told – do this – or do that and start now – instead we were told to go back to our Institutes to do what we were doing before, more intensively and more thoroughly, but ought we not to feel greatly encouraged and to realize that instead of one side of our work having been stimulated, it is the whole which has been given new significance.'[26]

At the time the conference was held, mobilisation was at its height and the war effort was being redoubled so some women wondered why there was such an emphasis on reconstruction when the war was not yet won and no one knew how long it would last. The answer was supplied by Dr Melville Mackenzie, the chairman of the Allied Medical Advisory Committee set up to deal with post-war problems. The Allies were endeavouring to benefit from the lessons 'so tragically taught at the conclusion of the last war when more individuals died from famine and disease than were killed in the war itself. This was to a great extent due to the fact that great chaos existed in relief work owing to the fact that no machinery had been set up before the end of the war to meet problems which must inevitably arise.'[27] What the medical profession most feared was an outbreak of an epidemic that would devastate populations weakened by severe undernourishment. He called on the WI to take food production as seriously as Miss Tennant had suggested but he also wanted the WI to be involved in specific projects, such as helping to feed and clothe students who would join training schools for midwives and nurses. And he appealed to the caring side of women's nature by painting a horrific picture of the plight of 300,000 orphans in Eastern Europe whose parlous state of health and lack of any decent housing had so shocked his committee. 'Special mention should be made of the difficulty of providing any form of entertainment or education for these great numbers of children and the value of toys could not be overestimated.'[28] He then delighted them by suggesting that tiny presents of packs of flower seeds would be appreciated more than they could ever know since the children could plant them and bring pleasure to other, older people in the population. This could be of inestimable psychological value in the rehabilitation of refugees. Mr McDougall, an economic adviser, was asked to spell out the current state of agriculture in Europe and to give his estimate of its state at the end of the war. It was of course a miserable picture. In western Europe alone 135 million people depended on agriculture and farming productivity had deteriorated as a result of the war. The majority of the population was surviving on two thirds of the food they should be eating to live adequately, with children and adolescents suffering the most. The harvest of 1943 would dictate the state of European food supplies for the future since all food stocks had been depleted during the harsh winter of 1942. Mr McDougall's committee estimated that Britain and America would be feeding Europe for two harvest seasons after the war.

Miss Vernon told the delegates:

> Although it is not urged at present, our speakers in showing us the immensity of the problems to be faced have been so inspiring that all of us here must feel more than ever before the worthwhileness of our Institute work and have a new incentive for doing it well. This feeling we must carry back to our members, so that they, too, will know that the humdrum job of looking after evacuees, growing more food, jam making, handicrafts and all the rest, have a very real part to play in fitting us to help in post-war reconstruction. After all it is the incentive that supplies the energy, and our motto as helpers in these days should be 'Be Prepared'.[29]

Just as Lady Denman had sought to manage expectations at the outbreak of the war, so now, in 1944, she wanted to have her say on the peace that she believed would come soon. She asked the women at the AGM to keep up their courage and faith as the final assault on the enemy was launched. But then she asked more of them:

> Despite all the difficulties and anxieties we have had to face, it is hard for us to imagine what countrywomen in other parts of Europe have suffered. We shall soon have our chance to help them, and our war task will not be done until we have done all in our power to feed and clothe the victims of Hitler's New Order. We cannot give them back their murdered husbands and sons, nor restore to life the children who have been starved to death, but we can at least relieve their physical suffering.
>
> With that end in view we will still accept rations and regulations and go on with the countrywoman's own task of growing and preserving food even after peace is declared. It has not been easy for countrywomen to carry on their many heavy tasks in wartime, and we all long for a real holiday and relaxation – but with peace in sight and the knowledge that we are able to help the women and children of other lands whose lot has been so terrible we shall all, I know, make a supreme effort to finish worthily the work which countrywomen have carried out so splendidly since the war began.[30]

As the war in Europe was drawing to a close, so Edith at Red House Farm in Smethcote seemed to be busier than ever. The WI had been asked to make pillows for homeless in Hackney and she spent time in March 1945 baking feathers to put in the pillows. She was also knitting coats for refugees in Europe and packing up parcels of books, magazines, eye ointment, toothpaste and stationery for Leonard. On 12 April she wrote: 'sudden death of President Roosevelt. Jack takes trap to blacksmiths.' By the middle of the month there were daily notes in her diary about the progress of the war in Germany and the success of the American and Russian armies in cutting the German army in two. Then, on 2 May, she wrote: 'Berlin fallen to the Russians. Officially reported Hitler is dead. Jack sows marigolds. Total surrender in Italy. WI meeting in Smethcote.' Six days later it was all over: 'Germany signed total surrender (oh joy). Thanksgiving service in church. We had bonfire on field.' The following evening there was a meeting about bringing electricity to Smethcote. No agreement was reached. They finally got electricity at Red House Farm in the late 1950s.

Mrs Milburn had followed the last few weeks of the war in Europe in her diaries but her real interest was in the fate of her son, Alan, and how soon he would be released from his prison camp. On 8 May she wrote: 'The morning's weather seemed symbolic. It was as if in the thunder one heard Nature's roll of drums for the fallen, then the one loud salvo of salute over our heads, and the tears of rain pouring for the sorrow and suffering of the war. And then the end of the orgy of killing and victory symbolized as the sun came out and shed its brightness and warmth on the earth.'[31]

At Bletchley Park Betty Houghton was in the cinema. 'The manager came onto the stage and said: "You'll be pleased to know that the war in Europe is over." There was no clapping, no noise, no triumphalism. Just dead silence and I sensed that everyone was thinking what I was, "Now what are we going to do?"' Betty went back to Chiddingly but she knew that life would never be the same as it had been before the war. Her brother had been killed in 1941. Their family life had been completely changed, as had so many other people's. The war in Europe had lasted for years, for the whole of Betty's late adolescence and early adulthood. She explained: 'We had put all our energy into winning the war and now it was over. So many men had been killed, so much had changed. The atmosphere among our age-group was one of "Whatever next?"'

Ann Tetlow remembered the end of the war in Europe. She was nine years old. 'We hung a Union Jack out of the window on VE Day and the blackout came down. We had a devil of a time removing the sticky tape from the windows. That had been put on to stop the glass shattering if there was an explosion nearby and it took months, if not years, to get the marks off the windows.' There may have been celebrations in the village but there was no jubilation in Bradfield WI. They were war weary and the message, as it had been up and down the country, was echoed in the words of Cecil Beaton who said: 'Victory does not bring with it a sense of triumph – rather a dull numbness that the blood-letting is over.' Mrs Ward minuted the June meeting, the first after the declaration of peace in Europe: 'Mrs Howlett took the chair and spoke a few words about this historic meeting, the first since the war in Europe had been won. The minutes of the last meeting were read out . . .' and life continued in Bradfield.

Miss Moore, in her editorial in *Home & Country*, looked towards the future and suggested that the WI would have to brace itself to carry on rather than allowing itself a rest after the long and destructive years of the war:

> VE day has come and gone. We imagine that the majority of our 88,000 readers celebrated it with quiet thankfulness and gratitude to all those who have saved Europe from the horrors of Nazi domination. Now we turn our faces forward to the problems of peace and the tremendous opportunities for action that are offered to the National Federation and to every individual member of every Institute. This brave new world of the countryside, how are we going to achieve it?[32]

The WI, always keen to look beyond its own borders, embraced post-war planning with enthusiasm. Lectures and slide shows on the economy, history and politics of European countries appear on the monthly programmes of institutes throughout England and Wales. After the end of the war in Europe the WI was indeed asked to supply surplus food, to make toys for children and knit clothes and send garments to women in France, Belgium and Germany. In addition a great deal of effort and help was extended to women's organisations whose lives had been so badly affected by the war. In June 1945 three WI members, Mrs Egerton from Yorkshire, Mrs Pick from Nottingham and Mrs James from the Isle of Ely, were invited to spend a week in France by the Entre Aide Française to see how the clothes and necessities collected by WIs were being distributed to peasant families in Normandy. 'This will, incidentally, give the WI representatives first hand information upon conditions in rural France today.'[33] Miss Deneke was among a small group who went to Germany to meet women's groups who were beginning to re-form and consider how best they could help their fellow countrymen. Interest in these and other such visits was intense and Miss Deneke wrote an article about her experiences on her return: 'Conditions of living in Germany are grievous. What can we eat? How can we get clothing? Where can we find shelter? These questions pre-occupy the average German woman. At home we are troubled with ration books, clothes coupons, and a housing shortage but in Germany distress is acute.' She described the extraordinary juxtapositions: farms with carefully cultivated and ordered fields, herds of brindled cattle yet 2 million refugees from Poland and nearly 9 million homeless Germans on their own soil. 'Men are scarce. Before POWs were released, women in Germany outnumbered men by 70 per cent and the disproportion will remain for a

> If family life is to be resumed after the war without conflict and distress, it must be on a basis of sympathy and tolerance. Don't expect to pick up the threads just where you dropped them. Particularly where a husband and wife are concerned it may be necessary to go back a bit – to get a little nearer your courting attitude, when you weren't quite so sure of each other and couldn't afford to take things for granted, but rather set out to please and to win the other's affection. All but the most fundamental difficulties (which would probably have arisen, war or no war) can be overcome where there is affection, sympathy and tolerance.[36]

At Coningsby and Tattershall's AGM, held in Lloyds Bank in Coningsby on 12 December 1945, their guest speaker, Mrs Fieldsend, spoke to the gathered membership about their role in the future: 'The war is over but there is still strife in the world. Now is the time of building and working for peace not only in our own country but throughout the world. We in the Institutes belong to a huge organisation both here and overseas, and our aim should be a better understanding of all nations.'

There was another aspect of post-war life that would require great strength and commitment and that concerned the return home of 4.5 million servicemen, the tens of thousands of women who had been drafted into the forces and into war work, and the remaining evacuee children from the countryside, numbering several hundred thousand. Families all over the country had to adapt to peace and to the return of fathers, sons, brothers, lovers, daughters. As at the beginning of the war there was major upheaval in the countryside. Now, six years later, there was another. And once again it was the women of Britain who were called on to take the strain, to rebuild family life and to cope with the future in what became known as Austerity Britain.

10

A FINAL WORD

> Peace is invisible.
>
> *Soviet delegate to the League of Nations, 1937*

We ended the last chapter on a note of understanding of just how high the cost had been to women who had battled through the war years and now had to face an austere future. Up to now this book has celebrated the great industry, energy, enthusiasm and determination of the WI not only to survive the war but to do as much as they could for their fellow Britons in the process. In this chapter I want to look at the WI from a slightly different perspective and celebrate it at a more private level.

Seen from the twenty-first century it is hard not to conclude that members of the Women's Institutes were thoroughly put upon during the Second World War. Actually, I think the picture is more complex and interesting than that. First, it is important to remember that WI members were not a separate species but were the mothers, wives, sisters, friends in the local village or community. They might also have been the village postmistress, the district nurse, the schoolteacher. They might have been married to the local doctor or policeman. Some like Dr Gwen Bark were the local doctor. During the war they could have held several offices or played their part in more than one voluntary organisation. In other words, they were part of the fabric of the community and as such represented women of all types on the rural home front. There was also a very wide spread of wealth, from the poorest women married to farm labourers or, in Northumberland, to miners and industrial workers who lived in villages or, in Cornwall, to fishermen through to the wealthy, landed county gentry, many of whom were as committed to the cause and belief of the WI as their founders in 1915.

Although it would seem that the government asked the earth of them, that they expected them to work for no pay on every conceivable aspect of civilian war work from knitting comforts for the troops to growing surplus vegetables and fruit to feed the nation, from bottling jam to collecting rosehips and foxgloves, from making toys to collecting salvage, or from mending socks to advising on post-war housing, they were accorded a degree of respect from ministers that came as a result of hard-won esteem earned by their twenty-four years of pre-Second World War history. Though others poked gentle fun at the WI and spoke patronisingly of their contribution, assuming them to be relied upon merely to serve tea and refreshment at events, the government knew better than to talk down to Lady Denman and Miss Farrer. Lord Woolton, in his capacity of Minister of Food, was aware that he, through one contact, had access to the largest voluntary women's organisation in the country and he did not abuse it, though I would argue that he made the most of it. Certainly he asked a lot of the WI but he was always careful to record his thanks, to explain why he was asking them to do so much and above all he made sure he was seen to be supporting them by turning up at centres or supporting VIP visits. Mr Hudson, in the Ministry of Agriculture, was similarly careful to keep on the right side of the WI and his speech at the 1943 AGM showed a depth of knowledge not only of the countryside but also of the role played by the WI in rural life. Those who showed less understanding and tolerance, such as the civil servants in the Ministry of Supply who made Miss Farrer's life so difficult in the middle years of the war, demonstrated an ignorance of the relevance of the WI which has in some instances continued to prevail. On a national level the Executive Committee had been desperate to keep spirits up and to emphasise the national importance of their work as praised by the likes of Lord Woolton. Thus an editorial in *Home & Country* published at the very beginning of the war set the tone:

> Without doubt, we Women's Institute members are a remarkable race. What with war, taxes, black-out, rationed cars, non-existent buses, Stygian railway trains, packed houses, double-shift dinners, anxiety, loss of jobs, and that inexpressible dreariness that besets all war work – the feeling that you are darning a sock painfully with one hand and cutting off the foot with the other – she thought the members might be too busy to write. That doubt is over. There is nothing whatever Institutes are not doing in this war, from leading the Land Army, like their Chairman, down to sharing a saucepan with a lonely London mother, like Mrs Jones down the lane.[1]

After the war the NFWI decided to commemorate the contribution made by women by commissioning a huge piece of needlework which was described in the first stages of its planning as a modern Bayeux Tapestry. The embroidery celebrates the work of women in wartime and took over 400 embroiderers four years to complete. It measures 15 feet 3 inches by 9 feet and represents contributions from every Federation. Eighteen medallions surround three large central panels showing women working on the land, in industry and in the services. The medallions depict all the different aspects of women's contributions that have been covered in this book but they also included WVS and ARP work, reflecting the fact that many members were involved in multiple organisations during the war. It is at once an enormous but modest celebration of women's contribution to the war. Its size is spectacular but it is not triumphal.

That was the public image. But what of the private?

The WI is made up of individual women. It is true that the National Executive was represented predominantly by well-connected women but Lady Denman was unapologetic about that. She used their contacts to the WI's advantage but she recognised that it was the women in the villages who represented the lifeblood of the organisation.

I would like to introduce one of them whose life was shaped and enriched by her forty-year association with the Women's Institute. Her name was Alex Toosey and she was my maternal grandmother. There is no doubt in my mind that the WI offered a place of refuge as well as the opportunity for her to make a contribution to improving village life. It gave her somewhere she could be herself, particularly during the war. She could assist but also relax during what for her, like many others, were difficult years. Her husband left home on 31 August 1939 and but for one brief visit, did not set foot in their house again until November 1945. For three and a half years he was a prisoner of the Japanese and in all that time she received only a couple of letters and postcards. She was on her own with her three young children for the entire war.

It is undoubtedly the case that Mrs T, as she was always known, felt very comfortable in the Women's Institute. Amongst women she could be herself in a way that perhaps only her grandchildren ever saw. She could laugh about her woeful cooking abilities, which were a joke within Hooton institute, but she could also share her love of growing flowers without feeling self-conscious. Although she probably never pushed a wheelbarrow or wielded a hoe she was known for growing magnificent hyacinths and the fact that flower arranging was one of her passions was underlined by her gift of a vase to the institute on its 21st birthday.

She represented the kind of woman who benefited from contact with the WI in a way that otherwise would have been missing in her life. She belonged to an era before women's liberation from the slavery of the home. Husbands dominated and the social hierarchy of the village counted for a great deal. This was a time when country families had pews in church and women wore hats to go shopping. Women had less help in the house than their mothers and grandmothers had done and mod cons were still a dream for many. As we have seen, a fridge was a newfangled luxury and few owned one. Until then the larder, north-facing with slate shelves and a chilly feel even in summer, was the repository for fresh ingredients and cooked food alike. Spring cleaning was an annual event and undertaken with method and vigour. Carpets were dragged outdoors to be beaten, walls whitewashed, winter clothes put away and summer clothes and hats brought out of storage, often smelling of mothballs.

My grandmother was a stickler for routine. On Thursdays, after the war, she would drive into Willaston, park her Morris Minor in front of the general store, regardless of the double yellow lines that were painted outside the shop in the mid-1960s, and buy 200 Kent cigarettes and a bottle of Gordon's gin. She would then very carefully turn the car around and drive home.

She wore her permed grey hair in a hairnet with white beads.

Coloured beads on her hairnet meant it was a special day. She hated anyone touching her head and particularly disliked it when the wind blew her hair. She wore powder on her face and I have a strong memory of the smell of this powder compact, which used to appear regularly, sometimes even at traffic lights while she was driving. She would scrutinise her face and apply the powder with a thin, cream-coloured sponge that lived inside the compact.

I learned not so very long ago that as president of the Hooton Women's Institute she would check her make-up and apply powder during the reading of the last meeting's minutes, which new secretaries initially found disconcerting. She adhered so rigidly to the formalities of WI rules for meetings that she once did not turn up to a meeting because the secretary, with whom she had agreed the date at the Executive Committee earlier that week, had failed to write her a letter inviting her to attend.

Underneath this rather fierce exterior was a woman who was as devoted to the Women's Institute movement as any member of the national council. She was actively involved from the day she joined Burton and Puddington WI in 1933 until 1972 when she retired from WI office at Hooton in her seventy-first year. One of her fellow members described her as someone who was great fun to be with. This surprised me and contrasts with many people's recollections of my grandmother. They shared my grandfather's opinion, which he expressed in his autobiography in 1970: 'we are all very frightened of her but respect her deeply. She is known as Mrs T. or the Regimental Sergeant Major.'

When the war broke out Mrs T was predictably defiant. Someone suggested that given the proximity of her village to Liverpool it would be safer for her to move or allow the children to be evacuated. She announced sternly that if Mr Hitler wished to kill her he would have to do so in her own bed. Throughout the Blitz on Liverpool she resolutely refused to sleep in a shelter and remained in her bedroom, though she did make the children sleep in the 'Bogey Hole' under the stairs, something my mother still recalls with horror. She also remembered that their uncle Stephen's car was on blocks in the garage throughout the war and Mrs. T kept it stuffed with tins of food, probably obtained on the black market.

Mrs T was not a confident cook and the children have memories of rabbit stew with little bones floating in grey gravy and stewed rhubarb with no sugar. She was, however, a good knitter and produced countless pairs of socks. In 1940 Burton and Puddington had a knitting party that resulted in 850 garments as well as 500 WVS armlets. The minute book records that by 1943 one member had handed in her hundredth pair of socks and that 1,001 had been knitted altogether. As well as knitting, garnishing camouflage nets and looking after the household, Mrs T worked at a WI canteen in Little Sutton making teas and meals for the American troops. Like hundreds of thousands of other women during the war she coped magnificently and like many others she found adjusting to the peace difficult. When my grandfather came back from the Far East she was deposed. She was expected to go back to being a housewife with domestic duties and social expectations and she found this hard to take. Burton and Puddington WI was an active institute during the war. Their membership dropped to twenty-five and they lost their hall to the military in 1939 so had to resort to twice-monthly working party meetings until March 1940 when they were able to get back into Gladstone Village Hall.

The WI continued to be a source of escape, entertainment and enjoyment for her. In fact in 1951 she and a group of women decided the time had come to set up their own, new, institute in the village of Hooton, where she lived, and this became an absorbing interest for her. She never spoke about it though. It was her private world and we only know how much it meant to her because of the Hooton minute book that shows almost 100 per cent attendance at meetings, and by the comments from members who remember her in those meetings and at WI parties.

When I came to write *Jambusters* I appealed to county federations and to institutes for information about their wartime activities. Several allowed me access to county and institute minute books and although they show snippets of life in wartime they are just records of events and decisions. Sometimes it is possible to read between the lines, such as on the occasion when Audlem decided to substitute 'Jerusalem' with 'God Save the King' to open their meeting to mark military triumphs in North Africa. Other minute secretaries allowed for tantalising glimpses into their social half-hour activities: 'Mrs Roberts put on a wonderful series of sketches about people in the village. They were anonymous but we were able to recognise everyone. It was one of the best evenings we have had this year.' Unfortunately we shall never know who Mrs Roberts was taking off, nor why it was so funny. But perhaps that is right. The WI has been described by many women as a safe haven and they regard it as private and not something to be made public.

In the Cheshire County Federation minutes for January and February 1941 the focus was on a forthcoming visit from Miss Cox. She was due to spend four days in Cheshire, visiting various institutes where she would inspect, advise, attend demonstrations and bring something of head office to Cheshire's most rural villages. It was an event as eagerly anticipated as any. Yet in the minutes of the May meeting, the month after the event, there was no mention of Miss Cox's visit, nor is there in any of the institute minute books I read. Attention had been focused forward to the manufacture of syrup from beetroot and advice on drying moleskins. Only *Home & Country* offered any hints of how people had taken part in, celebrated or enjoyed activities, but these were compiled by institutes and sent to the editor, who picked and chose what she wanted. The intimate was hard to find. Linda Oliver, Surrey's archivist, was hugely helpful in sending through brief memoirs and talks given by their members about the war years and that helped to get the ball rolling. Then the anecdotes began to come in.

A letter from Margaret Funnell of Bideford in Devon shed a little personal light on a wartime WI. She was an evacuee from Guernsey living near the Bude WI hall in Cornwall. When meetings were held she and her friends would climb up the outside wall to peep inside. 'One day a lady came out and invited three or four of us to watch a cookery demonstration. We were taken to chairs in the very front row and seemed to be given particular attention by the demonstrator. As she worked she stressed the importance of handling the mixture as little as possible and rolling out the pastry on one side only. Afterwards we were invited to taste her cookery – a treat in wartime!' Margaret was about ten years old at the time but she told me that when making pastry she can still hear and see that lady giving her advice, which she continues to follow even now, seventy years on.

Janet Melvin was born in 1938 and her mother was a member of Woodmansterne WI in Surrey. She remembered that the WI meetings were held in the local village hall. Once she was taken to a big meeting dressed up in her Sunday best with white gloves and her Easter bonnet. All the women present were dressed in their best clothes too. 'I was told by my mother that I was not allowed to move. A big imposing lady came to talk to us about WI jam-making.' Janet does not know who the lady was but as we spoke we both wondered whether or not it might have been Lady Denman herself.

Although trips and visits during the war were difficult to arrange because of the lack of fuel, Mobberley members did manage to get to make a farm visit in Derbyshire. The weather was terrible and Mrs Wright, wearing her WI badge, offered to go and ask at the old farmhouse whether they had come to the right place. When the door opened and the old lady inside saw the badge she grabbed her arm and pulled her inside, giving her chapter and verse on her own experiences with the WI during the last war. The rest of the women joined her for home-made tea and a walk around the farm, concluding that 'it was one outing we will all remember for it gave that old lady so much pleasure to have so many members around her'.[2]

Betty Houghton had joined her WI at Chiddingly in East Sussex at sixteen. She was not the only teenage member: 'You have to understand that there was not much else on offer for women in the villages at the time. I would say that most people living in cottages had some association with the WI. It is important to emphasise that the WI's role was and remains principally one of education. It taught women things, gave them skills, helped them to try something out that they might take further.' Betty, who was musical, remembered the social side of the WI in wartime. She used to take her gramophone to WI meetings and play classical music to the women during the social half-hour. She joined the WI choir in Chiddingly, which had a good reputation, and she remembered a high point when Dr Malcolm Sergeant, as he was then, came to adjudicate at a county-wide choir competition. 'Music kept people's spirits up, it kept people happy,' she said. Her mother was a good musician and used to play the piano to accompany the Chiddingly WI choir. Mrs Dayrrell felt that it was her role as president to conduct the choir but it was not her forte and Betty's mother used to conduct from the piano by moving her shoulders up and down to indicate when people had to come in. 'The WI was a great place to start something, to find out if you liked it and the great thing was that nobody would ever say "You are no good." The attitude was "You have a go."'

A letter from Alwyn Benbow in Shrewsbury shared a wonderful memory of her mother's wartime activities:

> Late evening my father would take the heavy metal cover off the large underground water tank in the yard. He would lean down with a bucket and scoop up the water. This was to fill the huge boiler in the kitchen. Then he would lay the fire for the next morning in the grate under the boiler. Several of my mother's WI friends would arrive the following day and using the canner, probably on loan from WI house, would fill and seal cans of seasonal fruit or vegetables from the orchard. I remember the noise and bustle and laughter of friends together. I also remember my fear every time my father bent down to fill the buckets, and even when we played games, we never dared to step on the heavy metal cover over the deep, dark tank.

So what happened to the women whose personal stories have featured in this book?

Lady Denman resigned from her position of Director of the Woman's Land Army in February 1945 in protest at the government's refusal to award the land army the grants and benefits that had been accorded to women who had been in the forces and Civil Defence. She continued as Chairman of the National Federation of Women's Institutes until 1946 when she was succeeded by Lady Albemarle. In 1951 she was appointed GBE in recognition of her war work with the Women's Land Army. She died on 2 June 1954 and her ashes were scattered at Balcombe Place. She had the pleasure of seeing the WI's own education college in

Marcham in Oxfordshire named after her. Denman College continues to thrive.

Miss Farrer was created Dame Commander of the Order of the British Empire in 1950 and continued as General Secretary to became the longest-serving to date, retiring in 1959 after thirty years in the post. She died in January 1977 at the age of eighty-one.

The German delegate at the 1939 annual general meeting, Gräfin Keyserlingk, had been on the national committee of the *Bund Deutscher Frauenvereine* from 1922, although the movement was banned by the Nazis in 1933. After her return to Germany she spent the war near Schweidnitz (now Świdnica in Poland) and was forced to flee before the Russians in 1945. Five years later she was elected an honorary member of the International Council of Women. She died in Baden-Baden in West Germany in February 1958 in her seventy-ninth year.

Mrs Milburn's son Alan finally rang her from Leamington Spa station at midnight on 10 May. She dressed quickly and drove to pick him up: 'At the station I saw the trellised metal gates closed at the entrance and in front of them were two figures, one in khaki in a beret and a figure in blue. The khaki beret wouldn't be Alan, I thought, but it detached itself, came to the car and said: "Is it Ma?", and so out I flung myself and . . . we had a good hug and a kiss and then soon were speeding home, talking hard.' For the next few days she made tours of the village and neighbourhood, exulting in his safe return and people's evident joy to see the family reunited: 'I had a special message from Berkswell WI Committee expressing their delight at Alan's return.'[3] Two days later she wrote: 'I walk about in a half-dream and the long bad years of war begin to fade a little as Alan's voice is heard . . . and the house is once more a real home. The intense relief at the ending of the European war is felt everywhere. No longer do we live under the strain of it, though we shall have it at the back of our mind, and its scars before our eyes, all our lives.'[4] Mrs Milburn's husband, Jack, died in 1955 and Alan was killed tragically in a car accident in 1959. Mrs Milburn died eighteen months later at the age of seventy-seven.

Peggy Sumner continued to share with her sister Marjorie the house in Hale where she and her parents had lived before the war. Once petrol rationing was lifted she was able to take her Morris 10 off the blocks it had been sitting on since rationing began. She remembered no major celebrations, just a gradual return of peacetime conditions, and of course she was free to attend WI meetings once again. She and her sister used to drive the Morris down to Cornwall on holiday and continued to do so until the car 'died of a broken heart – a valve went – in 1960'. The biggest changes in the WI for Peggy were the outings arranged after the war. 'We went to Reaseheath Agricultural College and Bodnant Gardens in North Wales. I went to Denman College in 1949. Then in 1951 we had a trip to London to visit the Festival of Britain and another one to a major craft exhibition at the Victoria and Albert Museum.' Peggy got drawn into more and more WI activities. She joined a WI choir, she went to dances and always tried to have a go when something new was suggested.

> The great thing about the WI is that you are one of a few who are all trying things out. You get drawn into it and that makes you want to encourage others to join. There is nothing you can tell a non-member to make her join. She has to appreciate what it can be, what it can mean to her, what it can do for her. I have seen members scared to open their mouths when they first joined who have ended up as President or on the county committee. Nowadays the WI has the feeling of an extended family for me.

Mrs Ward remained involved in Bradfield WI, occasionally as president, and the family went on farming at Copyhold Farm until Mr and Mrs Ward retired in 1976. After leaving school her daughter Dorcas went to Girton College, Cambridge to study history. When she left university she became a housing manager in London and ended up doing policy work. During the 1960s she worked for three years in Hong Kong. 'I missed the Beatles and the Swinging Sixties!' she said. She retired to Frilsham, not far from Bradfield, and contributed to a book published as a tribute to a local woman called Felicity Palmer, who was described as a 'farmer, natural historian and scholar'. In 2011 she published a history of Bradfield Village.

Mrs Sims remained as active as ever, taking on a variety of voluntary jobs and sitting on committees, including the WI, right up to when she died in 1996 at the age of ninety-two. Her daughter Ann studied at the Guildhall School of Music and Drama as a student in her twenties, having spent a few years working as a farm pupil and a secretary. She joined Bradfield WI in 1966 and has held most offices on the committee over the years. She is still an active member and says of the WI: 'it has been part of my life since I was a child. If you scratch my skin you'll see I'm WI through and through.'

Ruth Toosey lived at the White House almost until the end of her life. Her husband, a major in the army, was killed in Normandy in 1944. She became one of nearly 250,000 war widows who were left to bring up their families on their own after the Second World War. The WI provided continuity and a shared understanding in those circumstances. I remember her as a great character with a deep laugh and a wonderful twinkle in her eye. Her daughter, Caroline, had four sons and now lives in Nantwich in Cheshire.

Gwen Bark gave birth to a baby daughter, Mary, in 1946, at

which point she resigned from the committee of Tarporley WI in Cheshire though she continued to be a member for another twenty years. She joined her husband as a partner in the GP practice once the children were all at school. She always wore a tweed suit when working, Mary remembered, and was much loved and respected. She died in 1968 at the age of fifty-five.

After the war Sybil Norcott married Les, a tenant farmer like her father. Her wedding present from her parents were two in-gilt pigs and not long afterwards they had twenty-four piglets. Sybil took her exams in butchery via a grant given by the WI. The qualification for butchery was examined in Dolgellau and before she could teach she had to pass the test for pig curing. As petrol was still rationed she had to take her wares in a suitcase on the train. 'It was incredibly heavy. I lugged this great big suitcase across the platform and when people asked me what I had in there I told them books. But in fact I had a ham, picnic ham, cut from the shoulder, a side of bacon all cured with saltpetre and honey, and fresh sausages.' She passed her examination and returned to Cheshire with a lighter suitcase. She became ever more active within the WI, benefiting from any number of courses on offer, including public speaking. 'Les was marvellous. He never begrudged me going to the WI. On the contrary he encouraged it. He had his own interests. He was a great bowler and used to coach the young farmers' cricket team.' In 1976 Sybil became a TV star, featuring as a guest cook on Yorkshire Television's *Farmhouse Kitchen*. Could she have done all this without the WI? Unlikely. The WI had the structure to nurture her talent and the outlet for her to exploit that talent and put it to good use. From a wild country girl who liked nothing better than to dig her patch with her special spade and watch the barn owl rearing her owlets, she blossomed into an expert on the WI's national stage. She said, in summing up her seventy years in the

WI (and counting): 'If I had not been in the WI I would not have demonstrated for the NFWI at Earls Court. I would not have met the Queen three times and done a demonstration for her. I would never have done all this without the WI.'

Edith Jones continued to be a member of Smethcote WI. She and Jack retired to Church Stretton in 1947 and she remained an active member of the community. Her great-niece Chris recalled that she

> always made a bit of time to improve herself. She encouraged me to read and my brother and I were both great readers, probably as a result of her enthusiasm. She was always game to have a go at anything. The WI was an abiding interest and even when her husband was slipping away in 1958 she made sure that her cakes were delivered to the WI meeting before going into hospital to see him. As she got older and was less active my mother would go down to her cottage to help in the garden and would invariably find Edith sitting on the porch, chatting to passers-by. When she had a hip operation she had to come and stay with us at the farm to recuperate. One morning my mother heard a terrible crash at the bottom of the stairs and rushed to the hall to see Edith coming downstairs on her bottom having thrown her crutches down first. She had no intention of asking anyone to help her. She was a great character.

Edith died on 23 December 1980, just a few weeks short of her 97th birthday.

'The WI was a big part of Edith's life. When she left Smethcote and my parents took over the farm, my mother joined in her place and I too have been a member of Smethcote WI, so that there has been a family member in the Institute continually since it was formed in 1931,' Chris said.

It is difficult for us today to imagine what situation could arise that would call for and receive such extraordinary, unselfish and cheerful devotion to duty as did the Second World War. Although there was of course some grumbling, the vast majority of women who were involved in the wartime Women's Institutes rose to the occasion. However much the government asked of them they seemed to find the capacity to give freely and usually with humour and enthusiasm. I am constantly humbled by the thought of all that they achieved under what seem to me to be at times impossibly trying circumstances. Just keeping the household going, let alone adding a dozen extra tasks, would be trial enough, but to be cheerful through it all – that is probably the greatest achievement. And after the war was over? Well, those women had work to do. There was a country to rebuild, a college to found in order to continue to educate themselves, issues that had yet to be resolved: equal pay for equal work, analgesia for women giving birth in rural villages, piped water to every village, drains, electricity, more women police. The list was endless.

As one of their post-war chairmen, Lady Brunner, said,

> The history of the movement is one of *in*tolerance. *In*tolerance of burst pipes, children's horror comics, squalid newspapers and sordid litter. So long as there is cruelty or evil to harm children and young people, as long as animals are ill-treated, as long as there are ill-designed, shoddy goods on the market; as long as there is avoidable danger and hazard for young and old, whether on the roads, or by accidents in the home, or by food poisoning; as long as country people are badly in need of amenities they should share with townspeople – and as long as we are bound by fellowship, truth and justice we can afford to be intolerant of a lot of things.[5]

In amongst all the post-war campaigning and the adjustment to peace and another decade of austerity the WI had one other, private, role. It had to offer healing and refuge to those women who found life in post-war Britain a trial. Many took months or years to establish a comfortable relationship with their husbands; others had to come to terms with the loss of their husbands, sons and daughters, while more still mourned the return home to the cities of their evacuee foster children of whom they had become inordinately fond during the long years of war. In post-war Britain these issues were not discussed in public and seldom mentioned in private but women were aware of them and they helped one another in numerous, simple ways. The all-woman environment of a Women's Institute was a refuge from a different kind of existence after the war and it was one in which women, like my grandmother, could breathe. Elsie Bainbridge, who was a young widow, spoke about the difficulties she had mixing with other widows who were all much older than she was. She explained: 'I felt very uncomfortable amongst a lot of couples so I found the WI very much easier. I got used to going to meetings and getting to know people and mixing a bit.' Peggy Sumner talked of how the WI helped her when she was distressed after her sister's death. 'Marjorie died on the Sunday and I went to the WI on the Wednesday. There was no hugging, just a hand on my arm occasionally to say "I'm thinking of you." It was so reassuring. I always say to members who are widowed or who suffer a loss "Don't stay at home. Come. Come."'

I am not a member of a WI. I live in a city and thus do not qualify but my own association with the Women's Institute began in 1982 when, as a student, I was asked to give a talk on Bristol Cathedral. Ten years later I began to lecture more regularly to WIs and by 2002 I was a registered speaker in Oxfordshire. Delivering a lecture to a local institute is always fun. I tend to arrive during the business, so that I catch the tail end of the first part of the meeting and hear what is planned in the way of days out, theatre visits, demonstrations or county meetings. After a small amount of fiddling with the equipment I give my talk on whatever subject has been requested. Initially most of my subject matter had to do with exploration (Everest and Shackleton) or men in extremis (Japanese POW camps). I sometimes wondered how this would go down with women-only gatherings. I need not have worried. There is no subject that the WI is not prepared to tackle.

On one occasion I was asked to speak about the true story of the bridge on the River Kwai to a small institute in North Oxfordshire. An elderly lady in the front row smiled at me as I introduced the topic but the moment the first slide came up she closed her eyes and sat motionless. I carried on with the talk and at the end there were several questions. When it was all over I went to speak to her and began by saying that I hoped the subject matter had not bored her. She replied: 'Oh no, my dear, it's just that I couldn't see your slides. I have been going blind for some time but I'm now completely unable to focus on anything. However, I did so want to hear your talk as my late husband was a prisoner on that railway and as he never talked about it I thought I'd learn something more about it if I came to hear you speak.' I was deeply humbled by this and learned the important lesson that one must never assume anything when speaking to WI members.

Talking to a group at a half-yearly meeting in Cumbria was an experience of a completely different order. Five hundred women and one man, the Mayor of Kendal, were squeezed into a beautiful room in the Town Hall. At the beginning of the meeting we stood to sing 'Jerusalem'. I had not experienced a large gathering of women singing together since I was at school and the effect of 500 women belting out the familiar words to the even more familiar tune was utterly breathtaking. I am embarrassed to admit that I had tears in my eyes, so beautiful and uplifting was that experience. Fortunately for me there was some business to attend to before I had to stand up and speak.

I want to end with a beautiful letter published by a WI member anonymously in *Home & Country* during the war. She reflected on what the war had meant to her and her closest WI friends:

> What are the reactions of the ordinary person to these days? It is, of course, impossible to generalise, but those of our own circle are interesting. First then, our treasured possessions are no longer the same. The china on the mantelpiece, the old bits of furniture, even the house we have lived in happily for many years cease to be of real value. We know them to be unimportant, but family life, friendship, music, books: these remain our true possessions. Again the background of uncertainty seems to enhance our joy in the beauty of life; the summer morning with its long shadows, the dew-sprinkled flowers, the gentle chatter of swallows and their swooping grace. Life is more secluded, though not less full, and our occupations are changed. The hostess is cook and finds a fresh pleasure in hospitality, the artist becomes a practical gardener, and the gardener makes dug-outs. Each finds a new pride in a new achievement. Letter writing has come into its own again and we may have some enlightening records of daily life for posterity. We make the best of our next door neighbours, now that our movements are restricted, and find them pleasanter company than we had expected.
>
> Life is simplified; we cannot look forward or make plans, so that time seems to have ceased to exist. Perhaps after the rush and tension of these last years, these days may bring us single

> mindedness, an acceptance of life and of death, an inward peace. And the self concern which is our torment, whether we know it or not, must find an antidote when we let our imagination stray over the human misery now in the world. The common lot of men binds us to each other and if we will, we may pluck virtue from tragedy.[6]

The Women's Institute comprises some of the most remarkable women I have had the privilege to meet and I know that their wartime counterparts were equally as impressive.

NOTES

CHAPTER 1

1 Stamper, Anne, *Rooms Off the Corridor*, p. 16
2 Agricultural College, Guelph, December 1986
3 Goodenough, Simon, *Jam and Jerusalem*, p. 11
4 Walker, Collins and M. McIntyre Hood, *Fifty Years of Achievement*, Federated Women's Institutes of Ontario, p. 23
5 Stamper, p. 23, quoted from Roger Fieldhouse, *A History of Modern British Adult Education*
6 Robertson Scott, J. W., *The Story of the Women's Institute Movement in England & Wales & Scotland*, p. 19
7 ibid.
8 Stamper, p. 25
9 Robertson Scott, p. 22
10 Stamper, p. 25
11 Robertson Scott, p. 6
12 ibid., p. 40
13 *Home & Country*, June 1946
14 Jenkins, Inez, *The History of the Women's Institute Movement of England and Wales*, p. 16
15 Robertson Scott, p. 45
16 ibid., p. 46
17 Tribute in *Barrow News* by a friend

18 Lady Denman's address to the 22nd AGM, 1938
19 Robertson Scott, p. 107
20 Helena Clara Deneke, *Grace Hadow*, p. 32
21 Robertson Scott, p. 46
22 *Dictionary of National Biography*, Teresa Smith
23 Goodenough, p. 29
24 Jenkins, p. 42
25 Jenkins, p. 145
26 Stamper, Anne, p. 39, quoted from Piers Dudgeon, *Village Voices*, p. 46
27 Stamper, p. 33
28 ibid., p. 35, from Mrs Watt and Ness Lloyd, *The First Women's Institute School* booklet
29 Stamper, p. 35, from Watt and Lloyd
30 *Home & Country*, June 1919

CHAPTER 2

1 Andrews, Maggie, *The Acceptable Face of Feminism*, p. 30
2 *Home & Country*, April 1939
3 Sheridan, Dorothy (ed.), *Wartime Women*, pp. 73–4
4 Lady Denman, *Home & Country*, October 1939
5 Excerpts from a letter written by Lady Denman to the Ministry of Information, 5 September 1939
6 Miss Farrer to Lady Denman, 25 August 1939
7 Buckinghamshire newsletter, 'Our Monthly Letter', October 1939
8 *Home & Country*, November 1939
9 East and West Hendred WI minute books

CHAPTER 3

1 Dorset War Book, 1946
2 Mrs Constance Miles, Diaries, August 1939

3 NFWI Memorandum on Evacuation, November 1938
4 ibid.
5 Letter to *The Times*, 9 August 1939
6 Letter from J. M. Bush James to *The Times*, 12 September 1939
7 Harrisson, Tom and Charles Madge, *War Begins at Home*, p. 23
8 Roffey, James, *A Schoolboy's War in Sussex*, p. 18
9 ibid.
10 Harrisson and Madge, p. 313
11 Roffey, p. 27
12 *Home & Country*, November 1939
13 Walter Elliot, printed in *Home & Country*, December 1939
14 *Town Children Through Country Eyes: A Survey on Evacuation, 1940*, p. 3
15 ibid., p. 3
16 ibid., pp. 3–4
17 ibid., p. 4
18 ibid.
19 ibid., p. 5
20 ibid., p. 7
21 ibid., p. 9
22 ibid., p. 13
23 ibid.
24 ibid., p. 15
25 Sheridan, Dorothy (ed.), *Wartime Women*, p. 66
26 ibid., p. 67
27 *Town Children*, p. 18
28 ibid., p. 18
29 ibid., p. 20
30 ibid., p. 22
31 *Home & Country*, November 1940

CHAPTER 4

1 PRO, CAB 16/157, CID, Subcommittee on Food Supply in Time of War, FS 13, report of the Subcommittee on Rationing,

5 October 1936
2 Zweiniger-Bargielowska, Ina, *Austerity in Britain*, p. 1
3 Collingham, Lizzie, *The Taste of War*, p. 362
4 'The Effects of Severe Rationing', 18 March 1940
5 East Hendred WI minute book 1942
6 Collingham, p. 13
7 Donnelly, Peter (ed.), *Mrs Milburn's Diaries*, 18 January 1941
8 Longmate, Norman, *How We Lived Then*, p. 379
9 Blunt, Maggie Joy, Mass Observation Diary, 18 March 1941
10 Donnelly (ed.), 7 July 1941, p. 102
11 ibid., 28 July 1942 p. 147
12 Zweiniger-Bargielowska, p. 33
13 Letter from Denbighshire Committee for the Feeding of Rural Workers, Wrexham, to Trefnant WI president, 18 May 1943
14 Miss Farrer to Assistant Secretary (Defence), 16 April 1939
15 M. M. Squance of the Petroleum Department to Miss Walker, 24 June 1940
16 Mr Mackay to Miss Farrer, 1 January 1942
17 Cox, Vera, *Country Markets, A Pioneer Venture by the National Federation of Women's Institutes*, p. 22
18 'What the WIs Did in 1944', in *Home & Country*, January 1945
19 *Home & Country*, June 1941
20 ibid.
21 Cox, p. 25
22 ibid., p. 16
23 Oxfordshire Federation of Women's Institutes, 1942 Annual Report
24 Cox, p. 14
25 WI marketing subcommittee minutes, 2 July 1941
26 ibid.
27 Oxfordshire Federation minutes, April 1941
28 ibid., May 1941
29 Marketing Subcommittee minutes, May 1943
30 *Good Housekeeping*, August 1941

CHAPTER 5

1 *Home & Country*, July 1940
2 ibid., September 1940
3 ibid.
4 ibid.
5 ibid.
6 Jeff Walden, *Dictionary of National Biography*, entry on C. H. Middleton
7 ibid.
8 Middleton, C. H., *Digging for Victory*, p. 5
9 ibid., p. 18
10 ibid., pp. 35–6
11 ibid., p. 136
12 *Home & Country*, December 1939
13 Broad, Richard and Suzie Fleming (eds), *Nella Last's War*, 15 September 1941
14 Hookwood WI log book
15 Broadcast by Sir Reginald Dorman-Smith, reproduced in *Home & Country*, October 1939
16 Barham WI Annual Report 1944
17 *Home & Country*, July 1941
18 ibid., December 1942
19 Oxfordshire Federation minutes 1941
20 *Dictionary of National Biography*, entry on Dr W. O. James
21 Oxford Federation minutes 1941
22 Elizabeth Hess, 'Five Hundred Tons of Rose Hips for 1945', *Home & Country*, August 1945
23 W. King Wilson in *Home & Country*, July 1941
24 Editorial in *Home & Country*, October 1941
25 Letter from Mr Dawes to councils, 25 March 1942
26 ibid.
27 ibid.
28 ibid.

CHAPTER 6

1 McCall, Cicely, *Women's Institutes*, p. 31
2 *Home & Country*, November 1939
3 ibid. December 1939
4 Andrews, Maggie, *The Acceptable Face of Feminism*, p. 109
5 Editorial, *Home & Country*, July 1940
6 ibid.
7 ibid.
8 *Home & Country*, July 1940
9 Lord Woolton, quoted in *Home & Country*, August 1940
10 *Home & Country*, August 1940
11 Letter in *Home & Country*, October 1939
12 *Home & Country*, January 1941
13 Lord Woolton to Lady Denman, 31 December 1940
14 *Home & Country*, August 1940
15 *The Times*, 24 March 1941
16 Letter from Marion Hyde to Lady Denman, published in *Home & Country*, August 1940
17 News from the Institutes, *Home & Country*, October 1940
18 ibid.
19 Letter from an East Kent WI member to the editor of *Home & Country*, November 1940
20 ibid.
21 *Home & Country*, December 1940
22 McCall, *Women's Institutes*, p. 34
23 ibid., p. 35
24 ibid., p. 35
25 Cox, *Country Markets*, p. 20
26 Bowman, Jennifer, *Redlynch WI: the War Years* (Redlynch Review, 2009)
27 Oxfordshire Federation minute book, 1942
28 ibid., p. 20
29 *Home & Country*, June 1941
30 Lord Woolton broadcast, 6 June 1941
31 ibid.

32 ibid.
33 Donnelly (ed.), 18 July 1941, p. 103
34 *Home & Country*, January 1942, p. 1
35 ibid., March 1942
36 ibid.
37 Donnelly (ed.), 1 June 1941, p. 99
38 *Home & Country*, October 1943
39 ibid.
40 ibid.
41 ibid.
42 Letter from a jam centre supervisor to *Home & Country*, January 1945

CHAPTER 7

1 Letter from Mrs Hazelwood to Miss Farrer at the NFWI in September 1940
2 From letter to all county chairmen from Miss Farrer, 4 September 1939
3 P. G. Cambray and G. G. B. Briggs, *Red Cross & St. John: The Official Record of the Humanitarian Services of the War Organisation of the British Red Cross Society and Order of St. John of Jerusalem, 1939–1947*, p. 9
4 Gillies, Midge, *The Barbed Wire University*, p. 32
5 Cambray and Briggs, p. 586
6 Jenkins, Inez, *History of the Women's Institute Movement of England and Wales*, p. 91
7 Woods, Katharine, 'Headington WI memoir'
8 ibid.
9 Donnelly (ed.), 1 June 1941, p. 99
10 Longmate, Norman, *How We Lived Then*, p. 246
11 ibid., p.257
12 Zweiniger-Bargielowska, p. 47
13 Hansard HC Deb, 22 April 1943, vol. 388, cc1842–3W
14 *Home & Country*, October 1941

15 *Oxford Times*, July 1943 (not actually dated)
16 Donnelly (ed.), 17 July 1940
17 Letter from Mary Close, president of the Westbourne WI, to *Home & Country*, October 1939
18 'News from Institutes', *Home & Country*, February 1940
19 Letter to *Home & Country*, E. Hastings-Ord, February 1940
20 Miss M. Bowring, 4 March 1941, *Home & Country*, April 1941
21 *Home & Country*, September 1942
22 Letter to Miss Farrer, August 1942
23 ibid.
24 ibid.
25 Donnelly (ed.), 18 November 1941, p.115
26 *Home & Country*, October 1942
27 ibid.
28 Anne Stamper article 2003, 'Country Women in Wartime', paper delivered 2003
29 Letter from Clementine Churchill to Mrs Roberts, Trefnant WI, February 1942
30 Letter to institutes from county secretary, June 1943
31 *Home & Country*, 1943
32 Letter to county chairman from Edith Walker at NFWI, 29 March 1940
33 ibid.
34 Hampton, Janie, *How the Girl Guides Won the War*, p. 139

CHAPTER 8

1 Mrs D. Blewitt to James Blewitt, 9 June 1941
2 Lady Denman, message from our chairman, *Home & Country*, October 1939
3 *Home & Country*, November 1939, p.400
4 HM The Queen, speech to AGM, Albert Hall, 8 June 1943
5 National Federation of Women's Institutes personnel files
6 *Games for Women's Institutes*, 1941, p. 2
7 ibid.

8 McCall, *Women's Institutes*, 1943, p. 16
9 *Home & Country*, December 1939
10 ibid.
11 Audlem WI Minute Book, January 1941
12 *Home & Country*, October 1940
13 Donnelly (ed.), 15 November 1940, p. 67
14 ibid., 28 May 1941, p. 98
15 ibid., 21 March 1941, p. 86
16 Lady Denman, 22 January 1940
17 Tribute in *Home & Country*, January 1940
18 *Home & Country*, October 1940
19 ibid.
20 Wright, Gertrude, *The First Thirty Years: Mobberley Women's Institute*, p. 5
21 Oxfordshire Federation AGM, February 1942
22 Woods, Katharine, Memoirs of Headington WI, 1974
23 *Home & Country*, April 1944
24 'A Country Woman Looks About Her', *Home & Country*, August 1940
25 ibid.
26 *Home & Country*, January 1941
27 Wright, *The First Thirty Years*, p. 1728 Eileen Lloyd to the author, 3 March 2011
29 *Home & Country*, March 1944
30 ibid., October 1940
31 ibid., July 1940
32 Lady Tweedsmuir's address, Oxfordshire Federation AGM 1943
33 *Home & Country*, August 1940
34 ibid., June 1942
35 ibid., June 1944
36 ibid.

CHAPTER 9

1 Donnelly (ed.), 17 August 1944, p. 230
2 *Home & Country*, May 1941

3 ibid.
4 ibid., August 1942from broadcast on 21 June 1942
5 ibid., November 1944
6 Letter from Mrs Walshe to *Home & Country*, September 1942
7 'Managing an Earth Closet' in *Home & Country*, August 1944
8 'Turning on the Tap' by Cicely McCall, *Home & Country*, May 1944
9 ibid.
10 ibid.
11 *Home & Country*, November 1944
12 'Turning on the Tap'
13 24th AGM, Tuesday 8 June 1943
14 ibid.
15 *Home & Country*, June 1942
16 ibid., January 1943
17 ibid.
18 ibid., September 1942
19 ibid., July 1942
20 Evidence for the Central Housing Advisory Committee's Subcommittee on the Design of Dwellings, p. 1
21 ibid.
22 ibid.
23 ibid.
24 ibid., p. 2
25 Education questionnaire 1943, p. 4
26 Miss Nancy Tennant, NFWI conference on Post War Reconstruction in Europe
27 NFWI conference on Post War Reconstruction in Europe
28 ibid.
29 ibid.
30 Lady Denman message published in *Home & Country*, July 1944
31 Donnelly (ed.), 8 May 1945, p. 98
32 *Home & Country*, June 1945
33 ibid.
34 ibid., March 1946

35 Norah C. James, 'Back to Real Life', *Woman's Own*, January 1945, p. 15
36 K. M. Catlin, *Home & Country*, June 1945

CHAPTER 10

1 *Home & Country*, December 1939
2 Wright, *The First Thirty Years*, p. 15
3 Donnelly (ed.), 10 May 1945, p. 300
4 ibid., 12 May 1945, p. 302
5 Lady Brunner quoted in Goodenough, *Jam and Jerusalem*, p. 45
6 A WI member, letter in *Home & Country*, October 1940

BIBLIOGRAPHY

Andrews, Maggie, *The Acceptable Face of Feminism: The Women's Institute as a Social Movement* (London, Lawrence & Wishart Ltd, 1997)

Broad, Richard and Fleming, Suzie (eds), *Nella Last's War* (London: Profile Books, 2006)

Cambray, P. G. and Briggs, G. G. B. (compilers), *Red Cross & St. John: The Official Record of the Humanitarian Services of the War Organisation of the British Red Cross Society and Order of St. John of Jerusalem, 1939–1947* (London: Sumfield and Day, 1949)

Carey, Helen, *Bows of Burning Gold* (Kirby Malham: Alfresco Books, 2005)

Carter, David, *Tarporley Then and Now* (Tarporley: Rotary Club, 2000)

Collingham, Lizzie, *The Taste of War: World War Two and the Battle for Food* (London: Allen Lane, 2011)

Condell, Jenny (ed.), *The Day the War Ended: Voices and Memories from 1945* (London: Weidenfeld & Nicolson, 2005)

Deneke, Helen, *Grace Hadow* (London: Oxford University Press, 1946)

Donnelly, Peter (ed.), *Mrs Milburn's Diaries: An Englishwoman's Day-to-Day Reflections 1939–1945* (London: Harrap, 1979)

Gardiner, Juliet, *Wartime Britain 1939–1945* (London: Headline Book Publishing, 2004)

Gillies, Midge, *The Barbed Wire University: The Real Lives of Allied Prisoners of War in the Second World War* (London: Aurum Press Ltd, 2011)

Goodenough, Simon, *Jam and Jerusalem: A Pictorial History of Britain's Greatest Women's Movement* (London: Berkeley Publishers Ltd, 1977)

Hampton, Janie, *How the Girl Guides Won the War* (London: Harper Press, 2010)

Harrisson, Tom and Madge, Charles, *War Begins at Home* by Mass Observation (London: Chatto & Windus, 1940)

Hertfordshire Federation of Women's Institutes, *The Hertfordshire Village Book* (Newbury: Countryside Books, 1986)

Hertfordshire Federation of Women's Institutes, *Pride in our Past* (Newbury: Countryside Books, 2008)

Jenkins, Inez, *The History of the Women's Institute Movement of England and Wales* (Oxford University Press, 1953)

Kitchen, Penny (compiler), *The Women's Institute for Home & Country, War, Peace and Rural Life As Seen Through the Pages of the WI Magazine 1919–1959* (London: Ebury Press, 1990)

Lawson, John and Silver, Harold, *A Social History of Education in England* (London: Methuen & Co, 1973)

Livingstone, Sir Richard, *Education for a World Adrift* (Cambridge University Press, 1943)

Longmate, Norman, *How We Lived Then: A History of Everyday Life During the Second World War* (London: Arrow Books Ltd, 1973)

McCall, Cicely, *Looking Back from the Nineties* (Norwich: Gliddon Books, 1994)

McCall, Cicely, *Women's Institutes* (London: William Collins, 1943)

Middleton, C. H., *Digging for Victory* (London: George Allen & Unwin Ltd, 1942)

Nicholson, Virginia, *Millions Like Us* (London: Viking, 2011)

Richards, Guy and Dalton-Morris, Shirley, *Longcot: A Village in the Vale* (Faringdon: Shirley Dalton-Morris, 1999)

Robertson Scott, J. W., *The Story of the Women's Institute Movement in England & Wales & Scotland* (Kingham: The Village Press, 1925)

Roffey, James, *A Schoolboy's War in Sussex* (Stroud: The History Press, 2010)

Sheridan, Dorothy (ed.), *Wartime Women: A Mass Observation Anthology* (London, William Heinemann Ltd, 1990)

Stamper, Anne, *Rooms off the Corridor: Education in the WI and 50 years of Denman College 1948–1998* (London: WI Books, 1998)

Titmuss, Richard, *History of the Second World War: Problems of Social Policy*

(London: HM Stationery Office and Longmans, Greene and Co, 1950)

Townsend, Colin and Eileen, *War Wives: A Second World War Anthology* (Glasgow: Grafton Books for the Leisure Circle Partnership, 1989)

Tyrer, Nicola, *They Fought in the Fields: The Women's Land Army: The story of a Forgotten Victory* (London: Sinclair-Stevenson, 1996)

Waller, Jane and Vaughan-Rees, Michael, *Women in Wartime: The Role of Women's Magazines 1939–1945* (London: McDonald Optima, 1987)

Ward, Dorcas, *History of Bradfield in Berkshire* (Frilsham: Dorcas Ward, 2011)

Weightman, Christine, *Remembering Wartime Ascot, Sunningdale and Sunninghill 1939–1945* (Ascot: Cheapside Publications, 2006)

Zweiniger-Bargielowska, Ina, *Austerity in Britain: Rationing, Controls and Consumption 1939–1955* (Oxford: Oxford University Press, 2000)

PERIODICALS, REPORTS AND LEAFLETS

Beveridge, William, *Report of the Inter-Departmental Committee on Social Insurance and Allied Services (the Beveridge Report)* 1942

Elliott, Walter, *Transfer of Population in time of War*, broadcast on 6 January 1939 (Ministry of Health)

Ministry of Agriculture, *Allotment & Garden Guide, September 1945 Vo. 1, No. 9*

Ministry of Information, *Make Do and Mend* (London, Ministry of Information 1943)

Report of the Committee of Post War agricultural Education in England and Wales (HMSO 1943)

Town Children Through Country Eyes: A Survey on Evacuation, 1940 (Dorking, NFWI 1940)

Good Housekeeping, August 1941

Home & Country: The Journal of the Women's Institutes, monthly magazine with county supplements, 1938–1946

Dig for Victory Leaflet No. 11: *Bottling and Canning Fruit and Vegetables*

UNPUBLISHED SOURCES

Bowman, Jennifer, *Redlynch WI: the War Years* (Redlynch Review, 2009)

Cox, Vera, *Country Markets, A Pioneer Venture by the National Federation of Women's Institutes* (London, NFWI 1940)

Drage, Dorothy, *Pennies for Friendship* (privately printed, 1961)

Stamper, Anne, *Countrywomen in war time – Women's Institutes 1938–1945*, Paper delivered to the Second International Conference on the History of Voluntary Action, held at Roehampton Institute, University of Surrey, 9–11 September 2003

Stamper, Anne, *What the WI did in Wartime*

Walker, Collins and Hood, M. McIntyre, *Fifty Years of Achievement, Federated Women's Institutes of Ontario*, 1948

Woods, Katharine, *Headington WI Memoir: From Canada to Headington Fifty-Five years ago*, 1973

Wright, Gertrude, The First Thirty Years: Mobberley Women's Institute, 1958

Minute books and summaries from WI institutes: Arnside, Audlem, Barham, Barrow, Barthomley, Bickleigh, Burton and Puddington, Bywell, Coningsby & Tattershall, East & West Hendred, Feniton, Goostrey, Hookwood, Hooton, Leigh, Mobberley, Preston Patrick, Radley, Revesby, Ringmer, Smethcote, Tetney, Washington Station WI, Willaston

County Records and annual reports: Cheshire, Derbyshire, Dorset, Hampshire, North Lincolnshire, Oxfordshire, Surrey,

FROM THE WOMEN'S LIBRARY

NFWI Marketing Subcommittee Record Books

MISC 171 Item 2627 BBC Wartime Kitchen and Garden Interviews (1992–3)

5FWI/A/3/6-7 Box 46 Report on the AGMs at the Royal Albert Hall

5FWI/D/1/2/92 Women in Forces
5FWI/CT/1/3/2/1 Advice to Presidents on how to conduct meetings
5FWI/H/15 Personnel files
5FWI/H/16 Post-War planning
5FWI/D/1/2/84 Women Police 1939–45
5/FWI/H/15 1939–1945 War
5FWI/B/2/1/116 WI Movement – General 1944–1986
5FWI/B/2/1/115 Lady Denman
5FWI/H/14 Box OS72 Wartime Scrapbook of Miss Elizabeth Hess
5FWI/A/3/73 World War II and after, 1940–77
The Post-War Relief of Europe, report of the conference held in London on 11 March 1943

FROM THE IMPERIAL WAR MUSEUM

IWM 99/74/1 The papers of Mrs Constance Miles (b.1881)
IWM 08/20/1 Papers of Mrs Denys Blewitt

FROM THE NATIONAL ARCHIVES

cab/66/16/28 Rationing of Clothing (Memorandum by the President of the Board of Trade to the War Cabinet)
cab/68/7/2 Food Situation of the United Kingdom, July 1940 (Report submitted by the Minister of Food to the War Cabinet)
cab/68/8/54 Food Situation of the United Kingdom, July 1941 (Report submitted by the Minister of Food to the War Cabinet)
cab/68/2/39 Supply and Production October 1939 (Report submitted to the War Cabinet on the imports of wool)
cab/66/57/19 Tenth Report of the Shipping Committee, November 1944 (Report regarding imports of food, materials and munitions)
cab/67/5/34 The Effects of Severe Rationing (Report on the experiment conducted in Cambridge in 1939 to assess the effect of severely limiting food intake for the population)
cab/67/5/27 Standard Clothing (Memorandum by the Chancellor of

the Exchequer on the viability of issuing a range of standard articles of clothing at controlled prices)

cab/66/42/20 Post-War Reconstruction – Third Quarterly Survey 1943

cab/66/56/36 Supplies from North America in Stage II (note by the Chancellor of the Exchequer and the Minister of Production, 1944)

WEBSITES

www.bbc.co.uk/ww2peopleswar/
www.iwm.org.uk/
www.londonmet.ac.uk/thewomenslibrary/
www.nationalarchives.gov.uk/
www.oxforddnb.com/
www.thewi.org.uk

PHOTOGRAPH CREDITS

The author and publishers would like to thank the following copyright-holders for permission to reproduce images in this book:

The Mary Evans Picture Library: 1, 4, 5, 6, 19
National Portrait Gallery: 2
The National Federation of Women's Institutes: 3, 7, 26, 29, 30, 32
Mary Diggle: 14
Christine Downes: 8, 9, 9a
Caroline Dickinson: 10
Ann Tetlow: 12, 13
Dorcas Ward: 11
Peggy Sumner: 15
Getty Images: 24
WI Markets: 18, 22, 31
Sybil Norcott: 16
Mrs Milburn's Diaries: An Englishwoman's Day to Day Reflections, 1939-45: 17, 27

The author and publishers have made all reasonable efforts to contact copyright-holders for permission, and apologise for any omissions or errors in the form of credits given. Corrections may be made to future printings.

ACKNOWLEDGEMENTS

I am so very grateful to everyone who has been involved in *Jambusters* and for the enormously generous response from the Women's Institute. It has been a great privilege and fun in equal measure. First and foremost I would like to celebrate those women whose stories feature prominently in the book and who give it the voice from the war years: Caroline Dickinson, Mary Diggle, Ann Tetlow and Dorcas Ward talked to me about their mothers, Ruth Toosey, Dr Gwen Bark, Betty Sims and Miriam Ward respectively, bringing colour and humour to their stories. Betty Houghton, Sybil Norcott and Peggy Sumner told me about their own personal experiences of the WI in wartime, which provide vivid detail, and Chris Downes shared with me the glorious diaries and memoir of her great-aunt, Edith Jones. Thank you all so much.

I received wonderful encouragement from several ladies closely associated with the WI's archives and have pleasure in thanking them for their help: Helen Carey, Sue Cox, Virginia Lawrence, Edwina Oldham, Linda Oliver and Anne Stamper.

Every book needs a heart and this one, especially, has benefited from the generosity of Institute members who have delved into attics, boxes and memories on behalf of their wartime predecessors, and it is to them that I owe a great thanks: Jenny Andrews,

Sheila Arbuckle, Frances Armstrong, Christine Bailey, Elsie Bainbridge, Margaret Banner, Heather Bartlett, Heather Beaumont, Alwyn Benbow, Anne Bennett, Jill Bexon, Gillian Blake, Jeanette Booth, Jenny Bowman, Jill Broadley, Jeannetta Brodrick, Jean Burgess, Linda Carew, Yvonne Cherry, Celia Cleobury, Linda Cooper, Lilian Cowen, Bridget Crow, Mary Daniels, Sara Downey, Jane Finnerty, Margaret Funnell, Joan Grisedale, Margery Hall, Alison Hannaford, Marilyn Hawkins, Jenny Hayes, Mary Hodgson, Evelyn Hodson, Jenny Holloway, Anne Huddleston, Lesley Hunter, Janice Jones, Jean Lane, Eileen Lloyd, Annie Manson, Audrey McKinnon, Dawn McLaren, Janet Melvin, Gwyneth Moores, June Moran, Hilary Morris, Liz Nicholls, Pauline Norbury, Gill Offley, Anne Peacock, Chris Phillips, Brenda Powell, Gill Pratt, Jill Pratt, Betty Prickett, Val Reynolds, Jean Ridgeway, Joyce Ridgeway, Christine Salisbury, Joan Simpkins, Clare Slack, Margaret Smith, Charlotte Stead, Amaryllis Stock, Jan Talbot, Gill Tanner, Margaret Vivian, Jenny Warren, Sheila Westall, Heather Wilkin, Maxine Willett, Jane Williams, Christine Wootton, Elizabeth Wrigley, Jackie Wylie and Linda Young at the WI Markets. I would also like to mention Margaret Clephan of Goostrey WI, who was so supportive of the book and sadly died in 2012.

The Women's Library in London, which holds the National Federation of Women's Institute archive, provided a treasure trove of material and I am grateful to the librarians there who do such an outstanding job with important national collections on women's issues. The Department of Documents at the Imperial War Museum was as hospitable and helpful as ever and I thank them warmly.

Finally I would like to thank those who have helped with the production of the book: my agent Catherine Clarke, my editors Angela Herlihy and Mike Jones, my copy editor Martin Bryant,

Briony Gowlett and to those who gave me permission to quote from their own works or offered support and encouragement: Lizzie Collingham, Midge Gillies, Stephanie Hickish, Terry Mitchell, Penny Noble, Stephen Rockliffe, James Roffey, Dianne Shepherd, Nigel Stanley, Nigel Stoneman, Gillian Summers, Tim Summers, Erica Toosey, Michele Topham, Annabel Warburg, Maxine Willett, Ina Zweiniger-Bargielowska. Finally, thanks to my husband, Chris, and my sons Simon, Richard and Sandy who chip in and help with cheerful comments and chocolate biscuits to keep me going.

INDEX